Narratives of the Anglo-Zulu War, 1879

Narratives of the Anglo-Zulu War, 1879
A Compendium of Fifteen Personal and Authoritative Accounts from Extracts and Articles

ILLUSTRATED

H. O'Clery, J. R. M. Chard, H. Hook, C. Stein, A. Harness, J. H. Reynolds, F. E. Whitton, Mrs Stuart Menzies, Sir Hugh McAlmont, Arthur FitzRoy Hart-Synnot, Beatrice M. Hart-Synnot, G. L. J. Goff, D. Blair Brown, Archibald Forbes & P. A. Wilkins

Narratives of the Anglo-Zulu War, 1879
A Compendium of Fifteen Personal and Authoritative Accounts from Extracts and Articles
By H. O'Clery, J. R. M. Chard, H. Hook, C. Stein, A. Harness, J. H. Reynolds, F. E. Whitton, Mrs Stuart Menzies, Sir Hugh McAlmont, Arthur FitzRoy Hart-Synnot, Beatrice M. Hart-Synnot, G. L. J. Goff, D. Blair Brown, Archibald Forbes & P. A. Wilkins

ILLUSTRATED

FIRST EDITION IN THIS FORM

First published as individual articles or extracts

Leonaur is an imprint of Oakpast Ltd
Copyright in this form © 2023 Oakpast Ltd

ISBN: 978-1-916535-64-0 (hardcover)
ISBN: 978-1-916535-65-7 (softcover)

http://www.leonaur.com

Publisher's Notes

The views expressed in this book are not necessarily those of the publisher.

Contents

Facing the Zulus *By H. O'Clery*	7
Lieutenant Chard's Account of Rorke's Drift *By J. R. M. Chard*	19
Private Henry Hook's Account of Rorke's Drift *By H. Hook*	25
Rorke's Drift: An Overview of the Assault *By C. Stein*	33
The Zulu Campaign from a Military Point of View *By Lt. Colonel Arthur Harness. C.B, Royal Artillery*	49
A Critique whilst the War was being Waged *Blackwood's Magazine, March 1879, vol. 25*	65
Surgeon Reynolds' Account *By J. H. Reynolds*	91
The Defence of Rorke's Drift *By F. E. Whitton*	99
Lord William Beresford *By Mrs Stuart Menzies*	115
South Africa—1879-80 by an A.D.C. *By Sir Hugh McAlmont*	125
Zululand by a Staff Officer *By Major-General FitzRoy Hart-Synnot*	147

The 91st Argyllshire Highlanders in the Zulu War *By G. L. J. Goff*	215
Surgical Experiences in Zululand *By D. Blair Brown*	243
The Bravest Deed I Ever Saw *By Archibald Forbes*	269
Victoria Cross Recipients of the Zulu War, 1879 *By Philip A. Wilkins*	277

Facing the Zulus
By Harry O'Clery, Buffs, East Kent Regiment

O'Clery was present at the outbreak of hostilities and during the siege and relief of Ekowe now better known as Eshowe during the Zulu Wars.

It was at Canterbury, in July 1877, that I joined Her Majesty's forces. I was led to that step by Recruiting-Sergeant Jack Gavigan, who had the credit, while stationed at St. George's Barracks, of enlisting more men in one year than all the other recruiting-sergeants put together.

I was placed in the Depot M Company of the Buffs.

Having received a fairly good education, I soon afterwards sat for an examination, and having gained a second-class certificate—which was thought something of in those days, for men were not then up to the present standard of knowledge—I was appointed an assistant schoolmaster to the depot, with the remuneration of fourpence a day. It was my duty to take the two lower classes of the men; and I very frequently found myself in charge of the whole school, as the acting schoolmaster, a sergeant whose name I will not disclose, had frequently to repair to the mess for the purpose of refreshment.

About five months after enlisting, I learned that we were ordered to join the regiment at Pietermaritzburg; and soon afterwards we proceeded to Southampton, where we embarked on the ship *American*, and found ourselves in company with a detachment of the 87th Regiment, known as "The Old Fogs," or the "Faugh-a-Ballagh Boys," from the war-cry of the corps; "Fag-an-Bealoch" meaning "Clear the way."

During the voyage to the Cape, we heard this war-cry on several occasions, and the monotony of the voyage was varied by occasional fights between men of the two regiments, who probably considered that, as they were going out to fight, there could be no objection to a little practice beforehand; and I can speak from experience in saying that most of my countrymen enjoy nothing better than a lively argument, and a free fight to wind up with.

We encountered a gale off Cape Finisterre, and had to be battened down below; but at this time, I was afflicted with seasickness, from which I did not recover for seven days. The rest of the voyage was most pleasant and enjoyable.

We disembarked at Cape Town, and after a few days sailed from thence to East London, where we remained about a week, and then proceeded to Durban on *H.M.S. Himalaya*. Owing to the roll of the sea here, we had to land in surf boats. It was anything but a pleasant experience.

Fifteen or twenty men would go down the ship's side into the boat, and a canvas would be stretched over her to keep out the water. Then, in the dark, we found ourselves jerked and jolted, one against another, for some considerable time, until the boat was hauled to the beach, where we landed more dead than alive, for the rolling and pitching of a whole sea voyage was crammed into that brief trip in a surf boat.

After a short stay at Durban, we marched up the country to Pieterniaritzburg, a distance of upwards of fifty miles, which we accomplished in four days, being cheered towards our journey's end by meeting the band of the regiment, which played us into the town to the tune of a then popular comic song. On joining the regiment, I was drafted into the B Company.

While staying in the town we turned out to welcome the 24th Regiment, passing through on their way up the country. They stayed about a week, and I made the acquaintance of two brothers, Fred and George Conboy, both in the band.

Soon we learned that Cetewayo, the Zulu king, had been called upon to pay a fine of a certain number of bullocks, for some filibustering expedition which some of his young warriors had made into Natal; and the date of payment was fixed for the 12th January, which was about twelve months after we had left England.

On and before that particular day we were encamped upon the southern bank of the Tugela River, upon which the Royal Engineers, assisted by the soldiers told off for the work, were busily constructing a floating raft, or bridge, by the aid of which we were, if needful, to cross over into the enemy's country

We numbered in the camp between two and three thousand men, consisting of the Buffs, the 99th Regiment, Mounted Infantry, Naval Brigade, Royal Artillery, a native contingent, and some mounted volunteers from Stanger and Victoria—two small towns on the coast of Natal—who evidently thought they were out for a picnic, and brought with them several wagon-loads of bedding, tinned meats, comforts and luxuries, of which I shall say a word or two in the course of my yarn.

The river was very full, and some half a mile wide, and there were plenty of crocodiles in its waters. Two or three poor fellows, while at work on the raft, were snapped up on falling overboard, and seen no more. One was a friend of mine belonging to *H.M.S. Active*.

It was the day before the final pay-day, and away in the distance we could plainly see a body of natives, who were by many in the camp believed to be the people whose arrival we were awaiting. But the commanding officers, I suppose, thought differently, and sent a shell bursting among them to tell them we were there.

The next day we crossed the river, and then war began. The crossing of the river was accomplished this way—two companies, of about one hundred men each, marched on to the raft, and it was then hauled across by the Naval Brigade. As soon as the men landed on the opposite side, the empty raft was drawn back again for a fresh freight; and so, as it was a tedious job, the whole day was taken up.

From what I could learn of the plan, the British force was to invade the country in four columns. No. 1, nearest the sea, was under the command of Brigadier-General Pearson, numbered 4,200, and was to advance along the coast. No. 2 consisted of 3,000 natives, commanded by European officers under Colonel Durnford, R.E., who was to cross the Tugela at Middle Drift and march up the left side of the river to Rorke's Drift. No. 3, commanded by Colonel Glyn, was about 3,000 strong, and contained the first and second battalions of the 24th Regiment, numbering about 1,000 bayonets. And No. 4, under Colonel Evelyn Wood, also about 3000 strong, was to operate from Utrecht, in conjunction with Colonel Glyn's column.

We, in No. 1 column, learned now and then of the movements of the others, by the native runners, who were sent from one column to another with despatches. Poor chaps, they risked their lives for very slight remuneration, and it was dangerous work to play the spy as they did; for the Zulus, when it became known that we were marching on their capital, determined to make a stand for it

We were marched up country, and terribly wet weather it was, no mistake, for the first week or so. Not a single shot was fired by any of our skirmishers, who were on in front of us. The natives retired before us, keeping, as they went, a watchful eye upon our movements, but taking care to keep out of range. As a proof of their nearness, however, we found, upon coming to their camping-grounds, that the embers of their fires were still smouldering.

Every night we camped in *laager*. This consists of drawing the waggons into a circle and digging a slight trench all round it, the earth taken from the trench being thrown up on the outer side to form a breastwork

Our first *laager* was formed near the farm of an English settler named John Dunne, who had, I think, married a native woman, and suited himself to the customs of the country. He knew his way about the country, and some little while before we crossed the Tugela he joined our column, bringing with him his family and a large number of followers.

Another stopping-place was upon the banks of a river, and after that at another river. Crossing this at a shallow part, we continued our march, and noticed that traces of the enemy were becoming more and more frequent. This gave us hope of a brush with them.

We were halted to prepare breakfast at a place called Inyezane, when we heard firing in front, and found that our skirmishers were engaged with a Zulu *"impi."* On pushing forward to the brow of a hill, we found ourselves under fire. Puffs of smoke were appearing in all directions from the bush away in front of us, and we therefore lay down, and fired at every spot from which a puff appeared.

It was my first appearance on a battlefield. We were told by our officers to keep ourselves cool and steady, and fire low; and I tried not to get carried away by the excitement, but it's not so easy, when you know that each puff may mean a dose of death to you or the man next to you.

We had with us a naval brigade of two hundred and seventy blue-jackets and marines from the *Tenedos* and *Active*, and these had charge of the waggons and two Gatlings. The Zulus came on in fine style, but the steady fire we kept up prevented them coming to close quarters. They, however, attempted a flanking movement; but Colonel Panell led a spirited charge, and cleared the heights, and the enemy were driven off, leaving about nine hundred killed and wounded upon the battlefield. I think we lost in the action seven killed, and about twenty-seven wounded. These we took with us, but left the enemy where they fell.

We had had no breakfast before the fight, and as we had to reach a certain distance each day, we had no refreshment till 9 p.m.

Next day we were overtaken by a native runner, who was taken to the general, and in consequence of the news he brought we were hurried forward with as little delay as possible. These runners are strange individuals; they take to running when they are tired of walking, and I noticed they seemed to get their breath better by so doing.

On the following morning, eleven days after the invasion of the country, we arrived at the village of Ekowe, about forty miles due north of the River Tugela, where there was a mission-station; and here we set to work to build a fort around the church, which was intended to be used as an hospital if required.

We formed a *laager*, into which we went for safety during the night, the day being occupied in building a fort. Here, upon its completion, we took up our position.

This was how we built the fort. The church tower in the centre was a look-out post for our best marksmen; and around the church, at a considerable distance, we dug a trench, some ten or twelve feet deep, and about twenty feet wide, and into this trench we planted stakes pointed at both ends. The earth from the trench formed a high breastwork, with steps formed on the inner side of the fort; and outside, beyond the trench, we dug small holes, at regular distances apart, into which we drove sharpened stakes, upon which we stretched wire to entangle the legs of the enemy who might venture within the maze.

Our position being considered very secure, the native contingent, with the mounted volunteer picnic-party, were, to the surprise of many of us, sent back, as they could be of no service and would make a considerable difference in our commissariat department.

The mystery of the runner's message was soon cleared up. It turned out that he was the bearer of bad news. A British force had been attacked in camp at Isandlwhana, and literally cut to pieces. In confirmation of the terrible message, we happened to capture about this time a Zulu soldier, belonging to the Kandampemvu Regiment, who was wearing a jacket and carrying a rifle which had belonged to a man of the 24th Regiment.

We questioned him about the battle, and the account he gave was that the soldiers and volunteers retired, fighting all the way, and as they got into the camp the Zulus intermingled with them. One party of soldiers came out from among the tents, and formed up a little above the waggons. They held their ground until their ammunition failed, when they were nearly all *assegaied*.

As I said before, what a private soldier knows about the plan of campaign is what he picks up from hearsay.

It soon leaked out that our fort was itself surrounded by Zulus, in such numbers that there was no possibility of leaving the place, either to go backward or forward, until reinforcements arrived. We were therefore put on short rations, and the small allowance of meat and flour which was doled out to us we cooked in various ways. For drinking purposes, we had a small quantity of either tea, coffee, or lime juice; but we were altogether short of vegetables and tobacco.

I kept a diary while in Ekowe, and took note of the prices realised when the luxuries left behind by the mounted volunteers were put under the hammer, on the 22nd February 1879. Most of the goods were purchased by the officers, as prices were high:—

	£	s.	d.		£	s.	d.
1½ lbs. tobacco	£1	9	0	1 small bottle of sauce	£1	1	0
1 small bottle of curry	0	14	0	1 pint of ketchup	0	15	6
1 large do.	1	7	0	1 box of sardines	0	11	0
7 cigars	0	9	0	1 bottle of ink	0	7	0
1 tin of condensed milk	0	14	6	1 pot salmon	0	15	6
1 do.	0	15	6	1 pot herrings	0	13	6
1 do.	0	18	0	1 lb. dubbin	0	9	6
1 do.	1	0	0	1 small packet of cocoa	0	11	0
1 tin of lobster .	0	13	6	1 ham (12 lbs.)	6	5	0
1 small bottle of pickles	1	6	0				

The last item, I remember, was knocked down to an officer of the 99th Regiment, who invited the colonel to dine with him in the evening; but at the appointed time the feast was given up, for some person or persons unknown had stolen the joint!

We were now compelled to keep within the fort, except that occasionally we made raids in search of vegetables. Several times we visited native *kraals*, from which a few natives would fly on our approach, and here we sometimes found growing maize or pumpkins, which on our return we cooked and ate with much relish. But these raids were not unattended with danger, for frequently the Zulus would fire at us from the bush, and then there would be one or more wounded men to bring back, and place in the hospital tent. Each day, also, some of us were told off to guard the cattle outside the fort, and bring them back in safety at nightfall.

Doleful days were these; the rain used to come down in torrents, and we made our beds beneath the waggons, upon the damp ground, while creeping things crawled and ran over us as we slept. The officers used to sleep inside the waggons, and were, so far, a little more comfortable than the rank and file, but even they were roughing it.

We made the best of our time, now and then having an ope-nair concert, with choruses by all hands, at which times a few natives might be seen in the distance listening to our melodies; and now and then our marksmen would have a shot at them, for our rifles could reach them while theirs could not carry to us.

Sometimes the tables were turned, and frequently our mounted outposts would be attacked by Zulus, who crept up to them under cover of the long grass. One poor fellow rode back to the fort with more than a dozen wounds. How he managed to keep his seat and fight his way through the enemy I cannot tell. Those who fell into the hands of the Zulus were terribly mutilated, and left on the open ground to be found by their comrades on the following day, and carried back to the fort for burial.

That word "burial" reminds me of the funerals which so frequently took place, for typhoid fever came among us, and, despite the efforts of the doctors, carried off a good number of the men. The Rev. Mr. Ritchie, our chaplain, was a splendid man, and always hopeful and light-hearted. He attended all the funerals, none of which were very ceremonious; we simply wrapped the dead men in their blankets, and laid them in their graves without a parting volley, as ammunition was precious and we had no blank cartridges.

Time dragged wearily on, and there seemed no prospect of relief. Lieutenant Rowden, of the 99th Regiment, made several exploring expeditions, and ascertained the whereabouts of the Zulus; and on two or three occasions we captured from neighbouring *kraals* a considerable quantity of cattle, which were a welcome addition to our commissariat department.

Several of the engineers who were with us manufactured a home-made heliograph, and were continually flashing signals to inform Lord Chelmsford of the desperate position we were in. For a long time, these signals appeared to be unnoticed, but at last we learned that some reinforcements had arrived from St. Helena in *H.M.S. Shah*; and these, with a number of sailors forming part of the ship's crew, and others from *H.M.S. Boadicea*, together with 3,300 whites, 1,600 natives, and a small body of cavalry numbering about 160, with rocket tubes and nine-pounders, were marching to our relief under Lord Chelmsford.

To this encouraging information our men replied, cautioning the advancing army that a force of Zulus, estimated at about 35,000, were prepared to bar their progress.

I think it was about the 2nd of April when the relieving column arrived at Ginghilovo, three-quarters of the distance to Ekowe, and here they formed a *laager*, threw up earthworks, dug shelter pits, and prepared to spend the night. At daybreak the sentries observed the enemy stealing round the camp, apparently making observations; and within an hour or two they were seen advancing, in their usual skirmishing order, with the horns extended on either side, ready to sweep round the camp and attack it upon all points.

The 60th Rifles were prepared for them at the front, and opened a terrific fire, so that the Zulus, notwithstanding their courage and recklessness, did not get within three hundred yards of the camp. Then they changed their front, and attacked the side of the camp held by the 57th and 91st Regiments, making four fierce charges, none of which brought them up to the line of bayonets.

They then made a last attack on the left of the camp, where they came within ten or fifteen feet of the muzzles of the men's rifles, a few bold spirits even rushing forward and catching hold of the latter, and stabbing at the soldiers with their *assegais*. But the British lines stood firm, and as the enemy retired the handful of cavalry charged out upon them, worrying them as they fled.

We heard later on that the loss of the Zulus was close upon a thousand, while the British lost three killed, and had thirty-seven wounded

Though we could hear the fighting, we made no sortie, but simply waited until the relief came, and I shall never forget that relief as long as I retain my wits. It *was* good to grasp the hands of men who had risked their lives for us, and how we did enjoy a "square meal" and a smoke. Our friends had brought provisions, but had carefully avoided overloading themselves. Early the next morning we made a successful raid on the *kraal* of a chief named Dabulamanzi, situated a few miles from Ekowe, and having procured some provisions, with payment in lead, we set out on our return journey to the Tugela.

As we turned our backs upon Ekowe, in which we had spent between seventy and eighty days, the Engineers blew up the fort, so as to leave nothing of which the Zulus could take advantage. We made it a rule to destroy all *kraals* which we passed on our march, so that our track was marked with smouldering ruins

These *kraals* are built something like old-fashioned straw bee-

hives. Long thin sticks are stuck into the ground in a circle, and joined together at the top; grass, straw, and twigs are threaded through the sticks, like basket-work, until the whole is weather-tight, almost air-tight, I expect, except for the small hole through which one has to crawl. The word *kraal* stands for either a village or a hut, for the huts are seldom built singly.

We had no adventures on the return march; and camping once more at the Tugela, we waited while Lord Chelmsford continued his march to Durban for the purpose of arranging a general invasion of Zululand on a larger scale, with better organisation. For we had found the people more difficult to deal with than we at first expected.

Besting by the river-side we found time to talk over what had happened, and we then learned further particulars of the massacre at Isandlwhana

Some of us were fortunate enough to receive papers from home, and I suppose every paper was read and passed on for the benefit of others. No one but a soldier on foreign service has any idea of the full value of a newspaper.

At last Lord Chelmsford fixed the 2nd of June as the day for the second general advance, which was to be made in three columns much strengthened. The first, being that with which I served, was, as on the last occasion, to proceed along the coast-road, with Durban, Fort Pearson, and Ginghilovo as its bases of operation. The second, or central column, was under Lord Chelmsford; and the third, or flying column, was commanded by General Wood.

While on the march, we learned that Sir Garnet Wolseley was to be sent out to take command over Lord Chelmsford, and was on his way on board *H.M.S. Forester*. I happened to be stationed at Port Durnford, assisting in landing stores, when the vessel arrived off the shore, but on account of the heavy sea running she returned to Durban, and disembarked Sir Garnet at that port.

Before he arrived at our camp, we were paraded and ordered to fire a general salute in honour of a victory gained by the second and third columns, and the destruction of the Zulu capital on the 4th of July.

On that day, the two British columns having met—whilst No. 1 had not overcome all its difficulties—took up a position near Ulundi, forming a large hollow square, with Gatling guns in the centre. Colonel Redvers Buller, who, with his cavalry, had done splendid service in reconnoitring the country, advanced and set the smaller *kraals* on fire. This opened the ball, and the Zulus at once commenced their attack in such numbers that the cavalry were after a while compelled to retire within the square. All assaults of the enemy were repulsed by steady volleys, and finally, seeing them wavering, Colonel Drury Lowe led a charge by the King's Dragoon Guards and scattered them in all directions.

Nothing then remained to be done but to destroy Cetewayo's *kraals*, and while this work was in progress, Mr. Archibald Forbes, the special correspondent of the *Daily News*, set off on an adventurous ride of thirty miles through the enemy's country, to report that the war was practically over.

The enemy's loss was estimated at fifteen thousand, while the English lost under a dozen, which, however, included Captain Wyatt-Edgell, and eighty wounded. The king fled from his capital, attended only by a few faithful followers, and after a wearisome chase he was run to earth on the 29th of August, and escorted to Cape Town, where, with a few wives to share his captivity, he was allowed to reside as a political prisoner.

The Buffs were sent for two years to the Straits Settlements, and three years in Hong Kong; after which we returned to England, and I quitted the army.

Lieutenant Chard's Account of Rorke's Drift

By Colonel John Rouse Merriott Chard V.C.
(also published in 1889)

We must now turn to the incidents by which Lieutenant Chard's name has become connected with the memorable defence of Rorke's Drift. He was with the 5th Company, under Captain Jones, marching up the country from Durban towards Helpmakaar, when an order arrived from Lord Chelmsford, that an officer and four sappers were to be pushed forward as rapidly as possible, in order to join the column, then about to enter Zululand from Rorke's Drift. Chard, being the senior subaltern, elected to proceed in charge of the detachment, who were placed on light carts, and arrived at Rorke's Drift on January 21st.

He proceeded with his men early on the 22nd to Isandlwana, where he found that Lord Chelmsford had marched out with the larger part of the force, but had left orders that the sappers should remain in the camp, and that Chard should be stationed at Rorke's Drift, to fortify and maintain the post covering the crossing of the river, which was effected by means of ponts or ferries. He left his men as ordered (who all lost their lives in the disaster), and on the road back met Durnford on his march to the front. He informed that officer that the Zulus appeared to be threatening the camp, and was requested to convey a message to Captain Russell, who was about a mile in rear, to hurry up with his rocket battery. This he did, and then returned to the drift, where he was placed in command of the small party at the station, by Major Spalding, who was leaving for Helpmakaar.

In his report of what followed, he says:—

At 3.15 p.m. that day, I was watching at the ponts, when two men came towards us from Zululand at a gallop. They shouted out and were taken across the river, and I was then informed by one of them—Lieut. Adendorff, of Commandant Lonsdale's regiment, who afterwards remained to assist in the defence, of the disaster befallen at the Isandula Camp, and that the Zulus were advancing upon Rorke's Drift.

I gave instructions to strike tents, and to put all stores into the wagons, while I instantly made my way to the commissariat store, and there found that a note had been received from the third column stating that the enemy was advancing in force against our post, which we were to strengthen and hold at all costs.

A company of the 24th Regiment, under Lieutenant Bromhead, was at the station, together with some details and detached men. The following were also present:—Surgeon Reynolds, Acting-Commissary Officer Dalton, Assistant-Commissary Dunne, Mr. Byrne, Commissariat Department, Lieutenant Adendorff, of Lonsdale's regiment, and the Rev. G. Smith, with 131 non-commissioned officers and men. This formed the entire garrison. There had also been present a detachment of the Natal Native Contingent, under Captain Stephenson, but both officer and men left the post and made their way to Helpmakaar. After this desertion. Chard writes—

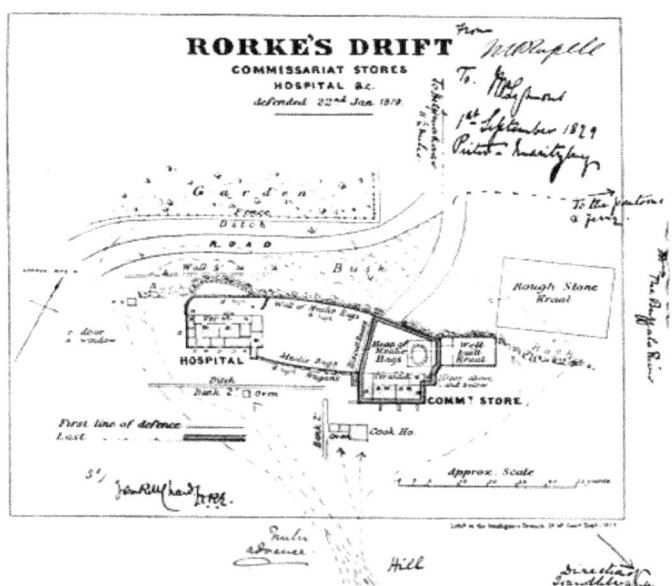

ORIGINAL SKETCH SIGNED BY CHARD

I saw that our line of defence was too extended for the small number of men now left, and at once commenced an inner entrenchment of biscuit boxes, out of which we had soon completed a wall two boxes high.

The post of Rorke's Drift was thus composed. There were two buildings, the store and the hospital, standing about 50 yards apart, running east and west, the store being to the east and projecting beyond the alignment of the hospital, thus flanking it. The inner side of the store was connected with the outer face of the hospital by a wall of mealie bags, with two wagons in the centre. Another of similar construction ran from the far corner of the inner face of the hospital, enclosing a considerable space and terminating at the further extremity of the store, where stood a well-built *kraal*, which was embraced in the general scheme of defence.

The wall of biscuit boxes built by Chard to reduce the extent of the space to be defended ran from the corner of the store nearest the hospital, to meet the wall last described, and, as events proved, was the means of securing the defence after that building was captured. The tale may be taken up in Chard's own words:—

> About 4.20 p.m. five or six hundred of the enemy came suddenly in sight around the hill to the south. They advanced at a run against our south wall, but were met by a well-sustained fire; yet, notwithstanding heavy loss, they continued to advance till within fifty yards of the wall, when their leading men encountered such a hot fire from our front, with a cross one from the store, that they were checked. Taking advantage, however, of the cover afforded by the cook-house and the ovens (these were detached buildings to the south of the post), they kept up thence heavy musketry volleys; the greater number, however, without stopping at all moved on towards their left, round our hospital and thence made a rush upon the northwest wall and our breastwork of mealie bags.
>
> After a short but desperate struggle these assailants were driven back with heavy loss into the bush around our works. Another body advancing somewhat more to the left than those who first attacked us occupied a garden in the hollow of the road, and also the bush beyond it in great force, taking special advantage of the bush which, we had not had time to cut down. The enemy was thus able to advance close to our works, and in this part

soon held one whole side of wall, while we on the other kept back a series of desperate assaults, which were made on a line extending from the hospital all along the wall as far as the bush All this time the enemy had been attempting to force the hospital, and shortly afterwards did set fire to the roof. The garrison of the hospital defended the place room by room, our men bringing out all the sick who could be moved before they retired. Private Williams, Hook, R. Jones and W. Jones of the 24th Regiment were the last four men to leave, holding the doorway against the Zulus with bayonets, their ammunition being quite expended . . . . Seeing the hospital burning and desperate attempts being made by the enemy to fire the roof of our stores, we now converted two mealie bag heaps into a sort of redoubt, which gave a second line of fire all along, Assistant-Commissary Dunne working hard at this, though much exposed, thus rendering most valuable assistance.

Darkness then came on. We were completely surrounded, and after several furious attempts had been gallantly repulsed we were eventually forced to retire to the middle and then to the inner wall of our *kraal* (this *kraal* was divided into two unequal rectangles by a division wall) on the east of the position we first had. We were sustaining throughout all this a desultory fire kept up all night, and several assaults were attempted but always repulsed with vigour, the attacks continuing till after midnight, our men firing with the greatest coolness, not wasting a single shot. The light afforded by the burning hospital proved a great advantage. At four a.m. on the 23rd January firing ceased, and at daybreak the enemy were passing out of sight, over the hill to the south-west.

Such is the succinct account of this memorable defence, as given by the chief actor therein. It requires no amplification or picturesque development to add to its impressiveness. As was well said of it by the *Cape Argus:*—

> The despatch is written by a simple subaltern of Engineers, and is couched in the plainest terms; but it reads with an eloquence words alone could not give, and tells a story that will go down to posterity among the glorious traditions of the heroes of the British race . . . . Any man may be a hero in the sense of doing a brave thing in a moment; but the highest degree of heroism

requires several qualities besides physical courage. Fortitude in the face of apparently overwhelming difficulties, strict obedience to duty, the calm courage that accepts labour, when necessary, as equal to fighting, endurance under seemingly crushing odds, these and other qualities were displayed at Rorke's Drift by Lieut. Chard and his companions.

It remains only to give the statistics of numbers and casualties. We have said that there were, all told, 131 non-commissioned officers and men present; but it must be remembered that of these thirty-five were sick in hospital, very few of whom were capable of assisting in the defence. The Zulus numbered about 3,000, and left behind them 350 dead. Their wounded were removed by them when they retired. Of the little garrison seventeen were killed and ten wounded.

It is no exaggeration to say that but for this heroic and successful defence, not only would the remainder of the third column, which had escaped the disaster of Isandlwana, have been cut off, but the torrent of Zulu invasion would have poured into Natal with results that are frightful to contemplate. Lieutenant Chard was promoted "to be Captain Supernumerary to the Establishment in recognition of his gallant services in the defence of Rorke's Drift Post against the attack of the Zulus," and in the same *Gazette* he was made a brevet major. He also received the Victoria Cross.

Private Henry Hook's Account of Rorke's Drift

Private Henry Hook, 24th Regiment, February 1905

Everything was perfectly quiet at Rorke's Drift after the column had left, and every officer and man was going about his business as usual. Not a soul suspected that only a dozen miles away the very men that we had said 'Goodbye', and 'Good luck' to were either dead or standing back-to-back in a last fierce fight with the Zulus. Our garrison consisted of B Company of the 2/24th under Lieutenant Bromhead, and details which brought the total number of us up to 139. Besides these, we had about 300 men of the Natal Native Contingent; but they didn't count, as they bolted in a body when the fight began. We were all knocking about, and I was making tea for the sick, as I was hospital cook at the time.

Suddenly there was a commotion in the camp, and we saw two men galloping towards us from the other side of the river, which was Zululand. Lieutenant Chard of the Engineers was protecting the ponts over the river and, as senior officer, was in command at the drift. The ponts were very simple affairs, one of them being supported on big barrels, and the other on boats. Lieutenant Bromhead was in the camp itself. The horsemen shouted and were brought across the river, and then we knew what had happened to our comrades. They had been butchered to a man. That was awful enough, but worse was to follow, for we were told that the Zulus were coming straight on from Isandhlwana to attack us. At the same time a note was received by Lieutenant Bromhead from the column to say that the enemy was coming on, and that the post was to be held at all costs.

For some little time, we were all stunned, then everything changed from perfect quietness to intense excitement and energy. There was a general feeling that the only safe thing was to retire and try and join the troops at Helpmakaar. The horsemen had said that the Zulus would be up in two or three minutes; but luckily for us they did not show themselves for more than an hour. Lieutenant Chard rushed up from the river, about a quarter of a mile away, and saw Lieutenant Bromhead. Orders were given to strike the camp and make ready to go, and we actually loaded up two wagons. Then Mr Dalton, of the Commissariat Department, came up and said that if we left the *drift* every man was certain to be killed. He had formerly been a sergeant major in a line regiment and was one of the bravest men that ever lived. Lieutenants Chard and Bromhead held a consultation, short and earnest, and orders were given that we were to get the hospital and storehouse ready for defence, and that we were never to say die or surrender.

Not a minute was lost. Lieutenant Bromhead superintended the loop-holing and barricading of the hospital and storehouse, and the making of a connection of the defences between the two buildings with walls of mealie-bags and wagons. The mealie-bags were good big heavy things, weighing about 200 pounds each, and during the fight many of them were burst open by *assegais* and bullets, and the mealies (Indian corn) were thickly spread about the ground. The biscuit boxes contained ordinary biscuit. They were big square wooden boxes, weighing about a hundredweight each. The meat boxes, too, were very heavy, as they contained tinned meat. They were smaller than the biscuit boxes. While all these preparations were being made, Lieutenant Chard went down to the river and brought in the pont guard of a sergeant and half a dozen men, with the wagons and gear. The two officers saw that every soldier was at his post, then we were ready for the Zulus when they cared to come.

They were not long. Just before half past four we heard firing behind the conical hill at the back of the drift, called Oskarsberg Hill, and suddenly about five or six hundred Zulus swept round, coming for us at a run. Instantly the natives—Kaffirs who had been very useful in making the barricade of wagons, mealie-bags and biscuit boxes around the camp—bolted towards Helpmakaar, and what was worse their officer and a European sergeant went with them. To see them deserting like that was too much for some of us, and we fired after them. The sergeant was struck and killed. Half a dozen of us were stationed in the hospital, with orders to hold it and guard the sick.

The ends of the building were of stone, the side walls of ordinary bricks, and the inside walls or partitions of sun-dried bricks of mud.

These shoddy inside bricks proved our salvation, as you will see. It was a queer little one-storied building, which it is almost impossible to describe; but we were pinned like rats in a hole, because all the doorways except one had been barricaded with mealie-bags, and we had done the same with the windows. The interior was divided by means of partition walls into which were fitted some very slight doors. The patients' beds were simple rough affairs of boards, raised only half a foot above the floor. To talk of hospital and beds gives the idea of a big building, but as a matter of fact this hospital was a mere little shed or bungalow, divided up into rooms so small that you could hardly swing a bayonet in them. There were about nine men who could not move, but altogether there were about thirty. Most of these, however, could help to defend themselves.

As soon as our Kaffirs bolted, it was seen that the fort as we had first made it was too big to be held, so Lieutenant Chard instantly reduced the space by having a row of biscuit boxes drawn across the middle, above four feet high. This was our inner entrenchment, and proved very valuable. The Zulus came on at a wild rush, and although many of them were shot down they got to within about fifty yards of our south wall of mealie-bags and biscuit boxes and wagons. They were caught between two fires, that from the hospital and that from the storehouse, and were checked; but they gained the shelter of the cookhouse and ovens, and gave us many heavy volleys.

During the fight they took advantage of every bit of cover there was, anthills, a tract of bush that we had not had time to clear away, a garden or sort of orchard which was near us, and a ledge of rock and some caves (on the Oskarsberg) which were only about a hundred yards away. They neglected nothing, and while they went on firing large bodies kept hurling themselves against our slender breastworks.

But it was the hospital they assaulted most fiercely. I had charge with a man that we called Old King Cole of a small room with only one patient in it. Cole kept with me for some time after the fight began, then he said he was not going to stay. He went outside and was instantly killed by the Zulus, so that I was left alone with the patient, a native whose leg was broken and who kept crying out, 'Take my bandage off, so that I can come'. But it was impossible to do anything except fight, and I blazed away as hard as I could.

By this time, I was the only defender of my room. Poor Old King Cole was lying dead outside and the helpless patient was crying and groaning near me. The Zulus were swarming around us, and there was an extraordinary rattle as the bullets struck the biscuit boxes, and queer thuds as they plumped into the bags of mealies. Then there were the whizz and rip of the *assegais*, of which I had experience during the Kaffir Campaign of 1877-78. We had plenty of ammunition, but we were told to save it and so we took careful aim at every shot, and hardly a cartridge was wasted. One of my comrades, Private Dunbar, shot no fewer than nine Zulus, one of them being a chief.

From the very first the enemy tried to rush the hospital, and at last they managed to set fire to the thick grass which formed the roof. This put us in a terrible plight, because it meant that we were either to be massacred or burned alive, or get out of the building. To get out seemed impossible; for if we left the hospital by the only door which had been left open, we should instantly fall into the midst of the Zulus. Besides, there were the helpless sick and wounded, and we could not leave them. My own little room communicated with another by means of a frail door like a bedroom door. Fire and dense choking smoke forced me to get out and go into the other room. It was impossible to take the native patient with me, and I had to leave him to an awful fate. But his death was, at any rate, a merciful one. I heard the Zulus asking him questions, and he tried to tear off his bandages and escape.

In the room where I now was there were nine sick men, and I was alone to look after them for some time, still firing away, with the hospital burning. Suddenly in the thick smoke I saw John Williams, and above the din of battle and the cries of the wounded I heard him shout, 'The Zulus are swarming all over the place. They've dragged Joseph Williams out and killed him.' John Williams had held the other room with Private William Horrigan for more than an hour, until they had not a cartridge left. The Zulus then burst in and dragged out Joseph Williams and two of the patients, and *assegaied* them.

It was only because they were so busy with this slaughtering that John Williams and two of the patients were able to knock a hole in the partition and get into the room where I was posted. Horrigan was killed. What were we to do? We were pinned like rats in a hole. Already the Zulus were fiercely trying to burst in through the doorway. The only way of escape was the wall itself by making a hole big enough for a man to crawl through into an adjoining room, and so on until we got to our inmost entrenchment outside. Williams worked desperately at the wall with the navvy's pick, which I had been using to make some of the loopholes with.

All this time the Zulus were trying to get into the room. Their *assegais* kept whizzing towards us, and one struck me in front of the helmet. We were wearing the white tropical helmets then. But the helmet tilted back under the blow and made the spear lose its power, so that I escaped with a scalp wound which did not trouble me much then, although it has often caused me illness since. Only one man at a time could get in at the door. A big Zulu sprang forward and seized my rifle, but I tore it free and, slipping a cartridge in, I shot him point-blank.

Time after time the Zulus gripped the muzzle and tried to tear the rifle from my grasp, and time after time I wrenched it back, because I had a better grip than they had. All this time, Williams was getting the sick through the hole into the next room, all except one, a soldier of the 24th named Conley, who could not move because of a broken leg. Watching for my chance I dashed from the doorway, and grabbing Conley I pulled him after me through the hole. His leg got broken again, but there was no help for it. As we left the room the Zulus burst in with furious cries of disappointment and rage.

Now there was a repetition of the work of holding the doorway, except that I had to stand by a hole instead of a door, while Williams picked away at the far wall to make an opening for escape into the next room. There was more desperate and almost hopeless fighting, as it seemed, but most of the poor fellows were got through the hole. Again, I had to drag Conley through, a terrific task because he was a very heavy man. We were now all in a little room that gave upon the inner line of defence which had been made. We (Williams and Robert Jones and William Jones and myself) were the last men to leave the hospital, after most of the sick and wounded had been carried through the small window and away from the burning building; but it was impossible to save a few of them, and they were butchered.

Privates William Jones and Robert Jones during all this time were doing magnificent work in another ward which faced the hill. They kept at it with bullet and bayonet until six of the seven patients had been removed. They would have got the seventh, Sergeant Maxfield, out safely, but he was delirious with fever and, although they managed to dress him, he refused to move. Robert Jones made a last rush to try and get him away like the rest, but when he got back into the room, he saw that Maxfield was being stabbed by the Zulus as he lay on his bed. Corporal Allen and Private Hitch helped greatly in keeping up communication with the hospital. They were both badly wounded, but when they could not fight any longer, they served out ammunition to their comrades throughout the night

As we got the sick and wounded out, they were taken to a verandah in front of the storehouse, and Dr Reynolds under a heavy fire and clouds of *assegais*, did everything he could for them. All this time, of course, the storehouse was being valiantly defended by the rest of the garrison. When we got into the inner fort, I took my post at a place where two men had been shot. While I was there another man was shot in the neck, I think by a bullet which came through the space between two biscuit boxes that were not quite close together. This was at about six o'clock in the evening, nearly two hours after the opening shot of the battle had been fired. Every now and then the Zulus would make a rush for it and get in. We had to charge them out.

By this time, it was dark, and the hospital was all in flames, but this gave us a splendid light to fight by. I believe it was this light that saved us. We could see them coming, and they could not rush us and take us by surprise from any point. They could not get at us, and so they went away and had ten or fifteen minutes of a war-dance. This roused them up again, and their excitement was so intense that the ground fairly seemed to shake. Then, when they were goaded to the highest pitch, they would hurl themselves at us again.

The long night passed and the day broke. Then we looked around us to see what had happened, and there was not a living soul who was not thankful to find that the Zulus had had enough of it and were disappearing over the hill to the south-west. Orders were given to patrol the ground, collect the arms of the dead blacks, and make our position as strong as possible in case of fresh attacks.

One of the first things I did was to go up to the man who was still looking over our breastworks with his rifle presented to the spot where so many of the Zulus had been. I went up to him, and saw that he did not move, and that he looked very quiet. I went nearer and said 'Hello, what are you doing here?' He made no answer, and did not stir. I went still closer, and something in his appearance made me tilt his helmet back, as you sometimes tilt back a hat when you want to look closely into a face. As I did so I saw a bullet-mark in his forehead, and knew that he was dead.

I went away, and was walking up the dry bed of a little stream near the drift with my own rifle in my right hand and a bunch of *assegais* over my left shoulder. Suddenly I came across an unarmed Zulu lying on the ground, apparently dead but bleeding from the leg. Thinking it strange that a dead man should bleed, I hesitated, and wondered whether I should go on, as other Zulus might be lurking about. But I resumed my task. Just as I was passing, the supposed dead man seized the butt of my rifle and tried to drag it away. The bunch of *assegais* rattled to earth.

The Zulu suddenly released his grasp of the rifle with one hand, and with the other fiercely endeavoured to drag me down. The fight was short and sharp; but it ended by the Zulu being struck in the chest with the butt and knocked to the ground. The rest was quickly over.

There was no time to sit down and mope, and there were the sick and wounded as well as the rest to look after. So, when the commander-in-chief arrived, I was back at my cooking in my shirtsleeves, making tea for the sick. A sergeant ran up and said, 'Lieutenant Bromhead wants you.'

'Wait till I put my coat on,' I said.

'Come as you are, straight away,' he ordered, and with my braces hanging about me, I went into the midst of the officers. Lord Chelmsford asked me all about the defence of the hospital, as I was the last to leave the building. An officer took our names, and wrote down what we had done. When the relief had come up the men of the column were sent out to bury the Zulus. There were 351 dead blacks counted, and these were put into two big holes in front of the hospital. The column made the Kaffirs who were with them dig the trenches, but although they dug the holes, they positively refused to bury the bodies. There were only a few badly wounded left, as the Zulus had carried off their wounded as they retired. A great many dead were found in a mealie field not far from the hospital.

As for our own comrades, we buried them. This was done the day after the fight, not far from the place where they fell, and at the foot of the hill. Soon afterwards the cemetery was walled in and a monument was put up in the middle. The lettering was cut on it by a bandsman named Mellsop, who used bits of broken bayonets as chisels. He drew a capital picture of the fight. Those who had been killed in action were buried on one side of the cemetery, and those who had died of disease on the other side. A curious thing was that a civilian named Byrne, who had taken part in the defence and was killed, was buried outside the cemetery wall. I don't know why, except that he was not a regular soldier.

Rorke's Drift: An Overview of the Assault
By C. Stein

At the end of 1878 there stood upon a rocky terrace on the Natal side of the Buffalo River two stone buildings with thatched roofs, which had formed a Swedish mission station, one of them having been used as a church and the other having been the dwelling of the missionary. These two humble edifices were destined to be, on the 22nd January, 1879, the scene of the most brilliant feat of arms performed during the whole Zulu War—a defence by a small determined force against the attack of vastly superior numbers, an exploit whose lustre, relieving a period of disaster, maintained the prestige of British arms, and whose success, there can be little doubt, rescued Natal from invasion when failure would have laid the colony open to the advance of a savage enemy.

So perfect was the conduct of the officers and men concerned in the episode, and so well-conceived and executed were the measures adopted, that even foreign military books quote the exploit as an example of the value of improvised fortifications when they are held by brave men.

When war was declared by Sir Bartle Frere, the High Commissioner for South Africa, against Cetewayo, the Zulu king, the conduct of operations was placed in the hands of Lieutenant-General Lord Chelmsford, K.C.B., as Commander-in-Chief. It was determined to invade Zululand, and all the forces available for this purpose were moved to the frontier. They were divided into five columns, of which three were to advance into the enemy's country from different points, with the intention of finally concentrating at Ulundi, the Zulu capital, while the other two were in the first instance to guard the frontier against possible Zulu raids. The third column, under the command of

Colonel Glyn, C.B., the centre of the three columns of invasion, was to assemble near Rorke's Drift and cross the Buffalo River at that spot, within a mile of the old Swedish mission station.

The river at Rorke's Drift was, like most African streams, an impassable torrent after rain, but the flood quickly ran off, and a passage could then be effected by the "*drift*," or ford. There had also been established two ponts, or big, flat-bottomed ferry-boats, each of which could transport an African wagon or a company of infantry.

Colonel Glyn's column crossed the river on the 11th of January, 1879, and from that time was engaged in operations in Zululand. Its line of communications with Pietermaritzburg, the chief city of Natal, was through Rorke's Drift to Helpmakaar, and thence by Ladysmith and Estcourt, or by the shorter, though more difficult, route through Greytown. Rorke's Drift, as the actual starting point of invasion, was formed into a depot of stores and a hospital. The deserted mission-station buildings were utilized for this purpose, the old church being converted into a storehouse and the missionary's dwelling forming the hospital.

As a garrison for the important post and to secure the passage across the river, Colonel Glyn left B Company of the second battalion of the Twenty-fourth Regiment, under command of Lieutenant Gonville Bromhead. With him were also Major Spalding, who was in general charge of the line of communications, Lieutenant Chard, Royal Engineers, Surgeon Reynolds, Army Medical Department, and other officers. This garrison was encamped near the store and hospital.

For some days after the departure of the third column, which was also accompanied by Lord Chelmsford and the Headquarter Staff, the quiet routine of duty was pursued. Letters were passed to and from the front, necessary stores and supplies were sent on, and the men wounded in the first engagements were received into the hospital. Among these last was one of the enemy, who had been shot through the thigh at Sirayo's *kraal*, and who was treated and nursed with the same care and attention as the Englishmen against whom he had fought.

On the 20th of January, however, a large portion of the second column, under Colonel Durnford, Royal Engineers, arrived at Rorke's Drift and encamped. Their stay was brief, for they were summoned to the fatal camp of Insandhlwana on the morning of the 22nd, Colonel Durnford leaving a company of the Natal Native Contingent, under Captain Stephenson, to strengthen the little post. It became evident from various circumstances that Colonel Glyn's column was encountering a stronger resistance than had been anticipated, and that, as the enemy were in force within a few miles, they might make a rapid descent upon the weakly guarded line of communications.

It was known that two companies of the First Battalion of the Twenty-Fourth were at Helpmakaar, ten miles distant, and Major Spalding resolved to go there at once in order to bring them up as a reinforcement to Lieutenant Bromhead's force. In his absence, Lieutenant Chard became senior officer at Rorke's Drift, and responsible for its well-being.

Although on the 22nd of January there was thus a feeling of uneasiness at the river post, nothing had occurred till some hours after midday to cause any special alarm to its garrison. We may believe that a general plan of action had been considered if an attack should be made upon it, but in the meantime all the officers and men were engaged in their usual employments.

Lieutenant Chard was at the ponts, and Lieutenant Bromhead was in his little camp hard by the store and hospital. Shortly after three p.m. two mounted men were seen galloping at headlong speed towards the ferry from Zululand. There is little difficulty in recognising messengers of disaster, the men who ride with the avenger of blood close on their horses' track, and Chard, who met them, knew that something terrible had happened. His worst anticipations were more than realised when the two fugitives—Lieutenant Adendorff, of the Native Contingent, and a Natal volunteer—told their story: the camp at Insandhlwana had been attacked and taken by the enemy, of whom a large force was now advancing on Rorke's Drift.

The Natal volunteer hurried on to give the alarm at Helpmakaar; but one man was enough for this service, and Adendorff—gallant fellow!—said that he would remain at Rorke's Drift, where every additional European would be a valuable reinforcement, and cast in his lot with its defenders. Chard at once gave orders to the guard at the ponts to strike their tents, put all stores on the spot into the wagon, and withdraw to the main body of the post. Now occurred the first incident which testified to the spirit which animated the small force on the banks of the Buffalo.

The ferryman—Daniells—and Sergeant Milne, of the Third Buffs (who was doing duty with the Twenty-Fourth), proposed that they should be allowed to moor the two ponts in the middle of the river, and offered, with the ferry-guard of six men, to defend them against attack—a brave thought, indeed, but it was put aside. Chard was too good a soldier to divide his few men in any way. He saw at once that the commissariat stores and hospital would require every available rifle for their defence, and that the safety of every other place was comparatively a very minor consideration.

While he was giving his orders an urgent message came from Bromhead asking him to join him at once. To Bromhead also had come several mounted men fleeing from Insandhlwana, bearing the same dread intelligence which Adendorff had brought to the ferry, and the trained officer of engineers was required to concert and decide upon measures of defence. But when the engineer joined the infantry subaltern, he found that the latter, aided by Assistant-Commissary Dunne, had already begun the necessary work, and that there was nothing to change, if much was still left to complete. The three officers held a hurried consultation, and prompt use was made of all ordinary expedients of war, while materials never before employed in fortification were pressed into service.

The store and hospital were loop-holed and barricaded, the windows and doors blocked with mattresses; but it was necessary to connect the defence of the two buildings by a parapet. There were no stones at hand with which to build a wall, and if there had been, there was no time to make use of them; the hard, rocky soil could not be dug and formed into ditch and breastwork; but there was a great store of bags of mealies, or the grain of Indian corn, which had been collected as horse provender for the army. Assistant-Commissary Dunne suggested that these should be used in the fashion of sand-bags for the construction of the required parapet.

Everybody laboured with the energy of men who know that their safety depends on their exertions. Chard and Bromhead, Surgeon Reynolds and Dunne not merely directed, but engaged most energetically in the work of preparation. When the alarm was first given, it was intended to remove the worst cases from the hospital to a place of safety, and two wagons were prepared for the purpose; but it was found that the attempt to move the patients at the slow pace of ox-teams when the Zulus were so close at hand would only result in offering them as easy victims to the murderous *assegai*. The two wagons were therefore used as part of the defences, and mealie bags were piled underneath and upon them, so that each formed a strong post of vantage.

The ferry-guard had joined the rest of the force at 3.30 p.m., and a few minutes later an officer of Durnford's Natal Native Horse, with a hundred of his men who had been heavily engaged at Insandhlwana, rode up and asked for orders. Chard directed him to watch for the approach of the enemy, sending out vedettes, and when he was pressed, to fall back and assist in the defence of the post. So far it seemed certain that when the threatened Zulu attack developed itself against the Rorke's Drift fortifications they would be found, though hurriedly devised and executed, to be adequately defended by the company of the Twenty-Fourth, Captain Stephenson's company of the Native Contingent, and about a hundred Basutos of the Natal Native Horse.

But if the gallant English officers who had striven so hard and with so much military genius to make their position tenable looked forward to this amount of support, they were destined to grievous disappointment and mortification. At 4.15 p.m. the sound of firing was heard behind a hill towards the south, and told that the vedettes of the Native Horse were engaged with the enemy. Their officer returned, reporting that the Zulus were close at hand, and that his men would not obey orders. Chard and his comrades had the sore trial of seeing them all moving off towards Helpmakaar, leaving the garrison to its fate. Nor was this all. The evil example was only too soon followed. Captain Stephenson's company of the Native Contingent also felt their hearts fail, and, accompanied by their commander, also fled from the post of duty.

For the Native Horse there is some excuse to be made. They had been in the saddle since daybreak; they were the survivors of a terrible defeat and massacre; they had seen a large number of their comrades slain, and they were demoralised by the loss of their beloved commander, Colonel Durnford. If on this occasion their valour failed them, it is to be remembered that they had behaved nobly in the early part of the day, and that in later episodes of the war their gallantry and self-devotion were proverbial.

But for the Native Contingent company nothing can be said. They were fresh, and as yet unscathed by war; they had the best example in the calm demeanour of their English comrades, and they had many causes of feud and quarrel with the enemy. But, as in all other occasions of the war where Natal Kaffirs were employed, they gave way in time of stress, and the greatest shame of the matter was that their colonial European officer now shared their misconduct.

The garrison at Rorke's Drift was now reduced to Bromhead's company of the Twenty-Fourth—about eighty strong—and some men of other corps, the total number within the post being One hundred thirty-nine, of whom thirty-five were sick or wounded men in hospital. The original scheme of defence had provided for a much larger force, and Chard recognised that it would now be impossible long to occupy effectively the range of parapets and loopholes which had been prepared. There was nothing for it but to form an inner line of defence, to which the garrison might fall back when the outer line became untenable.

He decided that, if necessary, the hospital must be abandoned, and that the defence must be restricted to the store and the space in front of it, including a well-built stone *kraal* or enclosure which abutted on it to the eastward. To carry out this plan he commenced an inner retrenchment, forming a parapet of biscuit-boxes across the larger enclosure. This was only about two boxes high when the expected flood of attack hurled its first waves against the frail solitary bulwark which stood between Natal and savage invasion.

About 4.30 p.m. five or six hundred of the enemy appeared, sweeping round the rocky hill to the south of the post, and advancing at the swift pace characteristic of the Zulu warriors against the south wall which connected the store and hospital. But they had to deal with stern men who were braced up for the encounter by feelings of duty, patriotism, and the long habit of regimental discipline and comradeship which makes each feel assured and confident that all are striving shoulder to shoulder, and that none will blench from his appointed place. From the parapet of mealie bags and from the hospital poured forth a heavy and well-sustained fire, which was crossed by a flanking discharge from the store. No man wasted a shot, and the aim was cool and deliberate.

Even Zulu valour and determination could not face the deadly leaden hail, and the onslaught weakened and broke within fifty yards of the British rifles. Some of the assailants swerved to their left, and passed round to the west of the hospital; some sought cover where they could, and occupied banks, ditches, bushes, and the cooking place of the garrison. But this first attack was only the effort of the enemy's advanced guard. Masses of warriors followed and flowed over the elevated southward ledge of rocks overlooking the buildings. Every cave and crevice was quickly filled, and from these sheltered and commanding positions they opened a heavy and continuous fire. It was fortunate that the spoil in rifles and ammunition taken at Insandhlwana was not yet available for use against the English, as at Kambula and later engagements, but the enemy's firearms were still the old muskets and rifles of which they had long been in possession. Even so, at the short range these were sufficiently effective, and, in the hands of better marksmen than Zulus usually are, might have inflicted crushing losses.

The first attack repulsed, a second desperate effort was made by the enemy against the northwest wall just below the hospital; but here again the defenders were ready to meet it, and again the assailing torrent broke and fell back. Such of the sick and wounded in the hospitals as were able to rouse themselves from their beds of pain had by this time seized rifle and bayonet and joined their comrades; but though every man was now mustered, the total number was all too small for the grim task before them.

The misfortune of the extreme hurry in the preparations for defence was now painfully apparent. In strengthening any position for defensive occupation one of the first measures taken by a commander is to clear as large an open space as possible round the parapet or fortifications which he proposes to hold. All ditches and hollows should be filled up; all buildings, walls, and heaps of refuse should be pulled down and scattered; all trees, shrubs, and thick herbage should be cut and removed; so that no attack can be made under cover, no safe place may be found from which deliberate fire may be delivered, or any movement can be made by an enemy unseen, and therefore unanticipated.

At Rorke's Drift, not only were the buildings and parapets overlooked and commanded to the southward by a rocky hill full of caves and lurking-places, but there was a garden to the north, a thick patch of bush which was close to the parapet, a square Kaffir house and large brick oven and cooking trenches, besides numerous banks, walls, and ditches, all of which offered a shelter to the enemy, which they were not slow to profit by. The post was encircled by a dense ring of the foe, and from every side came the whistle of their bullets.

Up till this time, though several men had been wounded, no one had been struck dead. Suddenly a whisper passed round among the Twenty-fourth, "Poor old King Cole is killed." Private Cole, who was known by this affectionate Barrack-room nickname, was at the parapet when a bullet passed through his head, and he fell doing his duty a noble end.

If the Zulu fire was telling, however, the steady marksmanship of the English officers and men was still more effective. Private Dunbar, of the Twenty-Fourth, laid low a mounted chief who was conspicuous in directing the enemy, and immediately afterwards shot eight warriors in as many successive shots. Everywhere the officers were present with words of encouragement, exposing themselves fearlessly and showing that iron coolness and self-possession which rouses such confidence and emulation in soldiery on a day of battle.

Assistant-Commissary Dunne—a man of great stature and physique, with a long, flowing beard—was continually going along the parapet, cheering the men and using the rifle with deadly effect. There was a rush of Zulus against the spot where he was, led by a huge man, whose leopard-skin *kaross* marked the chief. Dunne called out "Pot that fellow!" and himself aimed over the parapet at another, when his rifle dropped from his hand, and he spun round with suddenly pallid face, shot through the right shoulder. Surgeon Reynolds was by his side at once, and bound up the wound.

Unable any longer to use his rifle, he handed it to storekeeper Byrne, but continued unmoved to superintend the men near to him and to direct their fire. Byrne took his place at the parapet, and his bullets were not wasted. In a few minutes Corporal Scammel, Natal Native Contingent, who was next to him, was shot through the shoulder and back. He fell, and crawling to Chard, who was fighting side by side with the men, handed him the remainder of his cartridges. In his agony he asked for a drink of water. Byrne at once fetched it for him, and whilst handing it to the suffering soldier was himself shot through the head, and fell prone, a dead man.

While fighting was thus going on all round the post, a series of specially determined attacks was made against the northern side. Here the Zulus were able to collect under cover of the garden and patch of bush, and from that shelter were able to rush untouched close up to the parapet. Soon they were on one side of the barricade, while the defenders held the other, and across it there was a hand-to-hand struggle of the bayonet against the broad-bladed *bangwan*, the stabbing *assegai*. So close were the combatants that the Zulus seized the English bayonets, and in two instances even succeeded in wrenching them from the rifles, though in each case the breech-loader took a stern vengeance.

The muzzles of the opposing firearms were almost touching each other, and the discharge of a musket blew the broad "dopper" hat from the head of Corporal Schiess, of the Natal Native Contingent. This man (a Swiss by birth), who had been a patient in hospital, leaped on to the parapet and bayoneted the man who fired, regained his place, and shot another; then, repeating his former exploit, again leaped on

THERE WAS A HAND-TO-HAND STRUGGLE

the top of the mealie bags and bayoneted a third. Early in the fight he had been struck by a bullet in the instep, but, though suffering acute pain, he left not his post, and was only maddened to perform deeds of heroic daring.

The struggle here was too severe and unequal to be long continued. Besides the ceaseless attacks of their enemy in front, the defenders of the parapet were exposed to the fire which took them in reverse from the high hill to the south. Five soldiers had been thus shot dead in a short space of time. At six p.m. the order was given to retire behind the retrenchment of biscuit-boxes. When the defence of the parapet was thus removed, the dark crowd of Zulus surged over the mealie bags to attack the hospital; but such a heavy fire was sent from the line of the retrenchment that nearly every man who leaped into the enclosure perished in the effort. Again and again, they charged forward, shouting their war-cry "*Usutu! Usutu!*" and ever the death-dealing volleys smote them to the ground.

The story has now been told of the struggle during the first hour and a half about the storehouse and large enclosure, till the moment came when it was no longer possible to hold the whole of the defences as they were at first organised, and Chard was constrained to withdraw behind the biscuit-box retrenchment which his foresight had provided. All this time the enemy had been making fierce and constantly reiterated attempts to force their way into the hospital, which was at the west end of the enclosure. Here Bromhead personally superintended the resistance, and here deeds of military prowess, cool presence of mind, and glorious self-devotion were performed to be proud of.

It has been said that the building had a thatched roof, and the Zulus not only strove to force an ingress, but used every expedient to set the thatch on fire, and thus to destroy the poor stronghold which so long mocked at their attempts to take it. While many of the patients whose ailments were comparatively slight had risen from their pallets and taken an active part in the defence, there were several poor fellows, utterly helpless, distributed among the different wards; and it is difficult to conceive a situation more trying than theirs must have been, listening to the demoniac yells of the savages, only separated from them by a thin wall, thirsting for their blood. At every window were one or two comrades, firing till the rifles were heated to scorching by the unceasing discharge.

Bullets splashed upon the walls, and the air reeked with dense, sulphurous smoke. The combatants may have been excited and carried away by the mad fury of battle; but to men depressed by disease, weakened and racked with pain, truly the minutes must have been long and terrible in their mental and physical suffering. Shortly after five o'clock the Zulus had been able so far to break down the entrance to the room at the extreme end of the hospital that they were able to charge at the opening; but Bromhead was there, and drove them back time after time with the bayonet.

As long as the enclosure was held, they failed in every fierce attempt. Private Joseph Williams was firing from a small window hard by, and on the next morning fourteen warriors were found dead beneath it, besides others along his line of fire. When his ammunition was expended, he joined his brother, Private John Williams, and two of the patients who also had fired their last cartridge, and with them guarded the door with their bayonets. No longer able to keep their opponents at a distance, the four stood grimly resolute, waiting till the door was battered in and they stood face to face with the foe.

Then followed a death struggle. The English bayonet crossed the broad-bladed *bangwan*, the stalwart Warwickshire lads met the lithe and muscular tribesmen of Cetewayo, and the weapons glinted thirsty for blood. In the *mêlée* poor Joseph Williams was grappled with by two Zulus, his hands were seized, and, dragged out from among his comrades, he was killed before their eyes. But now it was known that the hospital must be abandoned, and as the usual path was occupied by the enemy, a way had to be made through the partition walls. John Williams and the two patients succeeded in making a passage with an axe into the adjoining room, where they were joined by Private Henry Hook. John Williams and Hook then took it in turn to guard the hole through which the little party had come, with the bayonet, and keep the foe at bay, while the others worked at cutting a further passage.

In this retreat from room to room, another brave soldier, Private Jenkins, met the same fate as did Joseph Williams, and was dragged to his death by the pursuers. The others at last arrived at a window looking into the enclosure towards the storehouse, and, leaping from it, ran the gauntlet of the enemy's fire till they reached their comrades behind the biscuit-box retrenchment. To the devoted bravery and cool resource of Private John Williams and Hook, eight patients, who had been in the several wards which they had traversed, owed their lives. If it had not been for the assistance of these two gallant men, all the eight would have perished where they lay. These, however, were only some of the hairbreadth escapes from the hospital, and only some of the deeds of stubborn hardihood performed in it.

A few of the sick men were half carried, half led, by chivalrous comrades across the enclosure to the retrenchment, but many had to make their own way over the space now swept by the Zulu bullets, and that that space was clear was due to the steady fire maintained by Chard, which prevented the Zulus themselves from leaving the spots where they were under cover. Trooper Hunter, Natal Mounted Police, a very tall young man, who had been a patient, essayed the rush to safety, but he was hit and fell before he reached his goal.

Corporal Mayer, Natal Native Contingent, who had been wounded in the knee by an *assegai*-thrust in one of the early engagements of the campaign, Bombardier Lewis, Royal Artillery, whose leg and thigh were swollen and disabled from a wagon accident, and Trooper Green, Natal Police, also a nearly helpless invalid, all got out of a little window looking into the enclosure. The window was at some distance from the ground, and each man fell in escaping from it. All had to crawl (for none of them could walk) through the enemy's fire, and all passed scatheless into the retrenchment except Green, who was struck on the thigh.

In one of the wards facing the hill on the south side of the hospital, Privates William Jones and Robert Jones had been posted. There were seven patients in the ward, and these two men defended their post till six of the seven patients had been removed. The seventh was Sergeant Maxfield, who, delirious with fever, resisted all attempts to move him. Robert Jones, with rare courage and devotion, went back a second time to try to carry him out, but found the ward already full of Zulus, and the poor sergeant stabbed to death on his bed.

It has been mentioned that a wounded prisoner was being treated in the hospital. So much had he been impressed by the kindness which he had received, that he was anxious to assist in the defence. He said "he was not afraid of the Zulus, but he wanted a gun." His newborn goodwill was not, however, tested. When the ward in which he lay was forced, Private Hook, who was assisting the Englishmen in the next room, heard the Zulus talking to him. The next day his charred remains were found in the ashes of the building.

That communication was kept up with the hospital at all, and that it was possible to effect the removal of so many patients, was due in great part to the conduct of Corporal Allen and Private Hitch. These two soldiers together, in defiance of danger, held a most exposed position, raked in reverse by the fire from the hill, till both were severely wounded. Their determined bravery had its result in the safety of their comrades. Even after they were incapacitated from further fighting, they never ceased, when their wounds had been dressed, to serve out ammunition from the reserve throughout the rest of the combat.

When the defence of the hospital was relaxed, it had been easy for the enemy to carry out their plan of setting fire to the thatched roof, and now the whole was in a blaze, the flames rising high and casting a lurid glare over the scene of conflict. The last men who effected their retreat from the building had as much to dread from the spreading conflagration as from the Zulu *assegais*. We have seen that, from the want of interior communication, it had been necessary for those who did escape to cut their way from room to room.

Alas! to some of the patients, it had been impossible for the anxious leader and his stanch, willing followers to penetrate. Defeated by the flames and by the numbers of their opponents, Chard records in his official despatch:

"With the most heartfelt sorrow, I regret we could not save these poor fellows from their terrible fate."

While in the hospital the last struggle was going on, Chard's unfailing resource had provided another element of strength to his now restricted line of defence, and had formed a place of comparative security for the reception of his wounded men. In the small yard by the storehouse were two large piles of mealie bags. These, with the assistance of two or three men and Dunne, who, severely wounded as he was, continued working with unabated energy and determination, he formed into an oblong and sufficiently high redoubt.

In the hollow space in its centre were laid the sick and wounded, while its crest gave a second line of fire, which swept much of the ground that could not be seen by the occupiers of the lower parapets. As the intrepid men were making this redoubt, their object was quickly detected by the enemy, who poured upon them a rain of bullets; but fortunately unhurt, they completed their work.

The night had fallen, and the light from the burning hospital was now of the greatest service to the defender, as it illumined every spot for hundreds of yards round, and gave every advantage to the trained riflemen of the Twenty-Fourth. The Zulu losses had been tremendously heavy; but still they pressed their unremitting attack. Rush after rush was made right up to the parapets so strenuously held, and their musketry fire never slackened. The outer wall of the stone *kraal* on the east of the store had to be abandoned, and finally the garrison was confined to the commissariat store, the enclosure just in front of it, the inner wall of the *kraal*, and the redoubt of mealie bags. But the steadfastness of the defenders was never impaired. Still every man fired with the greatest coolness.

Not a shot was wasted, and Rorke's Drift Station remained still proudly impregnable. At 10 p.m. the hospital fire had burnt itself out, and darkness settled over defence and attack. It was not till midnight, however, that the Zulus began to lose heart, and give to the garrison some breathing space and repose. Desultory firing still continued from the hill to the southward, and from the bush and garden in front; but there were no more attacks in force, and the stress of siege was practically over.

The dark hours were full of anxiety, and even the stout hearts which had not quailed during the long period of trial that was past must have had some feeling of disquietude for the morrow, lest wearied, reduced in numbers, and with slender supply of water, they should be called upon to meet renewed efforts made by a reenforced foe. The dawn came at last, and the eyes of all were gladdened by seeing the rear of the Zulu masses retiring round the shoulder of the hill from which their first attack had been made. The supreme tension of mind and body was over, and if the struggle had been long and stern the victory was for the time complete.

How bitterly it had been fought out was shown by the piles of the enemy's dead lying around, and by the silence of familiar voices when the roll was called. There was yet no rest. The enemy might take heart and return, for, though many of their warriors had seen their last fight, their numbers were so overwhelming, and they must have known so well how close had been the pressure of their attack, that they might well think that, with renewed efforts, success was more than possible. Patrols were sent out to collect the arms left lying on the field. The defences were strengthened, and, mindful of the fate of the hospital, a working party was ordered to remove the thatch from the roof of the store.

The men who were not employed otherwise were kept manning the parapets, and all were ready at once to snatch up their rifles and again to hold the post which they had guarded so long. A friendly Kaffir was sent to Helpmakaar, saying that they were still safe, and asking for assistance. About seven a.m. a mass of the enemy was seen on the hills to the southwest, and it seemed as if another onslaught was threatened. They were advancing slowly when the remains of the third column appeared in the distance, coming from Insandhlwana, and, as the English approached, the threatening mass retired, and finally disappeared.

Lord Chelmsford, Colonel Glyn, and that part of their force which, having been engaged elsewhere, had not been in the Insandhlwana camp when it was attacked and taken, had passed the night in sad and anxious bivouac among the dead bodies of their comrades and the debris of a most melancholy disaster. Full of disquietude about the fate of the post at Rorke's Drift, and the line of communications, they had pushed on with earliest dawn. Their advanced guard of mounted men strained eager eyes towards Rorke's Drift.

The British flag still waved over the storehouse, and figures in red coats could be seen moving about the place. But smoke was rising where the hospital had stood, and, remembering that the victorious Zulus at Insandhlwana had clad themselves in the uniforms of the dead, there was a moment of dread uncertainty to the officer who was leading the way. But surely that was a faint British cheer rising from the post! A few hundred yards more of advance, and it was known that here at least no mistake had been made; here courage and determination had not been shown in vain; and that here something had been done to restore the confidence in British prowess which had just received so rude a shock elsewhere.

What a sight was the spot in the bright morning sunlight! There lay hundreds of Zulus either dead or gasping out the last remains of life; there was the grim and grey old warrior lying side by side with the young man who had come "to wash his *assegai*"; there a convulsive movement of arm or leg, the rolling of a slowly glazing eye, or the heaving of a bullet-pierced chest showed that life was not quite extinct; and there were the defenders, wan, battle-stained, and weary, but with the proud light of triumph in their glance, standing by the fortifications which they had so stoutly held—fortifications so small, so frail, that it seemed marvellous how they had been made to serve their purpose.

The skeleton of the hospital still was there, but its roof and woodwork had fallen in, and in the still smoking pile men were searching for the remains of lost comrades. And there, in the corner of the enclosure, reverently covered and guarded, were the bodies of the dead who had given their lives for England and sealed their devotion to duty with their blood. Well might Lord Chelmsford congratulate the defenders of Rorke's Drift on the brilliant stand that they had made, and well might the colony of Natal look upon them as saviours from cruel invasion.

In telling the story of the events of the 22nd, it has been said that Major Spalding left Rorke's Drift to seek reinforcements at Helpmakaar. There he found two companies of the Twenty-Fourth, under Major Upcher, and with them he at once commenced to march to the river post. On their way they met several fugitives who asserted that the place had fallen, and when they arrived within three miles of their destination, a large body of Zulus was found barring the way, while the flames of the burning hospital could be seen rising from the river valley. It was only too probable that if they went on, they would merely sacrifice to no purpose the only regular troops remaining between the frontier and Pietermaritzburg.

Helpmakaar was the principal store depot for the centre column, full of ammunition and supplies, and it seemed best that its safety should, at any rate, be provided for as far as possible. The two companies were therefore ordered to return, and preparations for the defence of the stores were commenced.

According to the closest estimate, the number of Zulus who attacked Rorke's Drift was about four thousand, composed of Cetewayo's Undi and Udkloko regiments, and about four hundred dead bodies were buried near the post after the attack. The wounded were all carried away from the field. The loss of the garrison was fifteen killed and twelve wounded, of whom two died almost immediately.

The Zulu Campaign from a Military Point of View

By Lt. Colonel Arthur Harness. C.B, Royal Artillery

In taking upon myself the task of briefly noticing the strictures which have been made on Lord Chelmsford's conduct of the Zulu War, I wish it to be understood that I do not attempt, or presume to do so in the spirit of an advocate, but merely as one, who having been engaged, first throughout the Cape Colony War, and afterwards from the first invasion of Zululand to the end of the campaign, including the search for the king by the force under Colonel Baker Russell, had, perhaps, more opportunities of watching events, and forming opinions thereon, than many; and who is also, perhaps, owing to these opportunities, better able to appreciate and realise the position of affairs previous to the second invasion of Zululand, than those who came out after the disaster at Isandlwana on January 22.

Although aware that the Zulus possessed a standing army, a full account of which had been compiled by direction of Lord Chelmsford, and though the Zulus were known to have something of a military system, it was well-nigh impossible that, even with a knowledge of these facts, a proper regard for the reputed courage and endurance of the enemy could exist in the minds of officers or men who had taken part so recently in the war against the Cape Colony Kaffirs, and witnessed the absence of military qualities in them.

The fact alone of superiority in our weapons tended to produce a feeling of confidence, and at the commencement of the Zulu campaign I do not think many officers felt the necessity of forming laagers, or even of entrenching, where artillery and Martini-Henri rifles were opposed to *assegais* and muzzle-loading small arms. It is certain that none of us valued, to its proper extent, the many military qualities possessed by this savage nation: their discipline, their undoubted bravery, their disregard of life, and their powers of endurance.

It is to be observed that they also possessed the advantages of making war in their own territory, and of being but slightly encumbered with anything but their weapons and ammunition. All these combined rendered them a very formidable foe; but none of this was realised, or could well have been realised, until forced upon us by the dreadful events of January 22.

The adverse critics on the campaign seem never to consider the admirable, successful, and rapid conduct of the Kaffrarian campaign by Lord Chelmsford, nor his very natural expectation of being able to deal with the Zulu Army in a somewhat similar manner (though anticipating some superiority in his adversary) to that in which he had dealt with the Cape Colony Kaffirs. The Zulus also were savages—nothing could alter that—and therefore to be dealt with as other savage nations had been for centuries.

Mr. Forbes considers that the conduct of the Zulu campaign by Lord Chelmsford conveniently divides itself into four distinct period:—

1. From the inception of the preparations up to and including the catastrophe of Isandlwana.

2. From Isandlwana till the completion of the relief of Etshowe.

3. From the relief of Etshowe up to and including the combat of Ulundi.

4. From the combat of Ulundi until the acceptance of Lord Chelmsford's resignation by Sir Garnet Wolseley.

Let me deal with these periods in their sequence as he has done in his article.

1. From the inception of the preparations up to and including the: catastrophe of Isandlwana. Mr. Forbes acknowledges that Lord Chelmsford had no other course to pursue than to invade Zululand, but finds fault most severely with the division of the necessarily small invading force into four separate columns, for two reasons, the 'consequent individual weakness of the columns, and the impossibility of intercommunication and mutual support.' Yet he admits the desirability of the advance of a force from Utrecht in the direction of Ulundi, in addition to the force advancing over the Lower Tugela 'Drift,' and enumerates the obvious advantages to be gained thereby.

Now, it appears quite clear that had the force at Lord Chelmsford's disposal been thus divided, any intercommunication between, or mutual support of, these two forces would have been quite impossible, the distance between them being so great, and the country unknown. Whereas, by the formation of the intermediate columns, to enter at Middle Drift and Rorke's Drift, as was done by Lord Chelmsford, the power of communication and support shortly after crossing the border was made comparatively easy. It was also a point of some importance to traverse the country as much as possible, and, by capturing cattle, to strike the enemy on their most vulnerable point: both of which objects would be gained by the dispersion of forces.

As to the 'individual weakness' of each column by what is called 'this unsoldierlike subdivision,' it is by no means clear that each of these columns (No. 2 excepted) was not strong enough in itself to hold its own, and make good its own advance; and the defeat of part of No. 3 column at Isandlwana cannot be taken as a decided proof of their insufficiency.

As a matter of fact, Wood's and Pearson's columns did hold their own, but were brought to a standstill by the disaster at Isandlwana to Nos. 2 and 3 columns. Wood's column would have been in communication with the third column, had not the disaster occurred, very shortly after entering Zululand, and the two columns would have been in a position to render mutual support and assistance.

The difficulties occasioned by 'overcrowding and undue prolongation of a large force on one line' are a strong argument in favour of an invasion from several different points; and I cannot agree with the author of the article that Wood's and Newdigate's columns found no difficulty in marching on the same line, as is asserted, in support of the arguments against the subdivision of the forces. Where good grazing for horses, mules, and oxen has to be found, where drifts have to be made good, and broken-down waggons have to be repaired or removed, firewood to be collected, &c., &c., the advantages of a small force over a large one are soon recognised and appreciated by the working officers and men.

Mr. Forbes can hardly have been aware of these difficulties, and makes light of them; but I can bear testimony to the number of times I have myself lamented the indifferent water, the polluted camping ground, and the scanty remnants of good grazing left to us by the force moving immediately in front of us on the same line of advance.

In treating of the 'hostilities opened on January 11,' the author at once comes to the conclusion that Nos. 1, 3, and 4 Columns advanced into Zululand without having 'due relation to each other.' I discard, as he has done, No. 2 Column as 'trash,' although the fact of its being 'trash' was not known at the time that column was formed. On the contrary, our 'Black Auxiliaries' were looked upon, by many, as a great acquisition. But this is one of the many points on which it is easy to be wise after the experience of the past. How the above-mentioned conclusion has been arrived at, it is difficult to understand.

As one serving in No. 3 Column, I, with others, was certainly under the impression that a system of communication with the other portions of the invading force would be carried on shortly after the advance had commenced—a system to be matured and improved as the distances which separated them were reduced, or the country between each column became better known—and that the columns were acting under the directions previously designed by the general commanding. The fact alone that Lord Chelmsford and Colonel Wood met on the day on which the advance into Zululand was made disproves Mr. Forbes' assertion that the columns had no 'due relation to each other.'

The site of Isandlwana Camp is then described as one more 'inherently vicious than could ever have been found on the most industrious search.'

In reply to this assertion, I may suggest that, opposed to an enemy without artillery, and with the worst description of fire-arms, the use of which they little understood, the advantages of a site, well drained, and possessing the somewhat rare recommendations of good water and grass, may justly be taken into consideration in favour of a somewhat indifferent military position. Isandlwana possessed these advantages; and I have no hesitation in saying that the loss of the camp was *not due to the site on which the camp was placed.*

There are few who will not agree (and subsequent events tend to confirm this opinion) that the force left to guard the camp on January 22 was a sufficient one for the purpose; and had that force been kept together, as was ordered by the brigadier-general through his principal staff officer, and formed for defence, with its ammunition at hand (which there was ample time to do), there is little doubt that the Zulu Army would have been completely defeated at Isandlwana, in spite of its overwhelming numbers.

2. The 'second period embraces the operations extending from Isandlwana to the commencement of the final invasion.'

It would seem most natural that after the reinforcements had been applied for, the attention of the general commanding should be given to the consideration of protecting the Colony from the danger of an invasion, which it was thought more than probable would be made by the Zulus, elated by their success at Isandlwana, as well as to the accumulation of supplies and stores of all descriptions, in anticipation of the arrival of the reinforcements asked for, and also to replace those lost at Isandlwana, and in organising additional transport, and placing the troops in entrenched positions on the border.

I am, of course, not aware what Lord Chelmsford's views on the subject were; but there seems to be no reason to suppose that the opinions which influenced his decision in invading Zululand at several points ceased to exist after Isandlwana. Indeed, his preparations for the arrival of the reinforcements, his formation of a camp at Dundee, with a large supply of stores, show that he never swerved from his original intention as to this being the most desirable scheme of invasion.

The change of plan in taking Landsman's Drift as a point of entry, instead of Rorke's Drift, for the intermediate column, was one that was almost forced upon Lord Chelmsford, in consequence of the state of the roads between Greytown and Rorke's Drift, and the undesirability of marching a large force of cavalry and artillery through the unhealthy thorn country, which lies for some thirty miles between these two points, to say nothing of his possible desire to efface, by a change of route, the painful remembrance of Isandlwana to those who had been engaged in it.

This change of route has been a fertile source of criticism with those ignorant of the bearings of the case, and who had never ridden over the ground in question; Lord Chelmsford had traversed each road within the frontier several times, and, I believe, thoroughly appreciated the advantages and disadvantages of each. The road by Greytown and Helpmakaar lay within easy reach of the Zulu frontier and through a difficult country, and after Isandlwana it was found impossible to induce natives to accompany waggons by this route to Helpmakaar.

The road to Isandlwana from Helpmakaar, *via* Rorke's Drift, had been found by experience to be a very difficult one, with two terrible hills; and after crossing the frontier the ten miles or so which lay between the Drift and Isandlwana was found to be, even in dry weather, almost impassable for waggons, being constantly intersected by bogs and swamps; and for six miles it lay along a difficult close country (almost a defile in a military sense) in the most warlike district of Zululand. The road by Ladysmith, Dundee, and Landsman's Drift had no such disadvantages, and this line of advance and supply, although longer in actual distance, was virtually shorter and in every sense more secure.

The Free State was one great source of supply, and when, in consequence of the large increase to the army, much more extensive supplies were drawn from thence, Dundee was found to be a more convenient depot than Helpmakaar. It would seem that Lord Chelmsford was determined, after the relief of Etshowe, to await the arrival of the reinforcements from England, so as to run no risk, through an insufficiency of troops, as well as to secure the safety of the Colony until their arrival. There may have been a want of 'enterprise' in this determination; but the caution which is the result of experience should not be too readily condemned.

And here a few words as to the Court of Inquiry which was held during this period of 'aimless despondency,' and which is thus described by Mr. Forbes as:

> The Court of Inquiry, which did *not* inquire into the circumstances of the 'disastrous affair of Isandlwana.' This tribunal was a solemn mockery. It took the evidence, in some cases not even orally, in all without cross-examination, of eight witnesses. Neither Lord Chelmsford, nor any members of his staff, surely most significant witnesses, were examined. One of the members of the court, Colonel Harness, stood in common decency precluded from that position, in virtue of being the repository of most relevant evidence, which his appointment shut out. Major Gossett and Captain Lonsdale, whose evidence would have been of the utmost value, remained unexamined, as did numerous other available witnesses.

Mr. Forbes is evidently not aware that instructions were given to the Court to inquire into the '*loss of the camp on January 22*,' and not 'into the circumstances of the disastrous affair of Isandlwana.' To a careless, or indifferent, reader, there will not appear much difference between these two heads of instruction; but a little consideration will show that there is a wide distinction, and that 'the disastrous affair of Isandlwana' offers a much wider field of investigation than the 'loss of the camp.' The duties of the Court were, I hold to be, to ascertain what orders were given for the defence of the camp, and how these orders were carried out. When Mr, Forbes states that evidence, 'in some cases not even orally, of eight witnesses' was taken by the Court, he is quite inaccurate.

The evidence of *many* witnesses was taken by the Court, which evidence was recorded or rejected as the Court though fit. Those who had written their own evidence were personally asked by the Court if they wished to add to, or correct, any part of the written statements they had handed in; and the Court, in recording the most valuable evidence procurable at, or near, the place of assembly, and in sifting the evidence so obtained for the general commanding, carried out the object for which it had been convened. It is probable that even Lord Chelmsford himself is not aware what amount of evidence was heard by the Court, much of which was not considered sufficiently reliable to be placed on record. The Court was not called upon to give an opinion.

It was assembled solely for the purpose of assisting the general commanding in forming an opinion; and I can see no reason why my evidence on the subject should not have been received by the Court had it been thought desirable to take it. I repeat my assertion, that the Court was assembled by Lord Chelmsford for the purpose of collecting evidence for his own information. The idea, therefore, that he could be called upon by the Court to give evidence is simply preposterous; and it is not easy to understand in what way the evidence of Major Gossett or Captain Lonsdale could be required by the Court, as neither of these officers were in any way connected with the loss of the camp.

3. The third period extends from the 'relief of Etshowe till the combat of Ulundi.'

Here the critic proceeds to point out that the First Division, under General Crealock, was 'deliberately pigeon-holed, on or about the Lower Tugela,' and finally dismisses it as a 'non-efficient factor' in the 'scheme and execution of the campaign.' He throws doubt, too, upon any instructions ever having been given to General Crealock, and declares that 'if there were any, it devolves upon General Crealock, in the interests of his own reputation, to take steps that they may be produced.'

★★★★★★★★★★

General Crealock's reports, together with his written instructions from Lord Chelmsford, have been laid upon the table of the House of Commons, and speak for themselves, showing the difficulties of transport that officer had to deal with.

★★★★★★★★★★

General Crealock, in his address to his division before his departure from South Africa, stated distinctly what his instructions had been, and how they had been carried out by him. This appears to have been overlooked by Mr. Forbes. Can it be doubted that the position of a large body of troops on and about the Lower Tugela was of considerable assistance to the general in command in carrying out his scheme of invasion? As, although not taking any very active part in the offensive operations, from its strength and position this Division was the cause of much alarm to the enemy; the watching of it must have employed a large portion of the Zulu Army, thereby preventing a more combined attack on our advancing columns, and possibly also preventing a retaliatory movement into Natal from that quarter of Zululand.

It would be idle to attempt to deal with the author's remarks which follow this 'period,' so much personal animus is shown, the expression of which cannot but excite a feeling of indignation in those who have served with Lord Chelmsford and know his worth. Indiscriminate abuse can never be acceptable to just minds, and will never assist an argument with a generous-minded public; and Mr. Forbes cannot be surprised if the strong feeling displayed in this part of the article is felt to be unwarrantably unjust by many who possess minds capable of appreciating a strong sense of duty, with a desire of fulfilling it, in those in authority, and capable of understanding, in some measure, the great and many difficulties that had to be met and overcome.

4. Of the fourth period, which now comes under consideration, I quote from the Article:—

> The fourth period under consideration dates from the combat at Ulundi until Sir Garnet Wolseley's acceptance of Lord Chelmsford's resignation and the retirement of the latter from the army in the field. A simple statement of facts will demonstrate that, while up to the commencement of this period Lord Chelmsford's conduct of the operations had been erroneous, weak, and, capricious, the manner in which he acted after the Battle of Ulundi involves him in a yet graver culpability—a culpability that threw to the wind the results of the victory of Ulundi, devolved on another the work of finishing the campaign, and involved the country in a needless expenditure.
> On the afternoon of the combat of Ulundi, Lord Chelmsford retired his force into the laager on the Umvaloosi; on the next day he set forth on his return march. From Etonganeni he led the flying column back on St. Paul's over Kwamagwasa, which he reached on the 11th of July. Newdigate's division he sent

back towards the frontier by the line along which he had advanced. He made a clean evacuation of the whole theatre of his late operations beyond Fort Evelyn, in which he left his furthest advanced garrison; Fort Evelyn being some thirty-five miles short of Ulundi.

Mr. Forbes should have added that Lord Chelmsford remained at Entonjaneni three days, where he may have counted possibly on receiving instructions from Sir Garnet Wolseley as to his future movements; the fact of his having asked for them cannot be doubted. His march with the flying column to St. Paul's, and that of the 2nd Division to the Upoko River, where wood and supplies could be obtained, were deliberate and slow; and it is difficult to understand, even now, why the flying column was not halted by instructions from headquarters, if it was considered so all-important for a force to remain in the neighbourhood of Ulundi.

The word 'culpable' applied by Mr. Forbes to the conduct of Lord Chelmsford can hardly be used with propriety or truth towards one who certainly committed no voluntary error; and as to the accusation of having 'devolved' on another the work of finishing the campaign, and 'involved' the country in a needless expenditure, I may observe that it was doubtless possible for Lord Chelmsford to have remained in command of the field force after the arrival of Sir Garnet Wolseley, and to act under that officer's instructions; but most unprejudiced men, whether civil or military, would, I think, understand the extreme reluctance with which an officer of high rank and holding command, who had undergone the burden and heat of a campaign, would remain to perform duties in a subordinate capacity. But, in any case, whether Lord Chelmsford had remained or not, all *'responsibility'* in further operations must have rested with Sir Garnet Wolseley from the day of his assuming the chief command.

As to the question of 'needless expenditure.' It may be doubtful whether the expense of keeping a large force together so far to the front as Ulundi would not have caused an expenditure equally heavy as the maintenance of small detachments, such as Colonel Baker Russell's column, whose only object was the capture of Ketchwayo. *The campaign virtually ended with Ulundi.* The capture of the person of the Zulu king was to be the finishing and crowning event of the operations. From the very commencement of the campaign, it had been acknowledged, both by natives and colonists, that the taking of Ulundi and capture of the king would complete the overthrow of the Zulu nation.

The first accomplished, there remained but to prosecute the search for the king, for which duty only small parties were required. Lord Chelmsford, in the destruction of Ulundi, had accomplished the object that he had in view from the beginning of the campaign. He alone must have had the best knowledge of the state of his supplies; and doubtless their insufficiency was, as he states, a good and sufficient reason for his retiring from Ulundi. In the decision to retire, I have good authority for stating that the commander under Lord Chelmsford who had most experience in South African warfare cordially concurred.

After the victory of Ulundi, the force was hampered by about one hundred and twenty wounded, among them were many cases of a serious nature; the troops had no tents; the heat of the valley was great; and ten miles of bush country lay between the force and the large assemblage of waggons, with their native drivers and a small guard, in laager at Entonjaneni.

Except in the valley of Ulundi itself, the grass was exceedingly scarce; and, if I remember rightly, there was but a scanty supply of firewood. It was therefore absolutely necessary, having decided upon retiring from Ulundi (and what reason could there be for remaining there save, perhaps, a sentimental one; since it was neither a fortified place nor an important strategical position?), to move his columns to St. Paul's, and the Upoko Valley, in order to obtain grass and wood, and to be nearer to his base of supplies.

Mr. Forbes states that 'had Sir Garnet Wolseley not pushed up Clarke's column, Ketchwayo would still be loose, the Swazies would have assumed we had been beaten, and the Zulus would probably have gained heart to stand the fortune of another campaign.' I am at a loss to understand his grounds for making these assertions. Parties in search of Ketchwayo need not necessarily have been sent out from a main force at Ulundi, but could as easily have been despatched from such points as Fort Evelyn, St. Paul's, or other established posts in Zululand.

Regarding the assumption concerning the Swazies, and the Zulus 'gaining heart,' this can be purely a matter of speculation, which most of those, who rode through the country after the battle of Ulundi, and witnessed their complete subjection in the demeanour of the natives, and their evident acknowledgment of their inability to prolong the resistance they had so far carried on, will believe to be without foundation.

As far as I can discern, the only evil that has resulted from the retirement from Ulundi, has been some delay in effecting the capture of the Zulu king.

It is easy to say that the 'fruits' of the victory of Ulundi were to be gathered by the general commanding, after that victory had been won, and that he had but 'to stretch out his hand' to do so; but what were these fruits? I should like to be informed. Beyond a rather more speedy capture of the king, who was a fugitive, and not likely to remain in the neighbourhood of Ulundi after the result of the battle had been known by him, the 'fruits' appear to exist only in the imagination of adverse critics.

It is, no doubt, a grand, and at first sight an imposing idea, that after Lord Chelmsford had won his victory he should have called upon his soldiers to submit to some privations: to some 'stinting of their full rations,' and 'to go,' as the author so forcibly expresses it, 'without pepper, while beef held out,' and the idea is put forward as if there really was some glory in arriving at such a state of affairs; but I doubt if the author of the Article is at all aware of what many of the troops went through before, and during, the second invasion of Zululand—of the wet nights without tents, of the sickness and fever with but few medical comforts, which existed immediately after Isandlwana; and of the heavy outpost duties, the day fatigues, and night guards and picquets, which had to be undergone during the march to Ulundi; but Lord Chelmsford knows these things, and he also knows, and it requires no soldier to come forward to testify to it, that the troops under his command would willingly have endured whatever privations might have been required of them, and that, to a man, they would gladly have kept the field as long as he considered it necessary to do so.

Here it may not be considered out of place to touch upon the behaviour and discipline of the troops during the Zulu campaign, upon which points some differences of opinion have lately been brought to the notice of the public.

There is no doubt that the natural feeling of both officers and men, after Isandlwana, was one of caution; there also prevailed a feeling of determination that on no occasion should they be found unprepared. These feelings were strengthened by the disaster which befell a company of the 80th Regiment near the Intombi River; and the reinforcements, on their arrival from England, found the troops they had been sent out to assist, and with whom they were to work side by side, strongly under the influence of these feelings, which were probably at first regarded as extreme, and exaggerated by the new comers, but which were certainly very generally shared by them eventually.

The occasional false alarms that took place were partly the result of the cautious spirit pervading the army, and partly due to the intercourse with the friendly natives who were co-operating with us, ever ready to over-estimate the powers and tactics of the enemy, of whom they stood greatly in awe—awe, amounting almost to superstition. Perhaps such alarms would have taken place, whatever the material composing the force might have been. It may, however, be a matter of opinion as to how far the difficulty of allaying an alarm of this nature, once given, was increased, to those in command, by having to deal with young and untried soldiers, of which there was too large a proportion in the invading army.

As to the discipline which existed among the troops, I think all officers will acknowledge to a certain amount of difficulty in keeping non-commissioned officers and men steadily to their work for the first few days after their arrival at a town, or post where drink was obtainable; but it must be remembered that drink could only be procured at the base, and on the lines of communication with the border between Natal and Zululand; and, speaking for the 2nd Division of the field force, I do not think that a single instance of serious crime occurred in Zululand, where temperance was a necessity. Where drink is to be obtained and hard work has to be done, where officers, non-commissioned officers, and men are in such constant association as is unavoidable in camp life, offences resulting from intemperance are sure occasionally to occur, and doubtless did occur in South Africa.

Unwilling as all officers are to put into action the powers accorded to them by the law on the subject of corporal punishment, yet I feel sure that I represent the convictions of a large majority of officers who served in the field in South Africa, when I say it is the only means of maintaining that strict discipline which is so essential to the well-doing of an army, during active operations in time of war.

The public may rest assured that this punishment is only resorted to in extreme cases; and I conscientiously believe that were it not for the strong feeling of necessity for prompt and decided measures, a commanding officer would seldom be found ready to confirm a sentence of corporal punishment.

Of Lord Chelmsford's staff, Mr. Forbes writes as follows:—

Its inadequacy was flagrant. He commanded what was virtually an army corps, and an army corps, too, in detachments, and therefore demanding the services of an exceptionally efficient staff. Modern warfare has made apparent the inestimable value, to a general in command, of a good chief of the staff. But Lord Chelmsford would have no chief of the staff. He had indeed a military secretary, a man of proved capacity—in originating, stimulating, and perpetuating friction. His adjutant-general was respectable, and it may have facilitated the despatch of business that throughout the campaign he and the military secretary were not on speaking terms.

I am inclined to think that many general officers are not of the opinion here expressed as to the 'inestimable value' of a chief of the staff. If the heads of each department of the staff perform their own duties correctly, the creation of an additional staff officer might tend to increase labour and loss of time, and to render 'friction' more probable. With a distinguished general officer as inspector-general of the lines of communication and base, many will think that Lord Chelmsford acted wisely in thus dispensing with a chief of the staff, who is not only, as Mr. Forbes implies, a creation of modern warfare, but who, it must be remembered, has not yet been so entirely recognised as a necessary appendage to an English Army in the field as to have had definite duties allotted to the office. In point of fact, every general officer in command must arrange his staff to suit the peculiarities and exigencies of the campaign upon which he is entering.

Owing to my position as commanding a battery of artillery, I was frequently in communication with the officers on Lord Chelmsford's staff, more especially during the Kaffrarian war, and I can only say I invariably received from them the greatest consideration and assistance. A certain amount of formality is, of course, necessary in carrying on military duties, and this formality is frequently looked upon by those who are affected by it as useless and obstructive, and, possibly, as 'friction.' I doubt if any staff officer, however good and efficient he may be, ever carried on his duties, for even a short period, in the field without being regarded by many as obstructive, because he does not happen to fall in with the particular views of one and all with whom he has to deal.

The statement made in the latter part of the paragraph last quoted, to the effect that the military secretary and adjutant-general 'were not on speaking terms' is, I can assert, on the authority of the military secretary himself, *entirely* without foundation: I have been assured by him that no disagreement or 'friction' of any kind existed between himself and other officers throughout the eighteen months he acted in that capacity in South Africa. On learning the truth on these points, one cannot but feel strongly the great injustice that has been done to officers solely desirous of doing their duty to the best of their ability, and who spared neither time nor personal labour to achieve this end, and it is well to try to efface the false impression that has been so remorselessly given to the public by the remarks to which allusion has here been made.

On this subject I may add that the adjutant-general and military secretary are officers well known to the army in general, the junior of them having been connected with it for twenty-five years; and during that period having satisfactorily filled various positions on the staff. Doubtless the officers of the army who have been interested in this subject have made their own criticisms thereon, and it is highly improbable that their views will be changed by Mr. Forbes' remarks.

Hitherto I have carefully abstained from any mention of names, and I have avoided all allusion to the controversy that has been carried on with regard to the late Colonel Durnford's participation in the affairs of the campaign. I cannot, however, refrain from mentioning what will, perhaps, surprise many—that he remarked to an officer (from whom I have the information) shortly before leaving the base for the front, that 'Lord Chelmsford was a man for whom one would gladly lay down one's life.' Knowing Colonel Durnford as I did, I feel sure that this expression of feeling towards his general would be acceptable to him, as proving his loyal feeling which existed up to the date of his death.

Most military men have more than once in their lives, probably, been struck by the decided views expressed by civilians on military questions; and this is more particularly noticeable in men who have had the good fortune to accompany an army in the field, and who pride themselves, on that account, on their knowledge of these subjects. Mr. Forbes says, at the commencement of his article, 'In these days men read fast, think fast, and forget fast;' might he not have added, and *criticise fast*? With all due respect for Mr. Archibald Forbes' undoubted ability, I cannot but class him among those critics who are swift to find fault without due consideration; and I feel that he has made a mistake in taking up the challenge which he avers Lord Chelmsford has 'deliberately' and 'wantonly' thrown down.

Mr. Forbes undertook the task of proving Lord Chelmsford's incapacity as a general 'reluctantly' and 'compulsorily,' he informs us. Would it not have been better in every way, and more *really* public-spirited, to have left this self-imposed task unfulfilled, and not again to have agitated the public mind by recalling a past which is necessarily painful, while it cannot be truly said to reflect blame on anyone? The idea that a critic, in condemning the conduct of a general entrusted with a command, should suggest a 'preferable procedure' is not so absurd as Mr. Forbes would have us believe.

The critic, in condemning the conduct of a general, must have, in his own mind, a 'preferable procedure.' Why, then, should he not give it to the world as freely as he gives his condemnation? It is only by a comparison with his own ideas of what the campaign should have been that the value of his criticism can be fairly tested.

Arthur Harness.

A Critique whilst the War was being Waged

Blackwood's Magazine, March 1879, vol. 25

The success, exceeding our most sanguine expectations, which has attended our arms in Asia, has been cruelly dashed by a serious catastrophe to our troops in South Africa. A large body of soldiers, numbering nearly six hundred officers and men, has been completely annihilated, almost before a blow had been struck on our side, and before we were even able to realise that hostilities had actually begun. Scarcely less than the national sorrow for the loss of our brave soldiers is the feeling of regret that the colours of one of Her Majesty's regiments should have fallen into the hands of the enemy.

Seldom have British susceptibilities sustained such a shock. We must go back to the days of the first Affghan war for any parallel to the feelings which this disaster has inspired in the country; and even then, we doubt whether our prestige was felt to have suffered such an indignity as it has now sustained at the hands of a horde of savages. In the face of such a calamity, arty feelings can have no place. Between Liberal and Conservative there can be no difference of opinion as to the urgent necessity for now pushing this Zulu War to a speedy end, Exemplary punishment for the king who has dared to defy British power, to break the peace of South Africa, and to drag his wretched vassals into a contest where they must necessarily be the losers, is an object that supersedes all other considerations.

When our soldiers have retrieved their recent misfortune, it will be quite time to wrangle over the political objects of the expedition, and the means to be adopted for pacifying the Zulu country. We must postpone to the same event the very desirable inquiries that will doubtless be made into the unaccountable way in which the troops had been surrounded and decoyed from their position. All these and other subjects will claim attention in due course. At present we can have no thought and no desire but how most speedily and effectually we can avenge the slaughter of our countrymen.

For more than two years now, amid the disturbance of Eastern Europe and the dangers threatening our empire in Asia, we have been conscious of coming troubles in our South African Colonies, The fact that trouble is a chronic condition of these possessions, that one native difficulty is no sooner settled than another comes up for disposal, and that more or less fighting is always going on along our various African frontiers, has not on this occasion prevented us from seeing that a difficulty of more than usual magnitude was confronting Her Majesty's High Commissioner at the Cape.

All through the past year we have had unmistakable warnings of a coming collision with the Zulu kingdom, and ample proof that the commencement of hostilities was merely a matter of time, and we may say of convenience, to both sides. We knew enough of the Zulu character, and of the disposition of the Zulu king, to be aware that no pacific counsels would allay the war-fever which had seized on Cetywayo and his followers. We knew of how little avail it is to urge prudential considerations on savages, who do not count the cost, in comparison with the gratification of their tribal pride, or their desire to distinguish themselves in war. And we knew beyond all question that Cetywayo would have war with someone, and at all hazards, whatever force he engaged, or upon whatever quarrel he fought.

On our own side we have been clearly sensible that the military power of the Zulu nation was rapidly becoming dangerous to the colonists, as well as obstructive to the consolidation of our South African interests. In Natal on the one side, and in our new territory the Transvaal on the other, the strength of the Zulu king was a standing menace to progress and prosperity. What good was there in opening up farms, in building houses, or in buying herds, with a not remote prospect of Cetywayo sweeping across the country like a destroying angel, burning, slaying, and pillaging wherever he went? How was capital to be invested, enterprise to be encouraged, with such a cause of terror constantly in the background?

Writing in the columns of this magazine in the summer of last year, a distinguished British officer, who had had unusual opportunities of personally acquainting himself with this subject, spoke of the Zulu frontier as "that mine which may at any moment be sprung, bringing ruin and devastation to all within its reach." For the last eighteen months Sir Bartle Frere, Her Majesty's High Commissioner in South Africa, has been face to face with this difficulty, and no exercise of human ingenuity could have devised an escape that would be at once peaceful and productive of permanent security. We have recently seen how difficult it is to exert a pacific influence over Powers with more pretensions to civilisation when blood is up and arms in the hand, to be very sanguine about the success of diplomatic negotiations with such a sovereign as Cetywayo.

With the Zulu savage no arguments have force save those that are backed up by a pistol; and we can never have any security against his nation until it has tried its strength with the British power, and has learned such a lesson in the contest as will serve to impress it with the advantages of peace for the present generation. And it will be the fault of our government if the Zulu power should ever be allowed to reconstruct itself so as to cause anxiety to our colonists, or to necessitate further expenditure of British men or money to keep it within safe bounds.

To break the military power of the Zulu nation, to save our colonists from apprehensions which have been paralysing all efforts at advancement, and to transform the Zulus from the slaves of a despot who has shown himself both tyrannical and cruel, and as reckless of the lives as of the rights of his subjects, to a law-protected and a law-abiding people, is the task which has devolved upon us in South Africa, and to perform which our troops have now crossed the Tugela. This, broadly speaking, is the cause and object of the war. There are, of course, a number of events which have served as stepping-stones for the two parties taking up their present position; but we hold these to be of but secondary consequence compared with the evident antagonism which was bound to find some outlet sooner or later on Cetywayo's side.

On our part, the main point to be secured was, that the collision with the Zulus should take place at a time when we should be in a position to strike with effect, and with such a force as would reduce to a minimum the miseries which the Zulus would necessarily suffer in the struggle. This Sir Bartle Frere seems to have thought that he had provided for. He and Lord Chelmsford got together on the Zulu frontier such an army as, in the expectation of all the colonial authorities, was sufficient to speedily reduce the Zulu country. It was looked upon as a fortunate circumstance that the war should be undertaken at a time when the attention of her Majesty's Government was less distracted than it had been for some time back by more pressing anxieties nearer home.

And though the first step has proved a false one, we cannot permit ourselves to doubt that we shall speedily effect the settlement of what has been the most serious difficulty of South African administration, and that with the subjection of the Zulus, and the submission of Secocoeni, which has also to be secured, we shall have placed the native question upon a firmer basis, and reached the end of those little wars, which so unsettle the minds of our colonists, impede their prosperity, and burden the revenues of the mother country with expenses, from which at best we only derive benefit at second-hand.

The ostensible causes of quarrel with Cetywayo, though of secondary importance to the issues which we have indicated above, are still of sufficient interest, both as indicating the justice of our present course of action, and as showing how essential it is for the colonial population to be freed from the ever-increasing danger of a Zulu outbreak, to deserve brief recapitulation. We need not go into the general details of South African native policy, which not many months ago were explained with great minuteness in the columns of this magazine. We shall confine ourselves on the present occasion to the Zulu question and to those issues which more immediately spring from it, as affecting both our duty towards the colonies in their present straits, and the future tendencies of South African policy.

At the outset, we are bound to remark that the present Zulu panic contrasts rather sharply with the blind confidence in Cetywayo which the Natal Government, until quite a recent period, entertained. This confidence appears to have been based upon a belief that the Government, through its Secretary for Native Affairs, could always influence Cetywayo in the direction of its own wishes. Sir Theophilus Shepstone's great abilities, his unequalled knowledge of the Zulu character, his personal kindnesses towards Cetywayo, and the great respect which the Zulu king professed for him, went a long way to justify this reliance. But personal influence can at best only count for so much, eten when we have more responsible parties to deal with than savages.

We have no reason to suppose that our interests suffered in the hands of Sir Theophilus Shepstone, but it was unquestionably an error to trust so much to individual authority. The whole course of British policy towards the Zulus seems to have been made to depend entirely upon Sir Theophilus Shepstone's personal influence; and the system by which Cetywayo was at once kept in check and in humour was so much his own, that no other person has since been able to work it. In the present condition of the Zulu question there is, of course, a strong temptation to suppose that the Shepstone policy has broken down, and that this failure has naturally brought us into hostile relations with Cetywayo.

Until our recent dealings with the Zulu king have been more closely inquired into, it would be rash to return such a verdict upon Sir Theophilus Shepstone's policy towards the Zulus, In the meantime, we may point to the fact, which may or may not be of significance, that for the statesman who of all others was presumed to be the highest authority on Zululand and the Zulus, Sir Theophilus has kept himself much in the background during the present trouble. Apart from all the late disputes which have culminated in the present war, the fact is to be borne in mind, that Cetywayo's power had become dangerous to our colonies, and that a Kafir king, when he finds himself at the head of warriors, is never satisfied until he has tried his strength. Our career in South Africa has furnished us with many instances of this.

We have never yet found the Kafirs yield to any argument but physical force; and as soon as that was withdrawn, they have always seemed to feel that their obligations were removed at the same time. We have never yet had the experience that favours or protection constituted any claim of gratitude at their hands, unless we were in a position to make good our demands by the strong arm. In the case of Cetywayo, we are conscious of having deserved a better return for our benefits than his present outbreak. The Natal Government made him its special *protégé*, espoused his interests in his differences with his neighbours, and generally contributed to the establishment of that power which we now find it necessary to break.

When he came to the throne, the government extended a formal recognition to him that, we believe, had not been previously shown to any South African potentate. Mr. Shepstone, with a military escort, went into Zululand, and bore the principal part in the coronation ceremonials of the new king. Whatever anxieties the colonists may have felt—and the dread of native outbreaks is never long absent from the Natal settler—the Durban Government appears to have had implicit confidence in its own ability to influence Cetywayo.

We even, it is to be feared, encouraged him at the outset in the formation of that military force which has been the source of so much calamity both to him and to ourselves. It is alleged that the Zulu Army, and its threatening aspect towards the Boers, was turned to political account when reasons were wanted to justify annexation in the Transvaal; and if there is any foundation for this statement, we cannot be insensible to some appearance of retribution in our present difficulties.

With the annexation of the Transvaal, we took the place of the Boers as Cetywayo's chief enemies, and succeeded to the feud at which he had for so long held the Dutch republicans, The Zulus have for a good many years back complained of Boer encroachments, probably with more or less of just grounds; and they succeeded to some extent in interesting the Natal Government in their grievances. That Cetywayo refrained from forcibly asserting his territorial rights on the Transvaal side, was due to the counsels of the Natal Government and its Secretary for Native Affairs, who seems to have put off the Zulu king. with vague and indefinite, promises of seeing him righted on a future occasion. The Home Government, when the subject was brought to its notice, expressed an opinion adverse to interfering in territorial disputes between Cetywayo and the Boers.

The general conclusion, however, that we come to from the published despatches is, that Mr. Shepstone had encouraged Cetywayo to hope that his good offices would be exerted in effecting an arrangement favourable to Zulu interests, and that some such inducement had been held out to him to keep him back from war. On the annexation of the Transvaal, however, Cetywayo fancied that his hopes were farther than ever from being realised, and that the British were preparing to establish such legal title as would justify them in retaining possession of the tracts in dispute. This was a territory lying on the western border of Zululand, between the Buffalo and the Pongolo, upon which the Transvaal farmers had been allowed to graze their herds, and which they alleged had been formally granted to them by the Zulu king.

Soon after annexation, Cetywayo occupied a portion of the contested country, building on it a wattled *kraal* in token of his sovereignty; and wasted the farms round about, killing numbers of persons, and driving off their cattle. At this time, we had sufficient provocation to have justified those extreme measures which we have now been compelled to have recourse to; but an attempt was made, instead, to effect a peaceful settlement of Cetywayo's grievances, so that no reflection of injustice might rest upon our policy.

In October 1877 a meeting was arranged between Sir Theophilus Shepstone and Cetywayo's envoys, for the discussion of the frontier difficulty, and to settle if possible, some means of mutual reconciliation, Sir Theophilus had never before found the Zulu king intractable, but on this occasion Cetywayo's conduct in the preliminary negotiations forbade all hope of any accommodation on his side, The language used by the Zulu chiefs towards the Shepstones is said, on good authority, to have been most uncompromising: in the discussion on the disputed territory a chief is reported to have grossly insulted Sir Theophilus with menacing gestures; and the only terms that the Zulus would accept were the absolute and immediate cession of the whole country claimed by them.

Sir Theophilus broke up the negotiations, and returned to Natal in disgust; and from this time there appears to have been very little hope of persuading Cetywayo to come to a peaceable understanding. The king himself, however, again made overtures for arbitration to the Natal Government—but, chiefly for the sake of gaining time and of delaying the retribution which he could not fail to see must speedily overtake him for the numerous acts of violence committed by his followers in British territory, for his frequent raids upon our borders, and for the repeated insults with which all the warnings addressed to him by the colonial authorities were treated. That he had no intention of maintaining a peaceful attitude, or of containing himself within his own boundaries, the boasts of his tribe, and the threats thrown out to British traders in Zululand, afford unmistakable proof.

We may claim some merit for Sir Bartle Frere and his advisers, on the ground that though serious causes of complaint against Cetywayo were pending, and though fresh sources of grievance were constantly accumulating, the Government at once yielded to Cetywayo's request to appoint a Commission to settle the boundary difficulty. In this task they received little cordiality or assistance from the Zulus, The Zulus tendered no evidence of their own claims, and merely confined themselves to denying the assertions made by the Transvaal colonists, that Cetywayo had ceded to them the country between the Buffalo and the Pongolo.

The Commission gave a decision generally in favour of the Zulu sovereignty; and this cause of difference, which Cetywayo has for some time back alleged to be the only impediment to his friendship with the British, was removed in a manner that sets forth clearly the justice and liberality of our policy in South Africa. In December last this award was communicated to Cetywayo. The territory declared to belong to Zululand was to be at once marked off and made over; and the only reservation was the saving of the rights of *bonâ fide* British settlers, which our government was of course bound to protect from sustaining injury through the transfer.

But while we were thus doing all in our power to give Cetywayo his due, we were, on the other hand, vainly striving to induce him to redress our grievances against the Zulu State; and to remove the manifest danger arising from the maintenance of an extravagant military force, for which he had no employment, and for the sustenance of which he had no adequate means,

Before specifying the several outrages which have precipitated the quarrel between us and the Zulus, it may be well to say a few words about the boasted military organisation of Cetywayo's warriors. The Zulu nation is of comparatively recent importance in South-eastern Africa, having been raised from a small tribe tributary to the Umtetwas, by the ambition and military talents of the bloodthirsty Chakka, to be one of the greatest powers with which the Dutch *"voortrekkers"* or pioneers came into contact, Under Chakka the Zulus overran Natal and the Transvaal, making themselves dreaded all the way from Delagoa Bay to the frontiers of the Cape Colony.

The massacre of the Dutch emigrants by Chakka's brother and successor, Dingaan—still commemorated in the town of "Weenen"— made the Zulu name a terror to the colonists, which even the increasing strength of our Natal settlers, and their greater familiarity with Zulu Warfare, have perhaps, even at this period, not wholly removed.

The successors of Chakka and Dingaan, however, were not able to maintain the same wide sway. The British crept in upon them from Natal, and the Boers from the western side of their country. Other tribes which had been content to fight under the Zulu banner when it led to certain victory and plunder, fell off and became independent; new chiefs, like Moselkatze, were eclipsing the Zulu glories; and when the present king, Cetywayo, succeeded his father Panda as king of the Zulus in 1872, he mainly owed his position to British recognition, and to the zeal with which Mr. Shepstone used his influence in getting the chiefs of his country to accept his rule.

We seem to have had some view in those days of making Zululand a "model Kafir kingdom,"—a dream that, like most others of the same kind, generally changes to a reality of disappointment and difficulty. The good resolutions which Cetywayo made at his installation were speedily belied by his turbulent conduct towards other tribes, his cruel and tyrannical treatment of his subjects, and his evident ambition to make a name for himself in war. When he found that the

British Government were naturally disposed to discourage his bellicose disposition, he bitterly complained that we were infringing his dignity, because we would not allow him "to wash his spears" in the blood of his enemies, as became a sovereign of his dignity and nation. He turned all his able-bodied subjects into soldiers, forbidding them to marry until they had "washed their spears," and bound down his whole tribesmen to his will by laws of a most oppressive and despotic character.

As his military power increased, his arrogance and pretensions naturally grew in the same proportion. He was constantly reviving claims to all the countries which the Zulus had ever raided over; and if the area of Chakka's incursions be taken into account, this title would, if admitted, have placed him in possession of most ample boundaries. To maintain a force of from 30,000 to 40,000 fighting men was no easy matter; to provide work for them was still more difficult; and Cetywayo must have found himself placed in serious straits by his policy, which impoverished his country and discontented his people.

There was naturally a large war party; while a smaller number, comprising, however, some of the king's nearer relations, have counselled him to give up his mad schemes and yield to the wishes of the British. Unfortunately, Cetywayo soon allowed himself to get into such a position that it would almost have cost him his kingdom to retrace his steps, His military power had become scarcely less dangerous to himself than to his neighbours, and to have disappointed the expectations of his warriors would have been to run a considerable risk of having to deal with a revolution in his own country.

Moreover, the little wars that within the last few years we have been waging in other parts of South Africa, have naturally had an unsettling influence on a horde of armed savages standing by looking for an enemy; and we regret to say that in none of these cases has the punishment which we inflicted been either so prompt or so signal as to be likely to produce any very deterrent effect upon the Zulus.

In these troubles Cetywayo took a keen interest. He has sent encouraging messages to several chiefs who were in arms against the British. He egged on Secocoeni against the Boers of the Transvaal, and latterly against our own Government. He had become a source of danger, not merely to his own neighbours, but to the whole of the discontented races in South-east Africa, who were in danger of being misled by his emissaries.

He expelled missionaries from his country because they saw and bore testimony to his cruel treatment of his subjects, and endeavoured to take the part of those miserable wretches. Sir Bartle Frere tells us that the British Government has again and again had to check his purposes of aggression against unoffending tribes.

Cetywayo has, at the same time, formally and repeatedly requested the consent of the British Government to wars of aggression, which he proposed, not for any purpose of self-defence, but simply to initiate his young soldiers in bloodshed, and to provide a system of unprovoked territorial aggression by the Zulus, which had for many years been laid aside.

We come now to the *casus belli*—the quarrels which led to the recent *ultimatum*, and to the expedition into the Zulu country. The sketch we have given above of Cetywayo and his position will enable our readers to understand how these matters, not in themselves offences of the highest magnitude, should have come to be regarded as affording a legitimate and necessary basis for hostilities. Foremost among these come violations of British territory, and raids into the domains of tribes with whom we were in friendship, and who naturally looked to us for protection.

Another complaint was that two Zulu women had been forcibly carried away from British territory and put to death by stoning. The offender in those cases was the chief Sirayo, and Cetywayo met the demand for satisfaction by an inadequate offer of compensation. A number of assaults upon British subjects in British territories during the past year was also added to the charge, and more or less satisfaction demanded in compensation. In all these cases friendly efforts were made to induce Cetywayo to do justice, but in no instance with success. His replies to our representations are a good illustration of his character, being sometimes insolent, sometimes conciliatory, but always evasive.

The Natal settlers who neighboured the Zulu country appear to have known all the time that Cetywayo would not come into the views of the British authorities, but would keep playing with their demands so long as their patience lasted. Even after he was aware that the award had been given in his favour in his claims on the Transvaal frontier, his hostility to the British appeared to increase rather than diminish. Threats of coming war were openly uttered by the Zulus; and curiously enough, a favourite boast of Cetywayo's warriors was, that as the Queen of England had been obliged to send for "*coolie* soldiers" from India to enable her to hold her own at home, her troops would never be able to withstand the Zulus in Africa.

Traders have testified, too, that hopes of coming plunder from British territories, and from the countries of tribes friendly to us, have been indulged in to an extravagant extent in Zululand during the past six months, and have been held out by Cetywayo himself to keep his men in humour, and reconcile them to the harshness of his system.

It is important to note, that while all through the past autumn the South African authorities have seen that a Zulu War could not be postponed, Her Majesty's Government was doing its best to urge upon Sir Bartle Frere the necessity for "exercising prudence," and "by meeting the Zulus in a spirit of forbearance and reasonable compromise, to avert the very serious evil of a war with Cetywayo." This was in October last; and again, on 21st November Sir M. Hicks Beach, in acceding to reiterated urgent demands for reinforcements, writes as follows:—

> It is my duty to impress upon you that, in supplying these reinforcements, it is the desire of Her Majesty's Government not to furnish means of a campaign of invasion or conquest, but to afford such protection as may be necessary at this juncture to the lives and property of the colonists. Though the present aspect of affairs is menacing in a high degree, I can by no means arrive at the conclusion that war with the Zulus should be unavoidable; and I am confident that you (Sir Bartle Frere), in concert with Sir H. Bulwer, will use every effort to overcome the existing difficulties by judgment and forbearance, and to avoid an evil so much to be deprecated as a Zulu War.

Anything less like a "lust for aggression" and "imperialist tendencies" than the opinions and instructions sent by the Cabinet to the Cape it would be difficult to imagine. The Government conscientiously acted on the old adage, "*Si vis pacem, para bellum*." It provided for the safety of our colonists, while it impressed on the High Commissioner the necessity for doing all that could be done, with justice to our South African subjects and to the dignity of the British Government, to avoid hostilities with Cetywayo. In considering whether Sir Bartle Frere acted up to the "spirit of forbearance and reasonable compromise" prescribed to him by the Secretary of State, there are several points to be taken into account by critics who are removed from the scene of action.

It must be remembered that Cetywayo is not the only intractable chief with whom the South African Governments have to deal; that others are standing by watching the quarrel between the British and the Zulus with keen interest; and that any signs of weakness or hesitancy upon our part would simply be to bring a swarm of hornets upon us from every troubled point on the British border. We must remember, too, that to have given Cetywayo his due without exacting from him our own in return, would have at once been interpreted by the king himself as a sign of fear, and would have precipitated his invasion of our colonies, Sir Bartle Frere appears to have avoided all menace and threats in his negotiations with Cetywayo; and we may infer from the name which the Kafirs have given him, "*the dog that bites before he barks,*" that he has made use of no bluster or effort at coercion to influence Cetywayo's choice between peace and war.

On the 11th December, British Commissioners met Cetywayo's representatives on the Natal side of the Tugela, and delivered to the latter the text of the Transvaal award fixing the line of boundary as running from the junction of the Buffalo and Blood Rivers, along the latter to its source in the Magidela mountains, and thence direct to a round hill between the two main sources of the Pongolo River in the Drachensberg. The Zulu envoys received this part of the communication with lively satisfaction, and did not conceal that they had been dealt with more liberally than they had expected.

But as the High Commissioner's message went on to recite the offences committed by Cetywayo against British territory, to lay down the terms at which these were to be condoned, and to insist upon the king fulfilling those promises of good government which he had made to Sir Theophilus Shepstone at his coronation, the Zulus became visibly disconcerted, and did not scruple to admit that they had little hope of securing their master's compliance. Twenty days were given to Cetywayo to give up the men who had carried off the Zulu women from our territory, and to pay a fine of 500 head of cattle for the same offence; and also, to pay a fine of 100 head of cattle for an outrage on two of our surveyors.

Cetywayo was also required to surrender Umbaline, a Swasi refugee, who was harbouring with the Zulu king, and who had led numerous raids into our territory, killing many persons, and carrying off women and children and much booty. A strong recommendation to disband the Zulu Army, and to remove the restrictions on marriage which were operating so oppressively upon the people, was also given;

and that the king might have an assurance of the interest of the British Government in the proper management of his territories, as well as a security against annoyance from other tribes, a British officer was to reside in Zululand or on its border, "who will be the eyes and ears and mouth of the British Government towards the Zulu king and the great council of the nation."

Some journals have made the mistake, in criticising the terms of the ultimatum, of supposing that Cetywayo had only twenty days to accept or decline all these conditions, and have talked as if we were going to war because he refused to have a British resident forced upon them. This is not the case. The twenty days had reference solely to the delivery of the Sirayo raiders and the payment of the 600 head of cattle imposed as penalties. No specified period was laid down for carrying out the other wishes of the High Commissioner; and had Cetywayo agreed to these very moderate demands, we cannot doubt that ample consideration would have been shown him both as to the time and the manner of reforming his administration. The *ultimatum* was a simple and certain test of his disposition to choose between peace and war, and his treatment of it at once dispelled any doubts that might have still existed regarding his real intentions.

Assured as Sir Bartle Frere and Lord Chelmsford both were that there was no escape from a Zulu War, the question arises whether their military preparations were on a scale sufficiently ample for meeting Cetywayo and his 40,000 Zulus, Since the disaster near Rorke's Drift there has naturally been a feeling that we ought to have taken the field with more men and with a force of regular cavalry. On the other hand, the preparations were considered quite sufficient for overrunning the Zulu country by all the colonial authorities who have had experience of South African warfare. Lord Chelmsford apparently did not consider himself justified in formally asking the War Office for a regiment of cavalry, although he pointed out that dragoons would be of immense advantage.

Sir Bartle Frere, in recommending that cavalry should be sent out to the Cape, seems to have had as much in view the political effect of such a force on the natives generally as their special need in the Zulu campaign. The startling effect which the appearance of the 7th Dragoon Guards produced upon the Boers at Zwart Kopjies in 1845 is still an African tradition; and there can be no doubt that a cavalry regiment would have been of the utmost service, as well as of immense moral advantage, to us in the campaign. But on the other hand, we must not too rashly condemn the scruples of Lord Chelmsford to bring British cavalry into a region where the "horse-sickness" of the country may play such terrible havoc.

In the Secocoeni and other campaigns, we have lately had fatal experience of the imprudence of using "unsalted" horses—that is, cattle which have not already been seasoned by an attack of the disease. Those who desire more information upon this subject will find their curiosity fully satisfied in a recent book, which will be read with great interest at the present moment—*The Transvaal of Today*—by Mr. Aylward, who commanded the Boer forces against Secocoeni during the last years of the Republic's existence, and whose book contains a valuable amount of information on Zulu and Kafir Warfare.

From the 1st September to 25th May the climate of the Bushveld, or low country, under which classification falls a considerable tract of the Zulu territory, where our troops may have to operate, is fraught with danger both to men and horses, especially the latter. To guard against "horse-sickness," Mr. Aylward recommends travellers and troops:

> Never to permit their horses to bite grass or drink water until the morning mists, haze, or miasma, with which the low grounds are frequently covered, should have been first entirely dissipated leaving the *veld* dry. The horses consequently should be fed at night, and only allowed to graze at will during the later and warmer parts. of each day. This will be best effected by the English sportsman bringing proper nosebags and head-stalls with him, by the use of which, with great care and attention, I have seen delicate and valuable animals preserved, where there were no stables, during very bad seasons.
>
> It is the general opinion that the poison causing the fever is to be found in the dew. It is certain that horses eating dew-wet grasses during the sickly season almost invariably die. This is so firmly believed that I have known both Dutchmen and Englishmen to wash carefully every blade of grass or sheaf of oats coming from the damp air before it was admitted into their stables; and I must certainly say that this safeguard has been followed by good results.
>
> That there is something in the dew and miasma theory can be readily gathered from this fact: 'imported horses,' when properly stabled, and not allowed out except during the later and

warmer hours of the day, seem very frequently to escape the disease altogether; but to an imported animal so kept, one single night's absence from shelter during the unhealthy time will always prove fatal. So much for unsalted horses. With regard to the 'salted' ones, or those presumed to have passed through the sickness, I can speak with considerable certainty, as I have had in my charge at various times large troops of these animals, amongst which were some of great value.

We must exercise some caution, therefore, in concluding that Lord Chelmsford was insensible to the advantages of employing regular cavalry in the expedition. Dragoons without horses are the most useless of all troops; and had a regiment been hastily dispatched before the necessity for its presence was demonstrated, there would in all probability have been an outcry on the other side, had the cavalry suffered from horse-sickness, and the movements of the troops been impeded in consequence.

The recent disaster in Zululand does not appear to have been altogether owing to a want of cavalry; and if the promptitude with which the government is now hurrying out horse to the seat of war is reassuring, it is rather because the colonial authorities want an impressive military force at command to deter the other tribes from plucking up courage to attack us, than that we have great hopes of cavalry being of the first assistance to us in fighting the "rocks and caves of Zululand." The most reasonable regret to be indulged in at the present moment is, that a regiment which would have been so useful to us at the present moment as the Cape Mounted Rifles, should have been disbanded by Mr. Cardwell, to carry out a policy which seemed selfish to the colonists, and from which the Imperial Government cannot be said to have derived any economical advantages in the long-run.

The advance of the British into Zululand certainly took place under most favourable auspices. There had been plenty of time to make preparations; the force was a larger and better equipped body of troops than we had ever previously put in the field in South Africa; the provision for transport and for the preservation of communications was declared by the military and colonial authorities to be all that could be desired. The colonial journals prophesied a possibility of hard fighting, but the certainty of an early victory. We knew that the Zulus far outnumbered the expeditionary force; but any misgivings that were expressed on that account, seemed more than counterbalanced by the assurance that the Zulus would never meet us *en masse*.

On this point we must wait the issue of the contest, by which Lord Chelmsford's arrangements will be more fairly judged, rather than by any criticisms which we might be hastily tempted to put forth at present. Success in war will condone any blunder; while the most carefully laid plans, the most cautiously matured tactics, never come through the ordeal of failure with credit.

The advance into Zululand was made by four columns, acting simultaneously upon a concerted plan of operations, From the Natal frontier three forces crossed the Tugela and Buffalo Rivers, while a fourth advanced from the Transvaal border, crossing the Blood River, and keeping its base on the town of Utrecht. Colonel Pearson, with 2,200 Europeans and 2,000 natives, crossed the Tugela at Fort Williamson, not far above the mouth of the river, and was to advance by the coast-road into the heart of the country.

The two centre columns, the right under Colonel Durnford, and the left under Colonel Glyn, crossed the Tugela at Krantz Kop and Rorke's Drift respectively, and having rendezvoused in front of the latter place, were to advance by the principal road through Zululand towards the capital, which lies from Rorke's Drift in a north-easterly direction. At a point fifteen miles south of Ulundi, Cetywayo's principal *kraal*, the main body of the army was to be joined by Colonel Pearson's column.

An attack was then to be made on Cetywayo's *kraal* from the front, while the Utrecht column under Colonel Wood was at the same time to take the Zulus on their western flank. Such, roughly described, appears to have been Lord Chelmsford's proposed strategy; and it corresponds in the main with the course suggested in his memorandum, dated September 14, 1878, read by Lord Cadogan in the House of Lords. Lord Chelmsford's scheme also made arrangements for guarding the extensive Natal frontier, as well as that of the Transvaal, from Zulu incursions while our troops were engaged in the interior of the country.

The fullest accounts that can be put together regarding the disaster to the centre column are as yet sadly defective, and suggest a number of difficulties that we must trust to further information for removing. We know, however, that our right and left centres got safely across the frontier, and carried out their proposed junction in front of Rorke's Drift. They had apparently information of the presence of a large Zulu Army in front, but do not seem to have had cause for apprehending an attack on the rear.

A force consisting of five companies of the 1st battalion of the 24th Regiment, and a company of the 2nd battalion, with 2 guns, 2 rocket-tubes, 104 mounted colonials, and 800 natives, were left behind to guard the camp, which contained a valuable convoy of supplies, while Lord Chelmsford with the rest of his force advanced to clear the way. This was on the morning of the 22nd January.

Lord Chelmsford, it would seem, speedily found himself engaged with the enemy in the wooded and broken country in front. According to Lord Chelmsford's own account, which at present we are in justice bound to lay most stress upon, "the Zulus came down in overwhelming numbers" upon the camp, destroyed the great body of our troops, about 600, and apparently captured the whole of the valuable stores of provision and ammunition upon which our further advance must have mainly depended.

Our men must have made a desperate defence, for the Zulu loss is set down at 5,000, or nearly ten times that of ours. Such a disaster, so unexpected, so inexplicable, at once raises a feeling that "someone had blundered;" and the hurried language in which the commander-in-chief announces the event, gives a double force to the suspicion, Lord Chelmsford's words are:

> It would seem that the troops were enticed away from their camp, as the action occurred about one mile and a quarter outside it.

We must point out, however, that this mistake, if it was really made, could not have been the whole extent of the error, for the Zulus must in some way or other have been allowed to turn the flank of the main body before they could have fallen upon the camp behind, From Insandusana, or Insandula, where the disaster took place, to the point where Lord Chelmsford had been engaged in the front with the Zulus, was a distance of not more than twelve miles; and some explanation would seem to be required of how so large a body of men could be so utterly destroyed, and a booty so cumbersome and valuable carried off without apparently any diversion having been made by the main column in its favour, until it was too late to be of any use.

The official accounts bear out the opinion that the troops must have moved from the camp to attack the Zulus, probably on finding their communications with the main body cut off; and that they were surrounded and cut down in the forest which would be of the utmost assistance to the attacking Zulus. In justice both to the dead and the living, a more detailed and calmer examination must be made of the alleged breach of orders, as well as of the position chosen for the camp, than the hasty, and doubtless passionate, conclusions which the last Cape mails brought home. When Lord Chelmsford arrived on the scene of action, all was over—the camp—and its defenders slain.

Without provisions, means of transport, and ammunition, it was of course impossible for him to proceed; and the latest accounts represent him as having recrossed the Tugela and returned to Helpmakaar, which had been the base of the left-centre column before it passed the river. Here every preparation was being actively pushed on for another start, and we trust that before this time the centre of our, army has retrieved the unfortunate commencement of the campaign.

It is with very mixed feelings that we hear of the gallant advance of the other two columns from the Lower Tugela and from Utrecht into the Zulu country. If we were certain that they could succeed in effecting a junction and in destroying Cetywayo's *kraal* by themselves, we should feel that they had more than redeemed the misfortune of the central column. We have a sufficiently high opinion of British troops to hope that such a possibility is not too far-fetched to be gloriously realised. Colonel Pearson appears to have made excellent progress since crossing the lower Tugela Drift. At the River Inyoni, the first stream of considerable size after passing the frontier, Colonel Pearson was opposed by a force of 4,000 Zulus, whom he drove off after an hour's fighting, with considerable loss.

By the 23rd January, the same day as Lord Chelmsford had to retire, Pearson's force had reached Ekhowa, an important point on the road to Ulundi, about 25 miles from the Tugela. The Naval Brigade accompanying this column has rendered capital service, and is evidently destined to be of great use in the campaign. Ekhowa has been strongly fortified, and Colonel Pearson, by the latest accounts, was looking carefully after his communications. There is every reason to expect that a portion of the Zulu force which had opposed Lord Chelmsford will now be directed against our right wing; and the more the celerity with which the centre can again resume operations, the greater the chances of Colonel Pearson being able to continue his advance must be.

The latest news represents the Zulus as concentrating around Pearson's position, so that sharp fighting may be expected from the direction of Ekhowa. The Transvaal column, under Colonel Wood, engaged the enemy on 24th January, two days after the mishap at Rorke's

Drift, and scattered a force of 4,000 Zulus with only a trifling loss on our side; but he subsequently appears to have fallen back on Utrecht, probably in obedience to orders from headquarters. Of the encounters with the enemy which are reported from Rorke's Drift subsequent to the disaster at Insandusana, we cannot say much, except that they afford us a reassurance that we are still holding that position, and that the falling back of the force on Helpmakaar has not so damped the spirits of the troops that they are afraid to encounter a vastly superior force of the enemy. If we can hold the Zulus so well at bay with so small a force and such insufficient protection as Rorke's Drift affords, there is good hope that we shall find ourselves more than a match for them when Lord Chelmsford's columns again take the field.

So far as the meagre and generally conflicting reports show, the above is the position in which our troops, whether in Zululand or on the border, are now placed. The situation is full of anxiety, but by no means desperate. We have every confidence that we shall be able to confine the Zulus within their own territory, where Colonels Pearson and Wood will, we hope, presently find them occupation. On the vigour and decision which Lord Chelmsford displays in getting the centre columns again in motion, must depend not only his own reputation, but the issue of the war. His position at present is surrounded with difficulties into which we can all fully enter.

On the one hand, he must be naturally anxious that the other two columns should be allowed to advance, so that his own disaster might not have the appearance of having given a general check to the whole expedition; while, on the other, he cannot be free from a feeling of uneasiness as to their ability to hold their ground in the heart of Zululand without the immediate support of the centre columns. There will be also a strong. temptation to hold back until the reinforcements from England arrive to strengthen the army; but there is also the danger that the Zulus might gather both courage and strength from such delay, as well as that other discontented tribes might grasp at the idea that the British power had received a decided check.

These are difficulties amid which Lord Chelmsford must make up his mind. He is in a great measure free from the telegraph control which restricts so seriously the liberty of most commanders-in-chief nowadays in the field, while it can hardly be said to lessen their responsibilities. It has often been said that it is a higher test of generalship to retrieve a disaster than to follow up an advantage.

But though we cannot permit ourselves to look for any alternative except a successful termination to the war, we have been brought face to face with possibilities which compel us to wait the final issue with anxiety. We have a powerful enemy to conquer and a difficult country to overrun. Fatal experience has told us that bushfighting always costs us more men than do pitched battles; and the country by which Cetywayo's forces are covered will give them many opportunities of harassing us with impunity. Mr. Aylward, from whose book, *The Transvaal of Today*, we have already quoted, gives some very striking pictures of the disadvantages which European troops labour under when fighting a savage foe, who can turn every rock, every tree, and every cave into a point of attack for his enemy and of shelter for himself.

Along roads which defy ordinary means of transport, a force may march through the very heart of a Zulu or Kafir Army without seeing a foe until the signal for attack has been given. If anything could damp the spirit of the British soldier, it would be having to thus fight an unseen enemy; and that our men have behaved with such admirable bravery and patience in other African wars and in New Zealand, is even a higher compliment to the army than steadiness in open campaigns, where the soldier is more of a machine and less thrown upon his own wits than in such expeditions as that to the north of the Tugela.

In the present war the opening disaster at Rorke's Drift has given the army a motive for stern and decisive action which will carry it through all dangers and fatigue until the slight we have sustained has been more than avenged in the overthrow of the savage power that has forced us into hostilities. We trust, before many mails arrive from the Cape, to hear that Cetywayo has learned to estimate the danger of provoking British hostility, and that the Zulu power has been so thoroughly broken as to have finally ceased to be a source of fear to our colonists and native neighbours in South Africa.

But though the subjection of the Zulus is the first and most important matter in hand, it forms only a part of a very difficult subject that demands serious attention, and that will not be easily settled to the satisfaction of both the Home Government and the colonies, We must, by some means or other, put an end to the interminable series of little wars that are the great barrier to the progress of the South African Colonies, and that always end by causing trouble to the Imperial Parliament and expense to the imperial Treasury.

Even if we had no past experience to fall back upon in confirmation of our views, the present condition of affairs in South Africa justifies the opinion that we have been going upon an unsound system, or rather on no system at all, in the management of native affairs. When we have checked a native tribe, we have seldom set ourselves seriously to the task of consolidating it into the general body of our subjects, but have rather allowed it to remain apart under its hereditary chiefs, to be a source of disquiet, and perhaps annoyance, at some time when we were ill prepared to have it upon our hands, When we have punished them, it has been more in the spirit of a schoolmaster chastising a naughty child than of a government whose mission was to extend order and civilization along its confines.

We have had too much of the free-and-easy spirit of Sir Harry Smith in our policy, whose counsel to the native chiefs was;

Keep the peace; attend to your missionaries: then your cattle will get fat, and you will get to heaven.

Mistaken leniency has in more than one case offered premiums to rebellion and to encroachments on British territory; and the political disputes of the white races have not unfrequently been forwarded by intriguing with the black tribes. The present Zulu difficulty will have failed to teach us our duty to our South African Colonies, unless we effect far more secure arrangements for their safety all along our frontiers than have hitherto been carried out. The disarmament of all the native tribes who come under our protectorate is a duty that can no longer be shirked; and the illicit trade in selling arms to the savages, which has been so unblushingly carried on in all our South African Colonies, and which has contributed so much to render our position insecure at the present time, ought to be stamped out by all the power of the local governments.

Great complaints have been made regarding the trade in arms which the Portuguese settlement of Lorenzo Marquez, on Delagoa Bay, has been driving with the Zulus, the Swasis, and other savage nations; but it is more than probable that much of the outcry has been raised to divert blame from parties nearer home who were much more deeply implicated. To deprive the natives of such temptations to mischief as arms afford, must be one of the first steps towards the end of our South African troubles. Another is a better delimitation of our borders, so that the unfortunate territorial disputes which are constantly cropping up may be put an end to, and the natives taught to seek for justice in our High Courts, instead of taking it at their own hands upon the life and property of their nearest white neighbours.

It is, no doubt, a serious task to break powerful tribes from savagery to a settled and law-abiding life; but we can no more shrink from the task than we can contract the limits of our colonisation. Both in Natal and in the Cape Colony the natives who have settled on the "reserves" or "locations" have made great progress in civilisation, have acquired and set store by the rights of citizens, and have in a great number of cases shown anxiety to educate their children. Wherever we have supplanted the power of the chief by that of the resident magistrate, all goes well; it is only where the tribal feelings and the claims of chiefship are allowed to maintain their influence that we fail to make the natives peaceable. This native problem is undoubtedly the great question of the future in South Africa; and we cannot trust to having it settled by time, as in other parts of the world.

While the Australian aborigines, the Maories in New Zealand, and the Indians in America are dying out under white civilisation, the black races in our African Colonies are increasing rapidly, and at a far higher ratio than is known among the wild tribes, where war and starvation exercise of course a considerable check upon population, The Boers, on the whole, have given us scarcely less trouble than the blacks, and have been even more obstinate to deal with. Their bigoted aversion to British rule, and propensity for "trekking," have in most cases been the cause of our being compelled to extend our frontier far beyond the limits which our own colonisation demanded.

They encroached upon native territories; and when they had drawn down upon themselves the wrath of the chiefs, their weakness commonly compelled British interference in the interests of the general peace of the country. There is no question but the present war in Zululand, as well as that against Secocoeni, are largely due to the Boer encroachments, and have come to us as a *damnosa hereditas* with the Transvaal. We do not mean that the annexation of the Transvaal has of itself embroiled us with either Secocoeni or Cetywayo; for even though we had allowed that State to retain its independence, we should have been compelled to have fought both, to keep them from overrunning the Transvaal and slaughtering its farmers, who apparently found it difficult to hold their ground against even the less powerful of the two chiefs when acting by himself.

With the annexation of the Transvaal, we trust that there will be an end of the stubborn spirit of resistance to British rule which has worked so strongly against the unification of colonial interests; and that our new subjects will at last recognise the necessity for loyally aiding Her Majesty's Government in giving to all the races in South Africa under its sway a more assured protection, and a better meed of prosperity, than the divisions of the country have ever yet permitted them to enjoy.

The general subject of the defence of our South African Colonies is one that must inevitably come up for discussion, as soon as events in Zululand permit us to look a little ahead. In this respect, we are forced to the conclusion that the South African Governments have not realised their duty. They have contented themselves with applying temporary checks, and have trusted to the intervention of the Crown whenever affairs became too critical to be dealt with by colonial resources. We need not say that such a policy is not likely to earn commendation from the British taxpayer at the present moment. The claims of the colonies on the mother-country have always had due weight given to them in these pages; and we have steadily maintained that it was our duty to supply means of defence to every corner of the empire which was not able to protect itself.

We have always held that the abolition of the Cape Mounted Rifles and other colonial corps by Mr, Gladstone's Government, was an unwise and reprehensible measure, the evil effects of which are bitterly realised in South Africa at the present time. But with all our sympathies in favour of colonial claims on the Home Government for military assistance, we cannot deny the fact that the South African Colonies have leant too heavily upon the Crown in this matter. The present is not a fitting time to recapitulate the way in which the African legislatures have evaded the question of colonial defence—have bandied about from one to another the duty of providing for the protection of the borders—have sought to tide over difficulties by police, levies, "commandoes," and other makeshifts—and have almost invariably ended by falling back on the imperial government.

Most of all the African "little wars" could have been checked at the outset by the colonies themselves, at comparatively little outlay, compared with the expenditure that must be incurred when Imperial troops are put into the field. The cost to the mother-country of the Zulu campaign, apart from the sacrifice of British soldiers which has actually taken place and is still to follow, will inspire us with a more lively interest in South African confederation and inter-colonial defence than the home public have hitherto shown, and ought to give a powerful impetus towards a satisfactory settlement of these much debated matters.

The temper of the country on the Zulu War has expressed itself, both inside and out of Parliament, in favour of the course which Government has pursued. The despatches already published make clear that Government had no wish to wage war with Cetywayo, and no object to forward by such a step; but yielded because it felt bound to defer to the representations of imminent danger which came to it from all classes, and from every quarter of South Africa; and to the assurances which it received that we had no alternative but to choose between fighting the Zulus in their own country, and allowing them to overrun and devastate our colonies, and to bring the horrors of war into the homesteads of our settlers.

No Government could have turned a deaf ear to such warnings as Sir Bartle Frere and the colonial authorities sent home towards the end of last year. And when it became evident that war could not be evaded, it was nothing more than the duty of Government to the country to insist that Lord Chelmsford should limit his military establishment to the force absolutely necessary to effect his object. Between a general asking for troops in war time, and a nation grumbling over unnecessary military expenditure, a government has to hit a very fine mean if it is to please all parties.

Until the disaster at Insandusana the force under Lord Chelmsford was looked upon as amply sufficient for reducing Cetywayo; and the Government was considered by the colonial press to have behaved with great liberality in the matter of troops. Since the news of Lord Chelmsford's check, the zeal with which every department of the Government has thrown itself into the task of expediting the dispatch of reinforcements for Natal speaks for itself.

The task of Government is now rather to oppose itself to any panic which may break out, than to stimulate the public interest in its exertions to aid our army. We must look upon the Insandusana disaster as one of those catastrophes which, like the loss of the *Eurydice*, or the explosion on board the *Thunderer*, fall outside the boundary of the keenest human prevision, It is a sad calamity, but we cannot afford to lose our heads over it.

With such insufficient information as we possess upon the most material points of the situation, the Zulu War is not yet ripe for parliamentary discussion. The references in both Houses to African affairs, show that upon the merits of the questions involved parties have yet to make up their minds. Mr. W. H. Smith's powerful speech at Westminster, two days before Parliament opened, was the first public intimation of the spirit in which the Government had received the news of Lord Chelmsford's reverse; and it at once gave a tone to the feelings of the country, and paved the way for the Ministerial statements in both Houses.

The line taken up by Earl Granville does not indicate that the Liberal party have formed any decided opinions as to what course they are to pursue. He carped at Sir Bartle Frere's principles, which he said were "suspicious of any weakness in any line of defence, and not averse to immediate and energetic measures, not excluding war, to avoid possible future dangers." Such criticism, if not very generous, is not very damaging; and if Earl Granville feels that his duty to the Constitution requires him to malign an officer who is too far removed, and too hard pressed to have an opportunity of defending himself, we see no reason to stand in his way.

Sir Bartle Frere's conduct of South African affairs will no doubt be keenly canvassed afterwards, but we cannot admit that Her Majesty's Government are reflected upon when the Opposition choose to make him the subject of an attack. Lord Carnarvon, who has no disposition at present to justify the measures of Government, confessed that his experiences at the Colonial Office had convinced him of the justice of the Zulu War; while Lord Kimberley, who had also much official acquaintance with Zulu matters, seemed to think that we should have made war upon them long ago. In the Commons, Colonel Mure has evinced an interest in the Zulus explicable only by the instability of his seat for Renfrewshire; while Sir Charles Dilke contributed to the discussion a version of the difficulty, distorted by even more than his usual inaccuracy and extravagances.

But the member for Chelsea is apparently acting for himself, and without any definite support from the leaders of the Liberal party. The Opposition as a body are still, we. believe, sufficiently alive to their duty to the country in this crisis to refrain from any criticism that might obstruct the measures of Government for carrying through the Zulu War; and it must feel, besides, the hazard of committing itself to any particular line of censure until more definite information regarding the Zulu question, and the mode in which it has been dealt with by the colonial authorities, has been given to the public.

Perhaps the most notable fact in connection with the home aspects of the Zulu expedition, is the extraordinary reticence which Mr, Gladstone has shown regarding it. A whole fortnight has elapsed since the news of the Insandusana affair reached England, and up to the time of our going to press the ex-Premier had not uttered a word or written a post-card that could give the slightest clue to the view he meant to take of the disaster. This silence is so unwonted as to make us much more uneasy than if Mr. Gladstone had thrown himself into the breach in half-a-dozen monthlies and double that number of speeches.

In his case we have no reason to suppose that want of information has retarded his making up his mind as to the criminality of the Government, and its direct responsibility for a war which it has waged for purely selfish motives, and with the base view of influencing the constituencies at the coming elections. Whether he will go further, and recognise in Cetywayo the "Divine Figure of the South," the noble savage whose cause is the cause of liberty and benevolence, unjustly assailed by the unscrupulous Tory Ministry—the possessor of all those personal virtues which are so conspicuously missing in the characters of the Prime Minister and other members of the Cabinet—we scarcely care to predict.

Mr. Gladstone is presently posing before the public as the candidate for a Scotch constituency which demands more moderate views than the ex-Premier has been in the habit of advancing for some time back; and he may very naturally dread the risk of offending the tastes of his future supporters by launching out into a wild course of agitation such as he embarked upon two years ago. Whether or not his impetuosity of temper has been sufficiently subordinated to these prudential considerations, will most likely be seen in the coming discussions in Parliament.

Surgeon Reynolds' Account

By Surgeon J. H. Reynolds

Surgeon-General Woolfryes was still P.M.O. at the Cape when the invasion of Zululand took place. He then had under his command an average strength of sixty-nine officers of the A.M.D and eight officers of orderlies. A number of civil surgeons were also employed. At the commencement of the war the strength of the A.H.C. was 124. These were supplemented by drafts amounting to 310 during the campaign. The regulation field hospital of 200 beds was divided into eight separate units for convenience in dealing with small bodies of troops. Each of these units was allotted two M.O.'s. two A.H.C., a cook and a wagon orderly. The transport consisted of an ambulance wagon, a store wagon, a water cart and two pack horses. The authorised transport personnel was never supplied, and the service suffered from having civilian or native drivers.

The most advanced field hospital was usually made up of two of these units, but the medical officers were not increased. For every batch of ten patients after the first, a regimental orderly had to be demanded. The ambulance wagons were either the unwieldy country wagons used in the late campaign fitted with a spring floor, or converted store wagons. Later on, thirty regulation ambulances were sent from home. Regimental units had a M.O. attached, and two stretcher-bearers per company. Each soldier was supposed to carry a piece of lint and a bandage in his left-hand trousers pocket as a first field dressing. Base hospitals were formed at Durban, Pietermaritzburg, Ladysmith, Newcastle and Utrecht, and auxiliary hospitals and convalescent depots were subsequently added. Except where station hospitals already existed, these base hospitals seem usually to have been stationary field hospitals. The equipment of a stationary and a movable field hospital only differed in the fact that the former had twice as much clothing.

Towards the end of the war, a party of Netley nurses under Mrs.

Deeble was sent out, "whose example of devotion to duty had a most beneficial effect on the men of the A.H.C." Lord Chelmsford's force crossed into Zululand about January 6, 1879, in four columns, and at four different points, being formed of two infantry battalions, or the equivalent, a, detachment of mounted troops (mostly volunteers or irregulars), three or four guns and a native contingent. To each was attached a bearer party of 8 A.H.C., and 40 native carriers with 8 Ashanti cots, additional to its field hospital establishment.

The first news of the fighting to reach England was that of a serious disaster to No. 3 column under Colonel Glynn, which, advancing from Helpmaakar had crossed the Buffalo River at Rorke's Drift. At the latter a store depot was established, and a hospital of forty beds, in charge of Surgeon James Henry Reynolds, the garrison being formed by a company of the 2/24th Regiment. The remainder of the force proceeded to camp some twelve miles further east at the foot of Isandhlwana mountain. From here on January 22, accompanied by the commander-in-chief, Colonel Glynn led out part of the troops on a reconnaissance, leaving the 1/24th, a company of the 2/24th, a section of a battery, and some volunteers and native auxiliaries in the unfortified camp.

During the absence of the main body the Zulus appeared in great force, attacked the camp, and the defenders after a gallant resistance were killed almost to a man. Among the dead were Surgeon-Major P. Shepherd, Lieutenant and Acting-Surgeon Boué of the native contingent, Lieutenant of Orderlies A. Hall and eight men A.H.C. Six ambulance wagons and all the medical equipment were lost.

The commander-in-chief's party, on their return in the evening, bivouacked amid the wreck of the camp and the mutilated corpses of their comrades, without food, and almost without ammunition, expecting an attack at any moment. At 4 a.m. a start was made for the post at Rorke's Drift, about the fate of which there was the utmost anxiety. On approaching the spot, smoke was seen to be rising, but shortly, to everyone's relief, British cheers were heard.

De Neuville's picture of the defence of Rorke's Drift hangs in the corridors of many of our military hospitals, and the story is familiar to most of us. It is unlikely, however, that many of the present generation have had an opportunity of reading Surgeon-Major Reynolds' own account of the fight, which is to be found in the A.M.D. Reports, 1878.

At 1.30 a large body of natives marched over the slope of Isandlana in our direction, their purpose evidently being to examine ravines and ruined *kraals* for hiding fugitives. These men we took to be our Native Contingent. Soon afterwards appeared four horsemen on the Natal side of the river galloping in the direction of our post, one of them was a regular soldier, and feeling they might possibly be messengers for additional medical assistance, I hurried down to the hospital as they rode up. They looked awfully scared, and I was at once startled to find one of them was riding Surgeon-Major Shepherd's pony. They shouted frantically, 'The camp at Isandlana has been taken by the enemy and all our men in it massacred, that no power could stand against the enormous number of the Zulus, and the only chance for us all was by immediate flight.'

Lieutenant Bromhead, Acting-Commissary Dalton, and myself, forthwith consulted together, Lieutenant Chard not having as yet joined us from the pontoon, and we quickly decided that with barricades well placed around our present position a stand could best be made where we were. Just at this period Mr. Dalton's energies were invaluable. Without the smallest delay, he called upon his men to carry the mealie sacks here and there for defences. Lieutenant Chard (R.E.) arrived as this work was in progress, and gave many useful orders as regards the lines of defence.

He approved also of the hospital being taken in, and between the hospital orderlies, convalescent patients (eight or ten) and myself, we loop-holed the building and made a continuation of the commissariat defences round it. The hospital, however, occupied a wretched position, having a garden and shrubbery close by, which afterwards proved so favourable to the enemy; but, comparing our prospects with that of the Isandlana affair, we felt that the mealie barriers might afford us a moderately fair chance.

At about 3.30 the enemy made their first appearance in a large crowd on the hospital side of our post, coming on in skirmishing order at a slow slinging run. We opened fire on them from the hospital at 600 yards, and although the bullets ploughed through their midst and knocked over many, there was no check or alteration made in their approach. As they got nearer, they became more scattered, but the bulk of them rushed for the hospital and the garden in front of it.

We found ourselves quickly surrounded by the enemy with their strong force holding the garden and shrubbery. From all sides, but especially the latter places, they poured on us a continuous fire, to which our men replied as quickly as they could reload their rifles. Again, and again the Zulus pressed forward and retreated, until at last they forced themselves so daringly, and in such numbers, as to climb over the mealie sacks in front of the hospital, and drove the defenders from there behind an entrenchment of biscuit boxes, hastily formed with much judgment and forethought by Lieutenant Chard. A heavy fire from behind it was resumed with renewed confidence, and with little confusion or delay, checking successfully the natives, and permitting a semi-flank fire from another part of the *laagar* to play on them destructively.

At this time, too, the loopholes in the hospital were made great use of. It was, however, only temporary, as, after a short respite, they came on again with renewed vigour. Some of them gained the hospital verandah, and there got hand to hand with our men defending the doors. Once they were driven back from here, but others soon pressed forward in their stead, and, having occupied the verandah in larger numbers than before, pushed their way right into the hospital, where confusion on our side naturally followed. Everyone tried to escape as best they could, and, owing to the rooms not communicating with one another, the difficulties were insurmountable.

Private Hook, 2/24th Regiment, who was acting as hospital cook, and Private Conolly, 2/24th Regiment, a patient in hospital, made their way into the open at the back of the hospital by breaking a hole in the wall. Most of the patients escaped through a small window looking into what may be styled the neutral ground. Those who madly tried to get off by leaving the front of the hospital were all killed with the exception of Gunner Howard.

The only men actually killed in the hospital were three, excluding a Kafir under treatment for compound fracture of femur. Their names were Serjeant Maxfield, Private Jenkins, both unable to assist in their escape, being debilitated by fever, and Private Adams, who was well able to move about, but could not be persuaded to leave his temporary refuge in a small room.

The engagement continued more or less until about 7 o'clock p.m., and then, when we were beginning to consider our situation rather hopeless, the fire from our opponents appreciably slackened, giving us some time for reflection.

Lieutenant Chard here, again, shined in resource. Anticipating the Zulus making one more united dash for the fort, and possibly gaining entrance, he converted an immense stack of mealies standing in the middle of our enclosure, and originally cone fashioned, into a comparatively safe place for a last retreat. Just as it was completed, smoke from the hospital appeared and shortly burst into flames. During the whole night following, desultory firing was carried on by the enemy, and several feigned attacks were made, but nothing of a continued or determined effort was again attempted by them. About 6 o'clock a.m., we found, after careful reconnoitring, that all the Zulus with the exception of a couple of stragglers had left our immediate vicinity, and soon afterwards a large body of men were seen at a distance marching towards us.

I do not think it possible that men could have behaved better than did the 2/24th and the Army Hospital Corps (three), who were particularly forward during the whole attack.

Besides Lieutenants Chard and Bromhead, Surgeon J. H. Reynolds and five of the 24th received the Victoria Cross for their gallant defence of the hospital. Reynolds omits in his narrative the fact that during the most critical part of the struggle round the hospital, he crossed and recrossed the space between the building and the store to bring a fresh supply of ammunition under heavy fire.

The news of the disaster at Isandhlwana produced such consternation in England as it is at this date difficult to realise. It is not too much to say that the possibility of British troops being out-generalled and out-fought by half-naked savages, had never occurred to the public at that time. Reinforcements, which included, of course, medical personnel, were hurriedly pot ready. Meanwhile, Natal was put in a state of defence, and all the columns, except Colonel Pearson's, which entrenched itself at Ekowe, withdrew towards their bases. The remnants of No. 3 fell back on Helpmaakar, and Colonel Evelyn Wood, who was the mainstay of our considerably disheartened troops, established a fortified camp at Kambula, covering Utrecht in the Transvaal.

Ekowe was relieved by Lord Chelmsford, early in April. In March,

Wood's column did some hard fighting. His medical staff consisted of the usual field hospital detachments, with Surgeon-Major O'Reilly as S.M.O., and a party of native bearers. On March 28, a force of mounted troops and irregulars, part under command of Lieutenant-Colonel Redvers Buller, were surrounded, and nearly cut off on the Zlobane mountain. During the stampede back to camp, in which Buller earned his V.C., and during which many casualties occurred, Civil Surgeons Jolly and Conolly were the last in the retirement, pursued by several thousand Zulus, and frequently dismounting to assist wounded. In the attack on the camp next day, the whole medical staff and their orderlies won the approbation of the column commander.

During the hottest part of the fight, and in a very exposed part of the camp, Brown and Thornton, two regular surgeons, successfully amputated an arm. The enemy were utterly routed in the end, and pursued by the mounted troops. During May, the troops were concentrated in two very weak divisions, under Generals Crealock and Newdigate, and a flying column under Brigadier-General Evelyn Wood. The first division troops, of which Surgeon-Major Tarrant was S.M.O., were concentrated round Ginginlovo, and remained stationary in the unhealthy, low-lying country near the coast till late in June. The situation was aggravated by the absence of any sanitary efforts on the part of the troops in the camps of the colonial irregulars, and of the friendly Zulus.

Malaria, dysentery, and enteric were prevalent, and the medical staff and A.H.C. had a hard time. The hospitals at Fort Chelmsford and Fort Pearson were evacuated by road to Durban, except for the last fifteen miles, which was done by train. For this purpose, ten English ambulance wagons were employed, and rest stations in charge of A.H.C. non-commissioned officers were established on the road. From Fort Pearson to Durban is seventy miles. After the advance, the sea route from Port Durnford was available.

The second division, which, with the flying column, did most of the fighting during the second phase of the war, were more fortunate, as they were operating in the healthy upland country of central Zululand. Surgeon-Major Giraud was the S.M.O. On May 20 a junction was effected with Wood's flying column at Inceni mountain, and the combined force of 4,062 Europeans and something over 1,000 natives advanced eastward. The commander-in-chief, on whose staff was the Prince Imperial, accompanied them.

After the tragic death of the latter, his body had to be embalmed on the spot, and dispatched to the base in an ambulance. On July 4, Lord Chelmsford met the enemy at Ulundi. Taught by bitter experience, no mistakes were made this time. The force drew out in a square, against which the Zulu attacks were vainly expended, and a charge delivered by the 17th Lancers completed the victory. Our losses amounted to no more than nineteen killed and eighty-nine wounded. During the action, casualties were attended to at the field hospital, in the left rear of the square.

The evacuation of wounded and sick from the force, during its advance, was to Koppie Allein by sick convoy, whence the more serious cases proceeded to Ladysmith *via* Dundee, and the remainder to Utrecht.

The first division advanced no further than Port Durnford. The war ended with the capture of King Cetewayo, by the mounted troops, early in September.

The Zulu War having been brought to an end, an expedition was undertaken against a chief named Sekukuni, who had given constant trouble to the Transvaal Government. From our point of view it is mainly of interest for the employment of what has been described as the first bearer company. This company was trained in South Africa, by Surgeon-Major James Hector, the personnel consisting of 2 N.C.O.'s and 24 men of the 21st Regiment, the same number from the 94th, a serjeant and 17 men A.H.C. to perform the duties of No. 4 bearers, and 65 Kafirs. Surgeon-Major Hector commanded, and Surgeon Lloyd was the other officer.

The two battalions from which the bearers were taken represented the regular infantry at the assault on Sekukuni's town on November 28, 1879, and the fourteen stretcher squads, manned by Europeans, followed them up closely. The Kafirs, with their stretchers, formed a relay 150 yards in rear, and carried back the wounded to a dressing station supplemented by officers and personnel from the field hospital. Ambulance wagons then took the patients to the main dressing station. It will be observed that the bearer company on this occasion combined the duties of regimental stretcher bearers with their normal function.

The Defence of Rorke's Drift
By Lt. Colonel F. E. Whitton C.M.G.

The lonely little Swedish mission station, which stood on a rocky terrace on the Natal side of the Buffalo River, hardly knew itself in those early days of January, 1879. It had had greatness thrust upon it. About a quarter of a mile away there was a *drift*, or ford, over the river, by which Zululand could be entered, known to this day as Rorke's Drift. Four columns acting from the circumference of the country were to penetrate into Zululand and make for the Royal *kraal* at Ulundi, and of these columns, that known as Number 3—with which was the commander-in-chief, Lord Chelmsford himself—was to cross the Buffalo River and enter the enemy's country at this *drift* of which we have just spoken.

The actual ford was supplemented by huge ferryboats, or ponts, of a size sufficient to carry over a large Cape waggon or a company of infantry at a time; and to protect these and also some stores that were to be collected at the spot, as well as a hospital which was to be formed there, a small garrison was to be dropped when the Centre Column entered Zululand. The little mission station lent itself admirably for the purpose of a hospital and a commissariat store, and had, therefore, been requisitioned when the column came up from Natal early in January, 1879.

A large outhouse, some eighty by twenty feet, which the Swedish missionary, the Rev. Mr Witt, had used as a church, was turned into a store for mealies and boxes of biscuits, as well as for the ammunition; while the other buildings, the house where Mr Witt lived with his wife and their three children, was converted into a hospital. The dwelling-house was sixty feet by eighteen in size, and both buildings were constructed of brick and were thatched. Behind the mission station—to the south—were steep and lofty mountains through which ran the rough road to Helpmakaar.

In front—that is to say, looking in the direction of the river—was a fine orchard, and between this and the houses, which were about thirty yards apart, ran a natural step or ledge of rock three to four feet high, so that the buildings stood that height above the ground in the orchard—or 'garden' as it was usually called. Between the garden and this platform there was the wagon-track—the word 'road' is apt to convey a wrong impression—leading to the *drift*, and then, the rocky terrace was a strip, some twenty yards wide, of bush, which had not been cut down.

On the other, or southern, side of the buildings were a cook-house and two ditches with ovens—running at right angles to each other—the bank of each being two feet high, while beyond that again were the tents of the garrison of the post. The enumeration of these details may be wearisome, but before the African sun had swiftly set on the 22nd of January 1879, thatch and rock, cook-house and bush, were each to mean life or death to assailant or defender, to white man or to Zulu.

The actual garrison of the post consisted of 'B' Company of the 2nd Battalion, 24th Regiment under Lieutenant Gonville Bromhead, and a detachment—about equal to a company—of the Natal Native Contingent under a colonial officer with the temporary rank of captain. Further, in addition to some half-dozen details, there were thirty-three N.C.O.'s and men sick in the hospital. Bromhead and the colonial captain were not, however, the only officers stationed at Rorke's Drift. A subaltern of sappers—John Chard by name—was there in charge of the ponts.

Then there was the medical officer in charge of the hospital, Surgeon Reynolds of the Army Medical Department. There were also three commissariat officers—civilians in those days—and a missionary, the Rev. George Smith, who was acting as chaplain to the troops. Occasionally at the post was the staff officer in charge of this section of the line of communications, Major Spalding of the 104th Regiment, D.A.Q.M.G. As Rorke's Drift was on the Zulu border, it follows that it was at the moment the most advanced post of this line. To the south the nearest troops were two companies of the 1st Battalion of the 24th Regiment back at Helpmakaar, ten miles away.

It was a glorious day of South African summer, but although the little post was now free from the hustle and worry caused by the passage of the column across the river some days earlier, there was yet an atmosphere of tension and of strain. At dawn there had ridden in from the Zulu side of the river a young subaltern of the 95th who was in charge of 100 ox-waggons with the column. He had been sent back at midnight with a message from Lord Chelmsford to hurry up a column of native reinforcements under Colonel Durnford, R.E. He told how the column had gone into camp under the far side of a hill, nine miles away, called Isandhlwana, and that "a big fight was expected."

It had been a jumpy ride back in inky darkness, along a rough track intersected by steep *dongas* and through country that was known to be swarming with Zulus—especially for a twenty-year old subaltern. But this subaltern had the heart of a lion. His name was Horace Smith-Dorrien.

Having borrowed eleven rounds of revolver ammunition from 'Gonny' Bromhead, young Smith-Dorrien recrossed the river about half-past six and galloped off towards Isandhlwana. Then, after breakfast Chard obtained leave from Major Spalding to ride out to that place himself and ascertain if there were any fresh orders which would affect the service of the ponts of which he was in charge. Chard returned shortly before noon with the information that large bodies if Zulus had been reported working round the left of the camp at Isandhlwana, and he said that he thought it just possible they might be intending to ignore that camp and to "make a dash at the *drift*."

This was exciting news, but no one seems to have imagined for a moment that the post could be in any real danger. After all the column at Isandhlwana—about 4,000 strong, although more than half of these were natives, and very unreliable natives at that—with a battery of six seven-pounders, was only nine miles away from the drift, and Lord Chelmsford would hardly allow the Zulus to move unmolested against his advanced base. And if a battle then developed, who could doubt the result? There seemed therefore, nothing to worry about, and it is certain that no steps were taken to place the post in a state of defence.

Indeed, the Rev Mr Whitt, the Swedish missionary, who was still there, with the Rev. George Smith and Surgeon Reynolds, went up to the top of a neighbouring hill 'to see the fun' on the other side of the river, which, in the extraordinary clearness of the South African atmosphere, was quite feasible even with glasses of moderate power.

At lunchtime, however, it seems to have been decided that a reinforcement of the post might be desirable. A company of the 1st/24th ought to have arrived from Helpmakaar two days before, but for some reason it had not yet reached Rorke's Drift. Major Spalding, in supreme command of this section of the line of communications, decided to ride back himself and bring the belated company with him to the post. At two o'clock, therefore, he rode off, and before leaving told Lieutenant Chard that, during his—Spalding's—absence, he would be in command of the post.

So far as the two regular subalterns were concerned this was in order, for Chard was senior to Bromhead. But there was also another combatant officer present, of the Natal Native Contingent, with the rank of 'Captain'. As, however, both Chard and Bromhead were regular soldiers of more than eleven years' service apiece, and the captain had obtained his temporary commission merely a short time before, on the raising of the Native Contingent, Major Spalding did not worry himself about any titular claim to command which the colonial officer might have referred. It was just as well.

After Major Spalding's departure Chard rode down to the *drift*, where he busied himself with matters concerning the ponts which were his special charge. All was quiet at the river, but about 3.15 p.m. he was startled to see two mounted white men riding hell-for-leather on the Zulu side, heading towards the *drift*. In response to their shouts one of the ferryboats was sent across, and the horsemen proved to be an officer and trooper of a mounted irregular corps belonging to the column.

The officer, Lieutenant Adendorff, had a terrible tale to relate. The camp at Isandhlwana had been attacked that morning by 10,000 Zulus, and of the white troops there in camp, only a handful had escaped. It appeared that before dawn Lord Chelmsford had gone out with half the column to make a reconnaissance in force and to select a new camping-ground. There had been left behind at Isandhlwana some 1,800 officers and men, including six companies of the 24th Regiment, (5 companies 1st Battalion; 1 company 2nd Battalion), and about noon the Zulus, who had been reported earlier in overwhelming strength, advanced upon the camp in the form of an immense semi-circle, with the 'horns' gradually closing in.

The camp was in no way whatever prepared for defence. The tents were all standing. Not a waggon had been laagered; not a sod had been turned; not one stone had been placed upon another to form a breastwork. There had been, however, no question of surprise. The country was open, and for hours the Zulus had been observed by the outposts. But the outposts were too far out and too scattered, and when they were driven in upon the main body the situation became critical.

The native contingent immediately broke and fled. The 7-pounders continued gallantly in action, and the companies of the 24th, as the Zulus closed upon them, met the attack with a steady and discipline fire. Then the terrible thing had happened. The firing slackened, died away, and then ceased altogether. Ammunition had run out. Yet there had been no real lack of ammunition. There was all the reserve supply of the column—hundreds of boxes of it. (400,000 rounds. It was packed in the regulation wooden boxes; the lid of each box being fastened by 9 screws.)

But when the cry for "More ammunition" was raised, the screwdrivers wherewith to open the boxes could not be found; or, if found, the boxes could not be got at, for many of them were strapped on the backs of mules which were plunging or bolting in terror. The Zulus had suffered enormous losses, but now encouraged by the cessation of the rifle fire, they had rushed within *assegai* range, and what followed had been a massacre. Standing in groups, often back to back, the officers and men of the 24th, as well as the few white irregulars, had been killed almost to a man.

A few white men, provided with horses, at the last moment, dashed after the fleeing natives, but the horns of the Zulu *impi* had closed. As to what had happened to the detachment which had gone out with Lord Chelmsford it was impossible to say. By half-past one all was over at Isandhlwana. No sign whatever had been seen of Lord Chelmsford or of his force. Meanwhile thousands of Zulus were advancing rapidly towards Rorke's Drift.

Chard had been little over an hour in command at Rorke's Drift. Well might he have been dismayed by this terrible news, and any suspicion that the tidings had been exaggerated was discounted by the receipt of a note from Bromhead to say that a mounted infantryman had just come in with an urgent message, and to beg Chard to come up at once and take command. Chard instantly gave orders to pack up such stores as were at the *drift* and to bring them up to the post in the waggon. Of the two men who had crossed the river the trooper was sent off with the news to Helpmakaar, while the officer pluckily asked to be allowed to stay and help in the defence of the post.

Chard then galloped up to the post, where he found Bromhead feverishly engaged in loopholing the commissariat store and the hospital, and in connecting the two buildings by walls of mealie-bags supplemented by two waggons that were in the camp. Bromhead gave Chard the note—brought in by the mounted infantryman—in which it was stated that Zulus were advancing in force against Rorke's Drift and that the post there was to be strengthened and held at all costs. But in all orders, it may happen that circumstances may have completely changed since the order was issued.

The instructions to strengthen and hold the post at Rorke's Drift had been given before the force at Isandhlwana was attacked, and when it was even believed that the Zulus might pass by that place in their eagerness—as Chard himself had surmised—"to have a dash at the drift." It was one thing to hold on to Rorke's Drift when the whole of Number 3 Column was in being and but a few hours' march away: it was quite another to try and hold it with a mere handful of men now that half that column had been massacred and the other half might well have been massacred too.

Besides, since the note had been written, the strength of the Zulus had been enormously increased. It was known, at the outbreak of hostilities, that a proportion of them possessed rifles and guns, but now their complete victory at Isandhlwana had yielded them at least fifteen hundred more firearms and a practically unlimited supply of ammunition. In circumstances so startlingly altered prudence might well have recommended a short withdrawal from Rorke's Drift to some suitable defensive position in rear, where, at any rate, a good field of fire might be obtained, and where union with the company coming up from Helpmakaar might more certainly be effected.

But there was another point to be considered. If the detachment which had gone out under Lord Chelmsford from the camp at Isandhlwana could manage to fight its way back, then it was imperative that the stores at Rorke's Drift should be preserved. For, by the disaster, all the transport, all the supplies and all the reserve ammunition of the column had been lost, and at that very moment the detachment might be fighting its way towards the river, short of ammunition and in desperate need of food. To fall back to a defensive position in rear, although it might mean the safety of the garrison, would infallibly mean that the stores would fall into Zulu hands.

At all costs, therefore, even though the circumstances had since morning so dramatically changed, it was imperative to defend the post. Chard held a hurried consultation with Bromhead and with Mr Dalton of the commissariat, who was doing splendid work. It was decided that it was useless to try to hold the *drift* as well as the post. The two were more than a quarter of a mile apart; and, besides there were other fords in the vicinity which would certainly be known to the advancing Zulus. Every man, therefore, must be concentrated at, or immediately round, the post itself.

Chard accordingly galloped down again to the *drift* to hurry up the guard there of one sergeant and six men. On his arrival, the sergeant and the ferryman—a civilian—instantly volunteered to moor the ponts in the centre of the river and with a few men to defend the crossing with these improvised monitors. But Chard did not feel warranted in accepting an offer which would have meant a terrible risk to the men concerned, though he was cheered by the spirit in which it was made, and felt that it augured well for the fight which must now be at hand.

Back again to the post galloped Chard. He was not letting the grass grow under his feet, for little more than a quarter of an hour had elapsed since he had seen the two horsemen galloping to the *drift* with the news of the terrible disaster at Isandhlwana. It was now exactly half-past three, and shortly afterwards what seemed to be a welcome reinforcement arrived. This was an officer with about a hundred native horsemen of Durnford's force who had escaped from the massacre.

The officer asked Chard for orders, and was requested to send a detachment to observe the drifts and ponts, to throw out outposts in the direction of the enemy and to check his advance as much as possible; when forced to retire, the natives were to fall back on the post and to assist in its defence. Meanwhile the work of putting the place in a state of defence was proceeding with great activity. The tents had already been struck. The windows and doors of the hospital were blocked up with mattresses and tables, and loopholes were constructed in the walls of both this building and the storehouse.

The wall of mealie-bags was raised to a height of four feet, and continued so that a large rectangle was formed of which the bottom corners were filled by the hospital and store respectively. Of the sick in hospital many were able to turn out to play their part in the defence; an attempt was made to remove the serious cases to some place of safety, but when the two ox-waggons were brought up news had come in that the Zulus had been sighted. So, the two waggons were incorporated in the southern wall of mealies joining the hospital and the store. The water-cart in the meantime had been hastily filled and brought within the enclosure.

Every man was ordered to his post, and events now moved quickly. The Swedish missionary and his companions returned with the news that large numbers of Zulus had crossed the river by a *drift* about a mile away and were moving so as to take the post in reverse. In five minutes, they would probably be close at hand. Mr Witt then rode off to try to reach his wife and family, who had been sent back to a farm when the mission station had been taken over by the military.

About a quarter past four the sound of firing was heard behind the hills to the south, and just then the officer of Durnford's horsemen galloped in reporting the enemy close at hand, but reporting also that his men would not stand and were making off towards Helpmakaar. Chard looked in the direction in which the officer pointed, and there they were, about a hundred of them, galloping from the field. The sight was too much for the detachment of the Natal Native Contingent at the post. They, too, made off, and their officer, mounting his horse, galloped away likewise.

By this defection the total number within the post, was now reduced to, all told, 8 officers and 131 other ranks, of which latter number 33 were hospital patients. Of the figure 131 other ranks the 24th Regiment accounted for 110. Save for our or five natives in the hospital the defence of the post was now entirely in the keeping of white men.

Although possibly Chard and Bromhead were well rid of the fainthearts, it was now only too clear that the line of defence was too extended or the small number of men who remained. Chard, however, was equal to the emergency. There were wooden boxes full of biscuit in the store, and with these a retrenchment was at once begun, connecting the two parallel walls of mealie-bags at the storehouse end of the enclosure, so that what was virtually an inner work might be thus provided. Feverishly every man that could be spared worked at the task, but, before the wall was two boxes high, a murmur of "Here they come," from the southern wall of mealie-bags, sent every man hurrying to his allotted post.

Pouring over the right shoulder of the hill behind the mission station there appeared a dense mass of five to six hundred Zulus. On they came at the run, deploying as they advanced, making straight for the mealie-bags which filled the gap between the storehouse and the hospital. The attack was met with a steady and well-sustained fire; but although the old .577 Martini-Henty was a real man-stopper, and although Zulu after Zulu was knocked over, the survivors with rare courage got to within fifty yards of the wall. Here, however, they came under a terrible cross fire from the wall of mealie-bags and the loopholes of the storehouse, and the onrush was definitely stayed.

Some of the Zulus at once took cover behind the cookhouse and in the trenches where the field ovens were situated, and from this cover kept up a harassing fire. The bulk, however, swerved to their left, and, passing round the hospital, made a desperate attempt to rush the mealie-bags at the north-west corner of the enclosure. But the attempt was repulsed, and the baffled Zulus, now edging eastwards found cover in the piece of bush and below the rocky terrace on which the northern breastwork of mealie-bags had been erected.

The post was, therefore, threatened from both front and rear. But this was not the worst. The Zulus hitherto engaged were but the advanced guard. Thousands more could be made out lining a ledge of rocks and some caves overlooking the post four hundred yards to the southward. This main body for some minutes kept up a brisk fire which seriously inconvenienced the defenders of the post.

Mr Dalton, one of the commissariat officers, who had done splendid work in preparing the defences and had been continually moving along the breastwork encouraging the men, was now wounded. Unable to use his rifle any longer—though he continued to direct the fire of the men near him—he handed it to his storekeeper, Byrne, who, however, was almost immediately shot dead.

Meanwhile many of the main body of the Zulus had rushed forward from the rocks and caves behind, and, bearing well to the left, had passed the hospital, where they changed direction to the right, with the result that the northern face of the post was now in great peril. The garden on the farther side of the waggon track was soon occupied by a large body, and, taking advantage of some cover from view there afforded, the Zulus prepared to storm the northern breastwork.

With a wild rush they crossed the track and the belt of bush, and, scrambling up the rocky terrace, actually held one side of the breastwork while the men of the 24th held the other. Maddened with desire to kill the white men, the Zulus made several desperate attempts to swarm over the parapet, but every attempt was splendidly met and repulsed with the bayonet. Many Zulus actually grasped the bayonets of the defenders, and, in two instances wrenched them from the rifles, but they were instantly shot down.

One Zulu standing on the parapet fired at Corporal Schiess, of the Natal Native Contingent, the charge blowing the corporal's hat off. Schiess instantly jumped on to the parapet, bayoneted the Zulu, regained his place, bayoneted another, and then climbed once more upon the sacks and bayoneted a third. The corporal was a hospital patient, and, in addition, had been seriously wounded in the foot some time earlier in the engagement.

But the steadfast courage of the thin line of heaving, thrusting, sweating soldiers of the 24th who held that northern wall of mealie-bags could but delay the inevitable. A hand-to-hand fight in which the white men were enormously outnumbered could have but one end, and it was only a question of time before the corn-sacks would be torn from the breastwork and a wave of Zulus with their stabbing *assegais* would surge in among the defenders.

Nor was this all. In addition to the hand-to-hand combat in front, the defenders were still being fired upon heavily from the rocks and caves four hundred yards in rear. Although that fire had at first been wild and ill-directed it had now become much more serious, and within a few minutes five of the defenders had been killed by bullets from the rear. The company from Helpmakaar could not be expected for some hours, and it was most unlikely that it could force its way through the thousands of Zulus between it and the *drift*.

In these circumstances Lieutenant Chard gave the order for all the men who were holding the ramparts of mealie-bags to retire behind the entrenchment of biscuit boxes at the eastern end of the enclosure. But now the grave drawback of the position became at once apparent. The hospital at the other end was isolated. The post now resembled a sailing ship attacked by pirates' boats, the majority of the crew driven from the waist of the vessel to the poop, leaving its defenders completely cut off. The hospital building was now the forecastle; but the position was really worse than this; for in a forecastle the door would have opened on to the main deck, whereas from the hospital there was no egress on that side save by a small window high above the ground.

All this time the Zulus had been trying desperately to set fire to the thatched roof of the hospital, and scores of them leaped over the walls of the mealie-bags in their eagerness to get to the inner side of the building. Scores of them were mown down by volleys at a few yards' range from the rampart of biscuit boxes, but others took their place, yelling out their war-cry of *Usutu! Usutu!* Foiled in their attempt to fire the roof from the enclosure the Zulus redoubled their efforts at the farther end, where at any rate they were not exposed to those terrible volleys from the retrenchment. Soon they succeeded in their work, and, to the horror of the defenders of the eastern end of the post, a cloud of smoke rose from the hospital roof.

There were gallant deeds done at Rorke's Drift that day. But for courage and devotion to duty nothing can exceed the conduct of the half-dozen privates of the 24th Regiment left as the garrison of the doomed building. No office, no non-commissioned officer, was there to command and encourage them. The roof of the building was in flames; the place was filled with smoke; within it were at least a dozen patients too ill or too seriously incapacitated to take their place in the fight; the building with its separate and improvised wards was most unsuited for defence.

In one of the farther rooms two privates and a couple of patients held the door for more than an hour until their ammunition was expended, and then continued to guard the portal with their bayonets. With a fierce rush a band of Zulus at length forced an entrance, and Private Joseph Williams was seized by them, dragged outside and butchered before the eyes of his companions. The surviving private and the two patients were now cut off in the farthest room of the hospital, but, while the Zulus were busy dispatching their victim, the white men succeeded in making a hole in the partition with an axe and escaping into another room.

Here they were joined by another private of the 24th, Henry Hooke by name; and he and John Williams, one keeping off the Zulus with a bayonet and the other smashing holes into the adjoining room, relieved each other every few minutes. One patient ventured through one of the openings thus cut, but was immediately seized by Zulus and dragged away; the others, however, managed to scramble through the little window overlooking the enclosure, and run the gauntlet of the enemy's fire, most of them got safely within the entrenchment.

In another ward two privates of the 24th defended their post until six out of seven of the patients had been removed. The seventh was a sergeant who was ill with fever and delirious. One of the privates went back to try to carry him out, but the room was now full of Zulus and the sergeant had been killed. The last patients to escape were the more serious cases, and these had great difficulty in climbing up to the little window. Once through, they had to fall to the ground, and, being unable to walk, had to crawl to the retrenchment under the Zulu fire.

A few patients dashed out upon the verandah on the north side of the hospital and endeavoured to cross the whole length of the enclosure to gain the retrenchment, but two or three were *assegaied* in the attempt.

From behind their low rampart of biscuit boxes but thirty yards away the defenders of the retrenchment had witnessed with heartfelt sorrow the tragedy enacted under their eyes. But their own position was also one of the utmost peril. Flushed with their success at the hospital end, the Zulus were straining every nerve to fire the thatch of the storehouse roof. Chard's inventive mind was again equal to the emergency. There were in the retrenchment two large piles of mealie sacks, and by his orders these were hurriedly formed, under heavy fire, into an oblong and lofty redoubt from which a second and elevated tier of fire was obtained, and within which the wounded were dragged for safety.

So long as daylight lasted the redoubt immediately strengthened the defence; but in South Africa darkness comes swiftly, and soon the retrenchment and storehouse were completely surrounded. Several times the Zulus attempted to rush the position, and although every attempt was most gallantly repulsed, the defenders were forced back into the *kraal* at the eastern end of the retrenchment.

The Zulus were now to pay for their successful effort of firing the hospital roof. The burning thatch flared up, illuminating the scene for hundreds of yards around, and the light thus given was of priceless service to the defenders. At about 10 p.m., however, the fire had burnt itself out, and in the darkness that ensued the Zulu attacks were again renewed. But the indomitable and steadfast courage of the 24th never failed. The men behaved with the greatest coolness. Not a single shot was wasted, and there was always the bayonet to do the work when the Zulus tried to force their way over the low perimeter of the *kraal*.

It was not until midnight that the rushes and heavy fire of the Zulus began to slacken. But there was little rest for the defenders, now exhausted by eight hours' ceaseless fighting; for until nearly dawn a desultory fire was kept up from the caves and rocky ledge in rear, and from the bush and garden in front. At last, however, some respite came, and about 4 a.m., for the first time in twelve hours, the firing died away.

Shortly afterwards the first streak of dawn appeared and the little garrison was heartened by the sight of dead Zulus piled up in heaps round the walls of the mealie-bags and especially in front of the hospital; and cheered still more by the sight of the enemy retiring round the shoulder of the hill from which they had approached on the previous afternoon. Chard and Bromhead decided to send out some patrols to search the immediate vicinity of the post. These soon returned with about one hundred rifles and guns and some four hundred *assegais* left by the enemy on the field.

Meanwhile those left within the post were strengthening the defences of the place. But while the thatch was being removed from the storehouse a large body of Zulus suddenly appeared again on the hills to the southwest. The work upon the defences was instantly stopped and every man was ordered to his post. Chard scribbled a hasty not to Major Spalding begging him to bring help without a moment's delay, and this he sent off with a friendly Kaffir who had taken refuge in the post at dawn.

The Zulus came on in the same formation and with the same determination as before, and the garrison steeled itself for another contest against the same desperate odds. Suddenly, however, there was a check in the enemy's advance. The Zulu line seemed to waver; and then, slowly retiring, it disappeared behind the shoulder of the hill whence it had emerged.

****

We must go back to the previous morning and transport ourselves to the camp of No. 3 Column at Isandhlwana, nine miles across the river. Before dawn Lord Chelmsford had taken half the column with him as a reconnaissance in force and to select a further camping ground. Some brisk skirmishing with bodies of Zulus had taken place in the forenoon, and, while thus engaged, Lord Chelmsford had received more than one message to say that the camp at Isandhlwana was in imminent danger of attack by a large enemy forces.

These messages had been treated as merely alarmist; and when Lord Chelmsford—galloping to a hilltop—had seen with his glasses the tents at Isandhlwana still standing and men in red uniform moving about he had been completely reassured. Finally, however, messages of such grave import had been received that Lord Chelmsford had decide to march his force back to Isandhlwana, and, while *en route*, the terrible truth had been revealed.

An officer was met who had ridden back to Isandhlwana to make some arrangements about rations for his men; while riding unconscious of danger into the camp, with its "men moving about in red coats", he had been fired on; and almost too late had discovered that the redcoats were Zulus dressed in the tunics of the 24th. (At Isandhlwana were 21 officers and 581 other ranks of the 24th. All the officers and 578 other ranks were killed.)

It was pitch dark when Lord Chelmsford's force stumbled into the deserted camp. The silence of the tomb reigned everywhere. Patrols moving cautiously about came upon grisly evidence of disaster. Overturned waggons, looted stores and piles of mutilated corpses told their tale. There was nothing that could possibly be done but hold on for the night and make for Rorke's Drift at dawn. As the dispirited column wended its way to the river in the early hours of the 23rd a large force of Zulus was seen to the north about a mile away moving in the opposite direction. Each column silently held its course.

The Zulus—they were those who had been attacking the *drift* and had seen the approach of Lord Chelmsford's force—had learnt that every fight was not to be an Isandhlwana. In Lord Chelmsford's force the men were exhausted with the marching and fighting of the last twenty-four hours; they were without food; all the reserve ammunition had been lost; and the men had but fifty rounds apiece, And, so, right arm to right arm the two columns, Zulu and British, like ships that pass in the night, held each upon its way.

As the British force topped a rise a pillar of smoke could be seen rising from the *drift*. Too late! The news was whispered down the column and the men plodded dejectedly on, their hearts sinking at the thought of another charnel-house they were soon to find. Suddenly there is excitement at the head of the column, and there is hurried talk among the men that figures have been decried on the roof of one of the buildings at the *drift*, vigorously waving to the column.

A fierce roar of cheering bursts from the throats of these tired, hungry and exhausted men. A section of mounted infantry gallops down to the *drift*, crosses the river, and in a few moments is among the survivors of as gallant a defence as the annals of the British Army have ever known.

★★★★★★★★★★★★★★★

Of the 139 officers and other ranks engaged, 15 were killed and 12 wounded, two of the latter dying later of their hurts. The attacking Zulu force consisted of two regiments—the Undi and Udkloko—in all a total of nearly four thousand warriors. Of these, 371 lay dead around the little post at Rorke's Drift.

Although England was stunned by the tragedy at Isandhlwana she was quick to recognise the gallantry of the stubborn defence by which that tragedy had been in part redeemed. Lieutenants Chard and Bromhead received the thanks of both Houses of Parliament for their heroic behaviour and were advanced to the rank of major. Both these officers were awarded the Victoria Cross, as was also Surgeon Reynolds. Nor were those brave privates who had defended the hospital forgotten.

Upon six the Victoria Cross was conferred. Two of these brave soldiers deserve special mention. Corporal Allen and Private Hitch were holding near the hospital a most dangerous post which was raked by the enemy's fire from the hill. Both were severely wounded; but their determined conduct enabled most of the patients to be removed from the hospital. Incapacitated by their wounds from further fighting, these two soldiers did splendid service issuing ammunition to their comrades throughout the night.

In this duty the Rev. George Smith assisted, and for his work he received a commission in the Army Chaplains Department. Many of the Old Army who read this will remember 'Ammunition' Smith as he was always affectionately called. The number of officers and men of the 24th Regiment engaged at Rorke's Drift was 110 (of whom 22 were hospital patients), and between them they gained seven Victoria Crosses. This is a noble record.

If you see a battalion of the South Wales Borderers—as the 24th is now known—upon a parade at which the Colours are carried, you will notice on the pole of the King's Colour a silver wreath of immortelles. The Queen's Colour—as it then was—of the 1st Battalion was borne off the fatal field of Isandhlwana by the adjutant, Lieutenant Melvill, and he and a brother officer, Lieutenant Coghill, were killed by the Zulus at Fugitives Drift on the Buffalo River in a gallant attempt to save it.

The Colour was subsequently recovered, and, by Her Majesty's command was brought to Osborne for her inspection. The queen attached a wreath of immortelles to the pole, and later directed that, to commemorate the devotion displayed by Lieutenants Melvill and Coghill, and in memory of the noble defence of Rorke's Drift, a silver wreath should be borne for evermore upon the staff of the Queen's Colour of both Battalions of the 24th.

Lord William Beresford

By Mrs Stuart Menzies

In 1879 Sir Theophilus Shepstone had annexed the Transvaal. Sir Bartle Frere, as High Commissioner, explained to the Zulu King, Cetewayo, that there must be no more arguing about a certain strip of land claimed both by him and the Transvaal Republic, and to avoid further trouble he had better disband his army. This demand, stated as bare, undiluted fact and shorn of parliamentary terminology, sounds rather high-handed, but anybody interested in the history can read the matter up and form his then more mature opinion, as there were other matters of importance attached to the situation without which it would not be possible to form a fair judgment. At any rate Cetewayo, seeing "no sense in it," as an old retainer of ours used to say when requested to do anything he did not like, began the row by totally defeating the British troops at Isandhlwana on January 22nd, 1879, which was not a good beginning for us, and we felt rather small.

The horrors of that time must be still fresh in the memories of all persons alive now, who were old enough to read and think in 1879. Lord Chelmsford, who was in command, was greatly blamed for his plan of campaign, but he afterwards retrieved his mistakes to some extent by defeating the Zulus at the Battle of Ulundi and taking Cetewayo prisoner. That, however, was poor comfort to those whose dear ones had been sacrificed to his mistakes, that is to say if the disaster was attributable to his errors, which I am not competent to judge.

It was at this Battle of Ulundi that Lord William so distinguished himself and won the name of "Fighting Bill," appearing in *Vanity Fair* in September the same year under that title, though I cannot congratulate "Spy" on the production, for he represents Lord Bill as a "beery"-looking person, which is the last thing he ever looked in life, but in the picture it will be noticed more than any other of his pictures or photos the resemblance in the eyes and upper part of his face to his uncle, the Third Marquis.

Hearing of the unfortunate reverse at Isandhlwana, Lord William was "just mad," to use his own words, to go and fight in South Africa, and the kind, indulgent Lord Lytton again allowed him to go, this making the third time he had been permitted to leave his work on the staff to which he had been appointed. Doubtless His Excellency admired the spirit which prompted Lord William to again ask the favour, and six months' leave was granted.

Once more we see Lord William happy and "off to the war," his soul on fire. He succeeded in getting appointed to Sir Redvers Buller's staff, and left all his affairs in the hands of a brother A.D.C. with whom he had been sharing a bungalow, and who was a great friend, telling him to attend to all his business for him during his absence, and to open all his letters, adding, "If you find any of them beginning very affectionately you need not go on." The friend who received these instructions was Captain Charles Muir (now Colonel), at that time not only A.D.C., but also commanding His Excellency's bodyguard.

Lord William knew how to choose his friends, and felt he was leaving everything in safe and adequate hands, that his interests would be faithfully looked after, and all private affairs treated with tact and delicacy. It was an anxious and responsible position for Captain Muir. There were the private letters to be cared for, the official ones to be answered, the racing stable with its inevitable worries of horses going wrong, men going wrong, and the usual everyday matters to be carried out and adjudicated upon, all this requiring considerable discretion.

Lord William arrived at Durban about the middle of April, 1879, after a tedious journey from Aden in a coasting steamer, which, like excursion trains, seemed to stop everywhere with no particular object, and mostly at horribly unhealthy-looking places.

All around the roadstead were the transports that had brought troops from England. This thrilled Lord William to such an extent he could not wait to begin his fighting for queen and country—that was to follow—that was to follow so just to keep his hand in he indulged in a fight on his own account in the hotel at Durban, which was cram-full of officers in every branch of the service. This was fight No. 1, before he had reached headquarters or reported himself; that time-honoured institution he attended to later. Fight No. 2 was another private affair, between himself and a war correspondent named Mr. Fripps, who made some disparaging remark about General Buller,

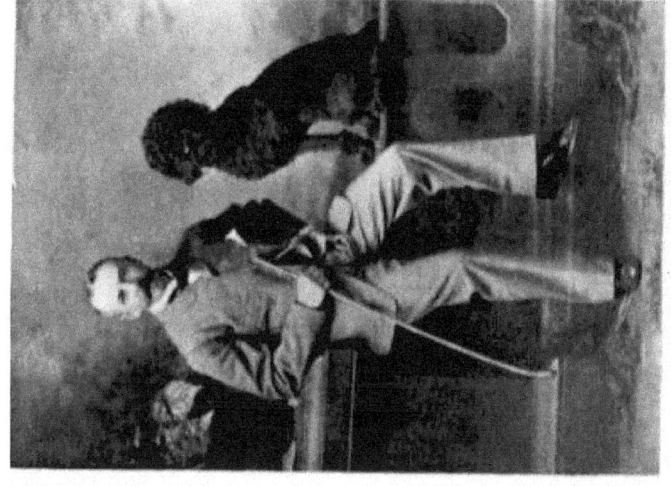

CAPTAIN CHARLES MUIR (NOW COL.), A.D.C. TO VICEROY AND COMMANDING HIS EXCELLENCY'S BODY-GUARD

LORD WILLIAM AND POSTO

when Lord William delivered a message, he had received orders to convey, and which caused the artist inconvenience.

Lord William could not stand this, and said he would not allow anybody to abuse his General, and if they did, he would thrash them. Mr. Fripps did not appear the least awed, and suggested when they got back to camp that night, they should settle the matter. Amidst the work and excitement of the day Lord William forgot all about the suggested thrashing: not so Mr. Fripps, who turned up before going to bed to see if it was convenient to His Lordship to carry out his threat. A fierce encounter ensued, and it was just touch and go who came out on top, when one of Lord William's arms got rather badly hurt; he wanted to go on fighting with only one arm, but chivalrous Mr. Fripps suggested finishing the fight another day, when he had both arms and it would be fair play. After this they were the best of friends.

Now came the official fighting. Lord William had been hoping for some staff appointment. His lucky star being in the ascendant, the wish was gratified almost immediately, as will be gathered from the above narrative, by General Redvers Buller (at that time Colonel Buller) appointing him, with the sanction of Lord Chelmsford, as his staff officer, in the place of Captain the Hon. Ronald Campbell, who had been killed in a recent battle when fighting against 20,000 Zulus.

Captain Campbell was a difficult man to follow, and Sir Redvers was rather in despair of finding anyone who could fill his place. General Marshall, who knew Lord William better than most people at that time, hearing he had arrived in the country, hastened to bring him to Sir Redvers' notice, knowing he would be invaluable.

It did not take Lord Bill long to collect his kit and start off on his long journey to join his new chief up country at Kambula, where he was in command of the irregular Volunteer Cavalry, forming part of Sir Evelyn Wood's splendid little fighting force, and it was here the Fripps fight already mentioned took place.

Lord William found he was the only staff officer with Sir Redvers, so his hands were soon full. The force of 8,000 under his chief were a strange but interesting crowd, made up largely of gentlemen not wanted elsewhere, run-away sailors, Australians, Canadians, and some of the undescribables from South African towns, in fact a cosmopolitan crowd who had volunteered for the period of the campaign for the sum of 5$s.$ a day as pay.

What made Lord William's work the more difficult was that there were several sub-commands which had originally been forces of their own, all of whom he had to keep up to the mark, work together, make efficient, and content. Every detail had to be arranged by him; also, the daily parades had to be inspected.

It was no sinecure being right-hand man to Sir Redvers, for he was a firm, silent martinet, ruling all under him with a rod of iron, and he considered it Lord William's place to wheel this heterogeneous crowd into line and order. Lord William was, in some degree, of the same way of thinking as his Chief. Both were born fighters, both, at any rate in theory, strict disciplinarians, but Lord William had the happy knack of always drawing the best out of people; his Irish wit, combined with his cheerfulness, was irresistible; even the most cantankerous, the worst funkers, the most lawless succumbed, and became his willing slaves.

June 1st saw Lord Chelmsford's Army in the Valley of the Umvaloosi, where across the silvery winding river could be seen the *kraal* of the Ulundi King, with all its minor attachments surrounding it. Two Or three days only had been allowed in which the Zulu chief had to decide whether he would do as we bid him or not. While the gentleman was making up his mind it was considered wise to find out what sort of ground was in front of our force, over which it was expected we should advance. The orders were that Sir Redvers was to make a reconnaissance across the river without aggravating Cetewayo unduly, before his days of meditation were concluded.

At the appointed hour Lord William and his Chief were to be seen in front of Sir Evelyn Wood's tent, waiting for the rest of the contingent, made up of all sorts and odds and ends.

Sir Redvers led the way, followed by the rest of the horsemen, Lord William bringing up the rear, to see all was complete. He then galloped forward to join and lead the Scouts, little thinking what stern adventure was awaiting him. General Buller followed with the rest of his party.

Cetewayo, not requiring time for consideration, having quite decided on his course of action, when hearing of our assortment of troops climbing down the bank of the Umvaloosi, at once commenced hostilities, a scattered fire from the Zulus greeting our horsemen. Nothing daunted, they forded the river on the left of a *kopje* which was evidently being held by the Zulus, and then bending again to the left took it in reverse. The late occupants were seen hurrying through the long grass out on to the open plain in front of our men, who thought they feared being cut off. Lord William and his scouts were pressing on the heels of the fleeing Zulus, some of them not reaching the *kraal* they seemed to be heading for.

It looked as if Sir Redvers and his staff officer were going to have an easy time and run straight into Ulundi. This was very exhilarating, and they galloped on close behind the Zulu chief, who was evidently in command of the fugitives, and possibly from design in their rear. He was a huge, powerful man and a veteran, which was proved by the ring round his head. Suddenly he turned round on the advancing scouts. Lord William being well in advance of the rest, leading his men, could plainly see the chief marking his distance preparing to use his *assegai*, and it came.

But his opponent was ready, and too quick for him, so dashing aside the *assegai*, he galloped with his sword up, the point fixed and rigid. The Zulu waited with his shield up. He did not wait long, the impetus given by the pace his horse was galloping carried Lord William's sword right through the shield and half through the man's body, entering his heart. He dropped dead, and the *assegai* was sent home to Curraghmore, where it decorated the corner of Lady Waterford's drawing-room.

I think we may take it the flight of the Zulus was only to lead our men on, and get them into a tight corner, for suddenly several thousand Zulus appeared out of the long grass which had entirely hidden a deep water-course in which they had been waiting. It therefore became necessary to retreat, and Sir Redvers Buller gave the order to fire a volley and then retire. Lord William and his scouts rode back, followed by many bullets. Two men were killed, and a third wounded, his horse getting away.

Always the first to lead the way into any danger zone, so likewise Lord Bill was the last to leave it. He had been taken by surprise, but was in no way flustered, and with that thought for others for which he was so remarkable, turned for a moment in his saddle, though hotly pressed by the enemy, to make sure all his living men were away and safe; he then discovered the wounded man whose horse had run away, lying helpless and dazed on the ground, but trying to rise.

He was a non-commissioned officer, Fitzmaurice by name, and at the mercy of the advancing hordes of savages who were perilously near. Quick as thought Lord William turned his Irish charger and galloped back, threw himself out of the saddle and tried to put Fitzmaurice up on to his horse, but the wounded man was as splendid as his preserver. Realising the delay only meant both being killed one might possibly escape, but two? It seemed impossible the Zulus were close on them, so he shook his head feebly, saying, "No," begging Lord William to leave him and save himself.

Of course, Lord Bill would have none of this, and, swearing mighty swear words, yelled at the man, "Come along, you b—— f—— (meaning I suppose "beloved friend"). If you don't I'll punch your b—— (beloved!) head for you."

How characteristic of Lord William. Those who knew him well will be able to picture the fierce way he would say it. Seeing Fitzmaurice was weak from loss of blood and unequal to any exertion, Lord William, though sadly impeded by the arm hurt in the previous private fight, with some difficulty lifted and shoved the man on to his horse, no easy matter on a highly-strung impetuous animal, but it was accomplished, and, hurriedly mounting behind him, galloped for life, but with little hope of escaping, the Zulus following closely.

What desperately anxious moments! made doubly so by the wounded man being unable to keep his balance from weakness and loss of blood, twice his weight nearly pulled Lord William out of the saddle, and he felt all was over. Just when beginning to fear he could not support Fitzmaurice any longer, help came in the shape of Sergeant O'Toole, who had seen their danger and rode out in hot haste to the rescue, shooting Zulu after Zulu with his revolver as they came within measurable distance. He then assisted Lord William with his now helpless burden.

It is interesting to note that both those brave men, Lord William Beresford and Fitzmaurice, were Irishmen, O'Toole, who came to the rescue, was Irish, and the horse which bore them into safety was Irish, each so splendid in their several parts; Lord William risking his life to save his countryman, he in his turn refusing to jeopardise his officer's life, then the plucky Irish horse straining every nerve in response to his master's bidding, though carrying a double burden of swaying riders. Again, the Irishman that grasped the situation, and without waiting for any word of command, lost not a moment in riding to their rescue, no precious time being lost in wondering what had happened, and if there had been a disaster. Truly a quartet of distinction.

It was hard to tell when they arrived at last in safety who was the sufferer, for all were bathed in gore. Mr. Archibald Forbes, the clever newspaper correspondent, tells the story of how on the afternoon of the same day, hearing Lord William was to be recommended for a V.C., he hurried to his tent to tell him the news, and congratulate him; finding His Lordship fast asleep, the sleep of exhaustion, he debated in his mind whether to awake him to hear the good news or let him sleep on and recuperate; deciding on the former, only to be rewarded by having a boot thrown at his head and being told to go to h— (heaven, I suppose).

Later on, hearing he really was to be recommended for the Cross for Valour, he remarked it would be no pleasure to him unless O'Toole received one also. I wonder how many men there are who would have thought of that? No doubt O'Toole's promptness had a good deal to do with the ultimate safety of the party, but it was due to Lord Bill's courage and kindness of heart that the episode occurred, and to him, assuredly, the greater glory.

In a letter written at this time by Lord William to Lady Lytton he says, speaking of his experiences:

"They were indeed two days' worth living for, and never to be forgotten. I was lucky in the day's reconnaissance inasmuch that I helped to save a poor man's life, whose horse fell with him, about 200 yards from 3,000 Zulus. He was half stunned and bleeding a good deal. I galloped back to him and with difficulty got him on to my horse (even more exciting than the gymkhana races two on one pony). The Zulus had come to within 50 yards of us when I managed to start off at a gallop with him, never thinking that the pair of us would get out alive, but we did."

It will be remembered that it was during this savage war that Prince Louis Napoleon lost his life.

When Lord Bill, or "Fighting Bill" as he was now called, returned to India, many people hardly knew him he was so altered in appearance, owing to his having grown a beard. It certainly entirely changed his face, and his friends were glad when he turned up one morning "in his right mind" as somebody expressed it, or, in other words, shaved, and as he was before he wasn't.

He was of course *fêted* and patted on the back, but fortunately he was not a nature this would spoil. At one regimental dinner given in his honour while being carried round the table on the shoulders of some of his old pals he espied in a corner of the room a doctor wearing the ribbon (V.C.), so the moment he could free himself from the affectionate attentions of his friends he made a dive for the doctor, and hoisting him on to his shoulders (regardless of the man's protests, who thought his last moment had come) ran round the room with him on his shoulders, all present now cheering lustily.

It is delightful to remember this sympathetic action of Lord William's, his blood still at fever heat, from the excitement and lust of battle and the appreciation and applause of his countrymen, yet in the zenith of his pleasure and congratulations on receiving the V.C., the moment he caught sight of the ribbon on another man's breast at once wished him to share in the applause and cheers of the evening. With quick perception and never-failing sympathy with others, he knew in a moment what memories had been stirred in the old hero's heart, perhaps a little bitterness for the forgetfulness of mankind, and that chivalrous action of Lord William's turned his night into day, all present drinking to the two V.C. heroes.

There are in this world a certain number of people who are by nature so jealous they cannot bear to hear anybody praised but themselves, who say when others have performed deeds of valour that it is purely a question of chance and luck, that of course everybody would have done the same if only they had the opportunity. No doubt many would like to do great deeds, give their souls for the opportunity, yet when the moment presents itself, fail to recognise it, and so the golden chance is lost. All are not blessed with a quick perception, dashing courage and an uncommonly human heart.

Deciding that a sight of the old country would do him good, Lord William thought he would finish up the remainder of his leave by dashing home. After figuring out the time it would take going and returning, he found he would have just eighteen clear days for enjoyment. They were a great eighteen days, but hardly restful, though certainly refreshing. The first to greet and congratulate him as the ship neared Plymouth was the Prince of Wales, who was in the Sound at the time with Lord Charles Beresford, and His Royal Highness was the first to convey the news to Lord William that the queen had been pleased to give effect to the recommendation for the V.C., and that he was commanded to Windsor to receive the reward at the hands of the Queen Empress. This was a happy beginning to the short but well-earned holiday. The prince was always a good friend to Lord William, indeed to all the Beresfords. It was seldom one of them was not in attendance in some capacity.

A very happy, light-hearted Lord Bill journeyed to Windsor to receive the modest looking but much coveted bronze Cross "For Valour," Her Majesty pinning it on to the hero's breast, but not before he had explained to his queen, he could not in honour receive recognition of any services he had been able to perform, unless Sergeant O'Toole's services were also recognised, as he deserved infinitely greater credit than any that might attach to himself.

The queen, appreciating this generosity and soldierly honesty, bestowed the reward also on Sergeant Edmund O'Toole of Baker's Horse, and Lord William was satisfied. He received a great ovation in London, being especially pleased with the congratulations of the Prince of Wales, who, while shaking him warmly by the hand, made one of those individual and graceful little speeches for which he was so deservedly popular.

When the Prince of Wales became King, he grew so weary of wrestling with the pins of medals which would not penetrate stiff material, that he designed a hook for fastening these on, to take the place of the pins, which makes it a much more simple and less fatiguing process. The hook is taken back after the hero leaves the "Presence."

After a great ovation in London, Lord William made straight for Ireland, going first to the Bilton Hotel in Dublin, then a fashionable resort. He asked his old friend the hall-porter if there was anybody he knew in the hotel, and was informed that Captain Hartopp, 10th Hussars, known to his friends as "Chicken Hartopp," was in the bathroom, so he quietly went upstairs and locked the door on the outside, then turned on the cold douche from the main source, giving the occupant a rather forcible shower bath. This was followed by strong language from inside the bathroom. Lord William was outside listening, and awaiting events. Presently he heard "I thought there was only one man in the world who would dare to do such a thing, and he is safe in Africa."

But he soon found out his man was not in Africa, but at home, very much at home in Ireland, where he was pleased to find he was not forgotten, but that if he hoped to visit all the kind friends who sent him pressing invitations, he would have to cut himself into a great many pieces.

While preparing to return to India, Lord William was staying with his mother in Charles Street. The Prince of Wales was dining quietly with her one night; Lord William came down without his V.C. medal. The prince at once noticed its absence and told him he believed his mother had given him the V.C., and he should remember it ought always to be worn when in the presence of Royalty. Lord William, of course, went and fetched it.

South Africa—1879-80 by an A.D.C.

By Sir Hugh McAlmont

Almost immediately after my arrival in London, orders came to hand for me to proceed out to South Africa on special service, to be employed in such manner as Lord Chelmsford, who was commanding the troops in the field against the Zulus, should think fit. I was to take out a draft of cavalry, and I proceeded to Ireland in the first instance for this purpose. But before I had arrived at the stage of taking the men over, orders came for me to return to London as Sir Garnet was proceeding to the Cape to assume command, and I was to go out as his A.D.C.

The situation out in Zululand, as far as one could make out, was none too satisfactory. After the disaster of Isandlwhana there had been a prolonged pause in the operations, while the reinforcements that were hastily despatched from England were on their way to Natal, while transport was being collected, while additional local forces were raised, and while preparations for the campaign were made on a scale more elaborate than those which had been thought sufficient at the outset.

There had been one or two minor contretemps, and the affair of the Zlobane Mountain had only been prevented from becoming a disaster by the gallant leadership of Buffer under circumstances of unusual difficulty. The undoubted reverse suffered on that occasion had, fortunately, been compensated for on the following day, when the Zulu *impi* attacked Evelyn Wood's entrenched camp at Kambula and was beaten off with great loss. At the time of our departure from England, Lord Chelmsford's forces were understood to be invading Zululand in two columns, which were to converge upon Ulundi, the *kraal* of Ketchwayo, the Zulu king; but their progress, as far as one could judge from newspaper information, appeared to be tentative and very slow.

I had to hurry back from Dublin on receipt of the fresh orders, and was off for South Africa in the end at only two days' notice, to find much the same staff going out with Sir Garnet as had been with him at the outset in Cyprus—Baker Russell, Brackenbury, Maurice, St. Leger Herbert, etc., and we all met on the platform at Paddington on the evening of the 29th of May to proceed by special train to Dartmouth and there to take ship in the *Edinburgh Castle*. Coffey was to join us in Natal as Chief of the Staff, coming from India.

We got a great send-off. There were swarms of people of note on the platform, and a crowd had assembled in the street outside the station who gave Sir Garnet quite an ovation when he drove up. Sir Michael Hicks Beach, the Colonial Secretary, travelled in the saloon-carriage with the Chief as far as Didcot, and as we steamed out of the station there was great cheering and hat-waving. There were a whole lot of us officers in the train, all bound for the theatre of war, as a number of special service men were going out besides the staff.

I wrote from on board the *Edinburgh Castle* next morning before she sailed:

> We arrived here at 4 a.m. There was a most enthusiastic farewell for Sir Garnet at Paddington, and at all the big stations there were enormous crowds, even up to 2 a.m. Sir Garnet was asleep, or tried to sleep, through it, and we had great work in the other saloon introducing fellows to the people as the real man. Before we got to Bristol, we dressed up Bushman, (Major, later Major-General Sir H. A., Bushman of the 9th Lancers), in a helmet, and pillow under his cloak in order to give him the appearance of an enormous sumac, and as the train entered the station he was to be seen seated on the table of our saloon, with sword drawn, and bowing to everyone. You never heard such cheering in your life, and I never laughed so much as at the efforts of the crowd—a most respectable one—to see him. Bush eventually went to the window and said he intended to put all straight on the Tugela, and on his return would take off the duties on tobacco, especially Bristol "Birdseye"! What Sir Garnet was thinking of all this time I don't know, but no one could have slept within half a mile of our carriage.
>
> We sailed from Dartmouth about midday and were accompanied out of the river by quite a crowd of small steamers and yachts, while the ancient castle at the mouth of the harbour was black with people,

all cheering like mad. It was evident that Wolseley's going out was extremely popular among the public, who were somewhat disgusted at the unsatisfactory course which events hitherto had taken in Zululand. We were an hour or two at Madeira, and we reached Cape Town on the evening of the 23rd of June, and there heard the tragic story of the death of the Prince Imperial. Sir Garnet, with Brackenbury and myself, went up to Government House and dined with Sir Bartle Frere, with whom the chief had a long conference next day.

That afternoon we continued our voyage to Durban in the S.S. *Dunkeld*, arriving there three or four days later. The news from Zululand that we had received at Cape Town was to the effect that Lord Chelmsford, with part of his force, was within twenty-five miles of Ulundi and was contemplating advance. When we arrived at Durban it was reported that he was now within fifteen miles of Ketchwayo's *kraal*.

Sir Garnet had been appointed Governor of Natal and High Commissioner of Eastern South Africa, in addition to his being military Commander-in-Chief, and he proceeded at once to Pietermaritzburg to be sworn in. He remained there a day or two, making various arrangements, interviewing native chiefs and so forth, and then returned to Durban. He had decided to proceed by sea to Port Durnford, on the coast of Zululand, in the neighbourhood of which General Crealock with the First Division was known to be, whereas Lord Chelmsford, with the Second Division and a special force under Evelyn Wood, was in the vicinity of Ulundi in the heart of Zululand, having advanced from Rorke's Drift on the frontier of Natal.

The chief embarked on H.M.S. *Shah* on the 1st of July; but there was a heavy swell on when he got to Port Durnford (which was quite an open roadstead) and, finding it impossible to land, he returned to Durban. He had already sent off a message to Lord Chelmsford to concentrate his forces, moving towards the coast; and he now decided to proceed to Port Durnford by land, so as to join General Crealock. But on the 5th, before he started, he received a telegram which Mr. Archibald Forbes had brought through to the Natal frontier, riding all night, announcing the victory of Ulundi on the previous day.

To us who had just arrived in the country, this news was by no means welcome, for it was evident that the Zulus had suffered a very serious defeat and it seemed doubtful whether they would be prepared to put up another fight. It looked, indeed, as if the war was to all intents and purposes at an end, and, although Ketchwayo was still at large and it took some weeks to catch him, this proved in due course to be the case.

Sir Garnet did not, however, change his intention of proceeding to Port Durnford, and he proceeded thither at once, accompanied by Colley who had turned up from India. I was at the same time started off with a convoy that was to take along the staff baggage, etc.—my first experience of a South African trek. I wrote on the 9th of July:

> We have had a fairly lively march. At the end of the first fifteen miles, I found there was a mistake about the wagons, owing to their being as usual two, if not three, masters; the consequence being that the wagons went along without calling at the place where our things were stored. These consisted of provisions and baggage belonging to the staff. The weather was very wet. The next day I received an order to take on all the ambulances and load them instead. There were ten ambulance wagons, with ten teams of sixteen mules each but only one driver, all the rest either drunk or absent. After a great deal of work, we started with four wagons. Today we have come thirty miles. Tomorrow, we cross the Tugela.

Eventually I went on to Port Durnford alone with Walsh and Barford, my soldier servant, as the caravan got stuck and there was a difficulty about escort after one passed the Tugela and got into the enemy's country. All the Zulus whom we met were, however, quite peaceably disposed.

After his victory at Ulundi Lord Chelmsford retired in the direction of the coast with his force in accordance with Wolseley's orders, and on the 15th of July Sir Garnet met him at a mission station called St. Paul's, somewhere about midway between Port Durnford and Ulundi. Lord Chelmsford, with Evelyn Wood, Buller and several other senior officers then proceeded home, while Sir Garnet returned temporarily to Natal, and I with a lot of wagons also marched back into Natal, and then moved on north-westwards on the Natal side of the Tugela and Blood River to Rorke's Drift. The chief proposed to move afresh into Zululand from that point, following the line which Lord Chelmsford had advanced by. I wrote of this trek:

"The march has been through most splendid country, and you get as good food everywhere as in England. It quite astonished me, coming from Armenia, etc., where there was often nothing whatever to be got. . . . It would amuse you to see Walsh. He has about ninety cartridges and a pistol, and he won't go a yard without them."

While at Rorke's Drift I found an opportunity to ride over the field of Isandlwhana, taking Walsh with me. The British officers and men who had fallen on the fatal day had all been buried some time before this, but there were still a good many skeletons of Zulus who had been killed in the fight to be seen above ground. I was busy making a sketch of the scene—the lofty *kopje* which overlooks the battlefield towers above it like a monument to the slain—when my attention was attracted by a queer sort of rattling noise that resounded from some little way off, and on looking to see what could be the cause of it I espied Walsh extremely busy over there at something or other.

Asked what he was after, he replied that he was engaged in collecting teeth. It was his inexorable method of handling the skulls of defunct Zulus that was making the drumming, and he carried off some forty of these ghoulish treasures in his pocket with the intention of sending them home as keepsakes to his many *inamoratas*. Headquarters moved forward into Zululand a day or two later, escorted by a squadron of the K.D.G., and on the way to Ulundi, which we reached on the 10th of August, we encountered a violent storm that caused a certain amount of havoc amongst our animals. It, moreover, did great damage amongst the oxen of a column under Colonel (afterwards General Sir Mansfield) Clarke, which had come up from near Port Durnford and which we found waiting near the king's *kraal* when we got there.

Headquarters remained some little time encamped at this spot, Sir Garnet in the meantime carrying on some negotiations with Zulu chiefs. One day I went out with a cavalry patrol to visit a locality where, according to native report, Ketchwayo had recently established a magazine and had set up a couple of military *kraals*. We found the *kraals* all right where we expected, and they proved to be full of mealies and of forage. While poking about in the vicinity on the chance of finding arms or stores hidden I lighted upon the two guns which the Zulus had captured at Isandlwhana, concealed under grass, and the gun-carriages were shortly afterwards discovered in a *donga* close by, and almost complete.

On our returning to camp with the news of the find a couple of gun-limbers were sent out to bring the guns and their carriages in. Another day some of us went out with Sir Garnet, accompanied by John Dunn (the colonist who had lived for years in Zululand, was the possessor of an assortment of wives, and was being utilised by the chief

THE FIELD OF ISANDLWHANA
(Site of British Encampment about x――x)

in his negotiations), to blow up a whole lot of powder that had been discovered hidden away in a cave. Then began the Ketchwayo hunt. Considerable doubt existed as to whereabouts the fugitive monarch was in hiding, and it proved most difficult to extract information on the subject out of the Zulus, who displayed a highly commendable loyalty to their fallen sovereign, in spite of the strong pressure that was brought to bear on them to give him away. I wrote home on the 20th of August:

> We have been having a great hunt after Ketchwayo. I accompanied the cavalry force as a spectator, which was not an agreeable position to find oneself in; but if we had only found Ketchy it would not have mattered so much.... On Wednesday a Dutchman arrived in camp saying he knew the king's whereabouts. This was at 1 o'clock. At 3.30 the cavalry and mounted infantry started, numbering about 300, intending to march all night and to surround the *kraal* at daybreak. The distance, however (forty miles), was underestimated in the first instance; the rate at which a column would travel over a Kaffir path in the dark was not thought about at all, for the cavalry officers were not consulted but were simply told to push on; and in the third place there was not the requisite rashness to push on with about twenty men.
>
> The consequence was that we arrived at the *kraal* at about 12.30 on the following day, instead of at 6 in the morning, and the bird had flown. No one was surprised. We went on again at 2, bivouacked on a mountain, and got the king's cattle the following morning. Gifford, in command of the scouts, had a good chase after two of the king's horses and servants, and during the day we got hold of one servant and three horses.
>
> We then had a halt for information and looted one or two *kraals*. Among other things I got a capital blanket off a kaffir, who eventually turned out to be a servant of Ketchy's. The blanket I took off the savage was most acceptable as I had nothing but a cloak, and the nights are cold although in the daytime the heat is oppressive enough. Bivouacked Friday night and pursued flying Royalty till 11.30 on Saturday night, by which time we had passed him in the bush. On Sunday I joined a party which went to the junction of the Black and White Umvoloosi Rivers, about twenty-five miles from where we were, as

there was a report that the king was on that line.

But, beyond a very fine hot ride through the bush and beautiful scenery, abounding with wild game, antelopes, zebras, etc., we got no reliable trail, and on the Monday, Herbert and I retraced our steps. My horse, after his five days' work, began to show signs of exhaustion towards evening, and I had to leave him in the bush. It then became dark and very wet and we had some difficulty in crossing a river. I found a way across which was really only up to one's knees, but in going back to show Herbert and (I quite forgot to mention) Mr. Walsh the way, I fell into deep water. Well, we then got across somehow and, as luck would have it, we found a *kraal*, a large collection of huts, on fire.

So we spent a comparatively pleasant night in spite of the rain, drying ourselves in front of the flames, and got in yesterday, having done about eighty miles in two days and a night. . . . .

A dead Zulu has just been found in the stream flowing by our camp, which accounts for a peculiarly delicate flavour I noticed in our tea at luncheon. It is very curious there are so few dead bodies on the field of Ulundi. I have been over and over the ground and can only see about forty. But people who were there assert that at least 400, some say 800, were killed on the field.

I went out again a day or two later with a small party of Basutos and an interpreter named Othro, a most invaluable fellow; he knew how to deal with the Zulus and had the real tracker's instinct. Had I been allowed to keep him I believe we might have caught the king, for we were well on His Majesty's track, and we did succeed in finding Ketchwayo's war dress at a place about forty miles from Ulundi; it consisted of 183 skins of monkeys and cats. We had got hold of a couple of prisoners, but found it quite impossible to elicit from them where their monarch was, although they evidently knew; so, I burnt the hut of one of the fellows and threatened to shoot him.

He promptly made a bolt of it, and we fired at him but—rather to my relief, I must confess—we missed him among us. The other sportsman then informed us where the above-mentioned Royal garment was to be found. Things were looking quite promising for my little party, when instructions arrived to the effect that friend Othro must return at once to Ulundi; so, there was nothing for it but to go back with the Royal fugitive's full dress, but without his person. It was about a week later that Major Marter of the K.D.G., who had gone out with a small force of British and native mounted men, succeeded in running the elusive Ketchwayo to earth. The king was brought into camp at Ulundi—a fine looking man—and was packed off from there to be interned at Cape Town.

The various Zulu chiefs had, in the meantime, been making their submissions, and Sir Garnet with his staff, now moved back into Natal, proceeding in the first place to Pietermaritzburg to attend to certain matters in connection with the civil Government of the colony. We arrived there early in September, and I was then laid up for a few days with a sharp go of fever—the result of having been perpetually out in the hot sun, day after day, in Zululand, followed by cold and wet nights out in the open. Those weeks of hunting after Ketchwayo had been enough to try anybody's health, although one worried along all right so long as one was on the move and was sustained by the excitement of the thing.

Sir Garnet, after a very few days, proceeded up to Pretoria by post cart, as his presence was much needed there in his capacity of High Commissioner. There was unrest among the Boers, who had never been satisfied at the annexation of the Transvaal by Sir Theophilus Shepstone two years before; but they had hitherto been prevented from too open outward manifestations of their objection to being included in the British Empire by their fear of the Zulus.

Now, however, that the Zulus were conquered and that their king had been captured and removed to Cape Town, the Dutchmen of the Transvaal were beginning to give Colonel Sir Owen Lanyon, the Governor, cause of anxiety—Lanyon had been in Ashanti in the 2nd West India Regiment and had succeeded me as A.D.C. to Wolseley when I was invalided home from Cape Coast Castle. Owing to being run down from fever, and also because there were various matters to attend to at Pietermaritzburg before going up to the Transvaal, I did not accompany the chief on his journey, but started about a week after him.

In those days this meant a trip by post cart a distance of over 400 miles, and I had looked forward to the journey with some concern; but it proved to be much less unpleasant and exhausting than one had anticipated. The cart, drawn by four horses which were changed at stages about fifteen miles apart as a rule, went at the rate of 100 miles a day, and there were fairly comfortable way-side hotels (which combined accommodation for travellers with stores to which neighbouring farmers and natives resorted to buy necessaries of all kinds) to put up in for the night.

Although the road was at most places no better than an ox-wagon track across the *veldt*, the jolting was not nearly so bad as one had been led to expect that it would be. I wrote home:

> A young lady of about twenty-four summers, who came out as a 'sister of mercy' was sent in my charge; she is supposed to look after the wounded out here, and I think that she will make a very charming nurse. At a place called Ladysmith I was received by all the doctors as a sort of surgeon-general. I took a leaf out of Sir Garnet's book with the wounded, always asking them how many they thought they had shot.

On arriving at Pretoria, I found that, besides trouble with regard to some of the Boers, the Chief was faced with difficulties in respect to the notorious Sekukuni and his people, who occupied a rugged, little-known region roughly about 150 miles to the north-east of the Transvaal capital. These natives had always been opposed to Boer penetration into their territory, they were a martial race who knew well how in time of war to make the most of the rocky hills and bush and forest in which they dwelt, and they had quite recently inflicted something uncommonly like a reverse upon a force that had been sent against them with punitive intent.

At the end of September, when I reached Pretoria, there seemed to be considerable prospect of a campaign in this quarter although Sir Garnet was doing his best to arrange the matter without fighting. What I wrote home was:

> He says now that he is a man of peace. I think he is beginning to fancy himself as a diplomatist, and certainly if things in South Africa can be brought to a successful issue without firing a shot on Sir Garnet's part, he will have a right to the applause of everyone in England.

Just at this time Colley was telegraphed for by Lord Lytton to go to India in consequence of the massacre of Cavagnari's Mission at Kabul, and of the fresh outbreak of warfare with the Afghans. I wrote home on the 8th of October:

> I am at the old game of looking after the butler, etc. There was

a levee yesterday, and we have a party every night, but it is a wretchedly small house for anything of the kind. The butler thinks himself a much bigger swell than the guests. I told him he was not liberal enough with the champagne. 'He should think anythink was good enough for the likes of 'em as drinks it,' said he, and you can imagine the deferential air with which he serves the unfortunate colonists.

It was growing hotter and hotter day by day, but just as one was beginning to feel utterly disgusted with Pretoria and the Transvaal, and the duties of A.D.C. to a High Commissioner in a one-horse little town inhabited mainly by Dutchmen, the negotiations which Sir Garnet had been conducting with Sekukuni broke down, and we found ourselves proceeding to that potentate's territories to bring him to reason by force of arms. I wrote from Fort Weber on the borders of the Sekukuni country on the 28th of October:

We have been on the march from Pretoria to the front off and on for the last ten days. We are now twenty miles from 'Sekukuni Town,' and some twelve miles from the passes where the fighting will be. I need not say that all 'hopes' of a peaceful solution of our misunderstanding with the chief are at an end, and we shall have to drive him out of his stronghold. The chief has the greatest contempt for white men. The last three expeditions against him failed—two undertaken by the Boers, and one under Colonel Rowlands last year.
The famous Buffer was Rowlands' second-in-command, but, notwithstanding, they retreated without firing a shot and were pursued for about ten miles by the natives. (This perhaps was too severe a way of putting the thing. The force was small and had great difficulty with regard to water.—C.E.C.) This business was kept very dark, though it is well known at the War Office. However, King Sekukuni saw the British soldiers retire, the place apparently being too difficult for them, and as the Boers had always told him not to fear the English as they were cowards, especially the soldiers, it is not surprising that the fellow had become cheeky.
The population of his territory is, roughly speaking, 30,000, of whom I suppose he can put 6,000 in the field. To attack him we have about 3,000 good troops and some Swazies, but the place is most infernal for fighting, composed of rocks and caves,

and the savages are well armed for this short range work and have any amount of ammunition. Moreover, it is a bad season of the year, and we have already lost a lot of horses from some sickness which gives this district an unenviable notoriety. We are, however, about 5,000 feet above the sea, and although the days are much too hot to be pleasant the climate on the whole is a magnificent one. . . . . The other night our horses took fright in one of the storms, about ten are still absent and are being tracked through the bush.

Mr. Walsh succeeded in losing two out of three horses on this occasion. The Transvaal is in a very unsettled state, it looks as if there may be an outbreak at any moment. It is, therefore, necessary to keep troops in the towns at present, and we want more—in fact all we can get—up here! It is a situation that requires a determined, clear head, and a cool hand to deal with. Before we left Pretoria, Herbert and I gave a picnic to the '*intombis*,' or unmarried ladies, of the place. We had a few matrons, of course. The whole thing went off in great style. We had the band of the 80th Regiment (an excellent one, by the way); the place was quite charming, called the 'Fontein'—the source of the mighty Limpopo, of which perhaps you never heard, a river all the same as big as all the rivers in Ireland combined. We larked about till darkness came on, and then all the servants were drunk and no one knew where the horses were.

A letter of mine of ten days later, also from Fort Weber, began:

> Nothing to me is more difficult than this writing in a tent. I have had my share of tent life, but the whole arrangement provokes me. First, there is nothing where it ought to be—pens and paper blowing about, and one is perpetually bothered by people interrupting you wanting to see the general. My object being to prevent these fellows bothering him, they think me a regular bear. If I go to the general he says 'O, damn the fellow, I can't see him.' I accordingly tell the man that if he will kindly put down his ideas in writing they will be carefully looked into. The fellow vanishes and either brings or sends a long rigmarole, which goes to the winds of heaven.
>
> The result is that, wherever we go, we are followed by a regular mob of insatiable office seekers, disaffected farmers and impecunious adventurers, who have come to regard me as a regular

blackguard. So much for one part of my duties as an A.D.C. The very last fellow I could only get rid of by telling him to come at 11 a.m. tomorrow, knowing that Sir Garnet was going on an excursion at 4 a.m.

The chief and I had in the meantime been for a trip to Lydenburg, where Bushman was in command. It meant a ride of some eighty-six miles, which we did in twenty-six hours, using two horses each. The first night there was a violent thunderstorm and we were both pretty well drenched. Just before dark we had to descend a very steep mountain side on foot and Sir Garnet's bad leg—bad owing to an old wound—gave out; he was regularly done up and had to rest for two hours, during which the rain poured down on us. The chief had scorned the notion of carrying stimulants, but I had brought a good ration on my own account, and he was uncommonly glad to partake of a generous nip from my flask. At about 10 p.m. we mounted and rode through the forest till 2 a.m., when we lay down and slept on the *veldt* till 4-30. Starting afresh at that hour and riding off and on all day, we got into Lydenburg in the evening.

> I made some soup, which we agreed was the greatest filth we had tasted under that name. I had brought some hard-boiled eggs, but the result of putting them in a saddle-bag was that when we came to eat them, we could find no eggs, the only trace of them was a sort of yellow pipe-clay which enveloped the clothes and everything else in the bag. Coming back, we had a pleasant time as regards weather, but our guide lost his way and we were fooling round for a long time in the woods. On the ride we passed several great *kraals*, towns in fact, ensconced in the mountain sides, teaming with natives, neutral at the present juncture. The hills resounded with their chants. They are the blackest fellows I have seen. There are as many, if not more, shades of colour among the black races as amongst the whites; there are, in fact, fair blacks and dark blacks, but it would turn the devil's hair grey to see some of these fellows.

The attack on Sekukuni's fastness was being delayed owing to our allies, the Swazies, not having come up. I wrote on the 9th of November:

> *Pour encourager les autres*, there is carrying drill going on. That is, a lot of fellows are at work pretending to carry about wounded

men on stretchers. It is a pretty arrangement in appearance, but how it will work in actual practice in all the confusion inseparable from a real bloody row such as this will be at Sekukuni, remains to be seen.

Billy (W. H.) Russell, the famous war correspondent, whose campaigning experiences in many lands carried back to the days of Sebastopol, had come out to South Africa with us on the *Edinburgh Castle*, and we had been seeing a good deal of him at various times since landing in Natal. He was crossing a *spruit* one day on the confines of the Sekukuni country, when his crock stumbled and his teeth fell out, to disappear for good and all in the turgid flood. They are not the sort of adjunct that one can replace at a moment's notice when out in the wilds, and the eminent journalist had to make shift as best he could with what was left of the originals till our present operations had come to an end. But the misadventure did not improve his temper, and he was not disposed to appreciate the humorous side of the episode quite so readily as we did.

The storming of the stronghold did not come off for nearly three weeks after that, the attack actually being delivered on the 28th of November under the command of Baker Russell. Although Sir Garnet was present as a spectator he left the tactical execution in the hand of his subordinate, who managed things very well. The force consisted of the 21st and 94th Regiments, with two companies of the 80th, some guns, some rockets, and a party of Royal Engineers with explosives.

Besides these, there was a mounted force of local troops under Commandant Fereira, another force of local troops and natives under Major (afterwards Major-General Sir F.) Carrington, and some 10,000 Swazies. Carrington's and Fereira's local troops pushed on from Fort Weber to within a very few miles of the stronghold after a successful skirmish on the 23rd, while the regulars remained near Fort Weber. But it was fully foreseen that we should encounter no really serious opposition until such time as we came face to face with the positions from which Sekukuni had defied the Boers for years past.

The British troops were held back till the last moment, and, as a matter of fact, they only arrived on the scene on the afternoon of the 27th, after a somewhat trying march, and Sir Garnet and staff reached the encampment of Baker Russell's main forces about the same time. But although these main forces had approached Sekukuni's lair from the south-west, *via* Fort Weber, a not unimportant body of warriors

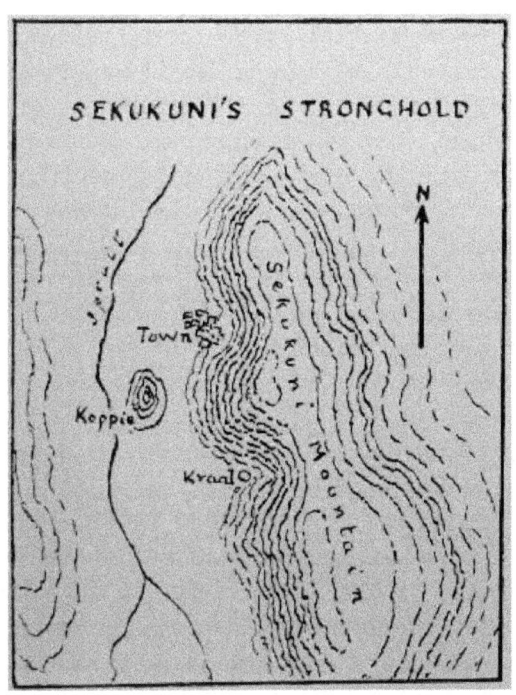

who were to participate in the fray had come from the south-east, starting from Lydenburg. This body, which was under Bushman, was composed of two companies of the both, two companies of the 94th, and of the Swazies, and it also arrived at a point about five miles from the objective (but on its further side) on the afternoon of the 27th and from there established communication with Baker Russell.

Everything tended to show that the enemy intended to offer a determined resistance, even if hitherto little effort had been made on the part of our antagonists to bar the way at the time when the forces assembling for the attack on the stronghold were advancing towards it from two different sides. But the approach of both columns had taken place, for a good part of the way, across more or less open *veldt*; and experience in the past had taught Sekukuni and his legions that they were always at a serious disadvantage when they opposed antagonists armed with rifles and supported with guns, on that kind of ground.

Sekukuni's town, Sekukuni's *kraal* and Sekukuni's "Fighting Koppie" were situated on the eastern side of a valley running north and south, and at the foot of a big flat-topped mountain which was some two or three miles long from north to south and about a mile wide. The town (the more northerly locality of the two) and the *kraal* were planted down in re-entrants running into the mountain side, and they were about half a mile apart. The Fighting Koppie an irregular mass of rock forming an extended oblong in plan and about 200 feet high, reared itself up out in the valley a few hundred yards from the mountain and formed, as it were, a detached salient between the town and the *kraal*. Bushman's force spent the night of the 27th-28th in bivouac on the east side of the mountain, while the rest of the troops encamped to the west of the stronghold. It was decided to commence operations at dawn next morning.

Baker Russell's plan of attack contemplated two distinct phases. The first phase was to consist of securing possession of the flat-topped mountain, the town and the *kraal*. The second was to consist of storming the Fighting Koppie from all sides. The first phase was carried out by three separate columns converging from the north, the south and the east. Carrington, with the Border Horse, the Transvaal M.I., some British M.I., and 700 natives attacked the town from the north, working along the sides of the mountain through awkward scrub, and the 700 natives showing no great stomach for battle at the outset. Fereira coming up from the south attacked the *kraal*, also working along the side of the mountain, and having some tough fighting before he gained his objective.

Bushman's force was to ascend the mountain from its eastern side, was to secure the whole top of it and was to co-operate with Carrington and Fereira from above; but, when it came to the point, the Swazies, who were adorned with head-dresses of dense plumes and with leopard skins, absolutely refused to stir before daylight, and the consequence was that this part of the programme was not carried out quite as had been intended. Carrington's and Fereira's columns had, however, pretty well accomplished their task when the Swazies at last appeared at the edge of the mountain overlooking the town and *kraal*, and the first phase of the operation had been satisfactorily completed, pretty well according to plan, by 7.30 a.m.

The British regulars had hitherto played practically no part in the combat, as Baker Russell was deliberately holding back the 21st and the six companies of the 94th who had come from Fort Weber to act as a reserve during the first phase, with the intention that they should play a leading role in the storming of the Fighting Koppie, while the companies of the 80th and 94th under Bushman, coming from the east, had been delayed by the Swazies' refusal to start at the proper time. The Fighting Koppie, it will be understood, was now surrounded; Carrington's and Fereira's forces, together with those under Bushman, having possession of all the ground to the north, east and south of it, while the 21st, 94th, and the four guns with the force, were on its western side ready to act. Baker Russell's plan for the storming of the rocky fastness was that the British infantry should attack the *koppie* from the north, that Carrington should attack it from the south-east, and that Fereira should attack it from the west; and the signal was given for assault at 8 a.m.

The guns were brought into action within 450 yards of the *koppie*, but being only seven-pounders, they had little effect against a mass of rocks and boulders which gave the defenders excellent cover, while these, moreover, had numbers of caves to retire into at the worst. Sekukuni's braves offered a most determined resistance and they proved by no means easy to tackle owing to the crannies that they were occupying. But the stormers would take no denial. They fought their way up from terrace to terrace till the whole eminence was in our hands, although numbers of natives were still lurking in the caves who refused to surrender.

I had been a spectator of the first phase of the operations from some little distance and was afraid that I should have to remain a spectator of the second phase as well; but the general gave me leave to bear a hand in the fighting as the troops were working their way up the *koppie*, and, being fresh, it did not take me long to get well up to the front in spite of its being a stiff climb. I wrote home:

> The fight at the town was an exceedingly pretty sight, I was out of it all till the very last. Then Sir Garnet gave me leave to join in the assault with Fereira's men, and it was about the best ten minutes possible. Going up the *koppie*, one savage as nearly as possible got me; how the shot missed I cannot make out. I pinned him with my revolver; and there were some others, but I cannot say for certain whether I shot any more of them. Mr. Barford was with me in the assault, part of the time, and did well. We had had very hard work. The night but one before the fight I spent in the open in pouring rain trying to get the road clear of baggage? and the night before the fight one got no rest either. The tents were struck at 2.30 a.m. and the fighting began at 4 and lasted till midday.

The contest was by no means completely at an end even after the cheering assailants had crowned the Fighting Koppie in triumph. Small parties of the enemy, as well as a number of individual warriors, had literally to be blown out of caves and crannies with explosives because they would not surrender. That night the *koppie* was ringed round with a girdle of troops, and natives on several occasions came rushing out from bolt-holes amongst the rocks and endeavoured to burst through the cordon. Sekukuni's braves had undoubtedly put up a gallant fight, and had lost very heavily both on the *koppie* and during the earlier struggles around the town and the *kraal*.

The Swazies, moreover, managed to kill some of them after they had surrendered, as well as a few women and children. These dusky allies of ours were out for blood, but they had showed no great eagerness to shed their own; they had, indeed, refused absolutely to budge during the early stages of the combat for possession of the *koppie* until they saw the white troops launched to the attack.

Sekukuni himself had not been present on the field, we soon learnt; but on the day after the action information was received as to his whereabouts. Thereupon Major Clarke, R.A., who was well acquainted with the natives of the country owing to having been acting in a civil capacity in the Transvaal since its annexation, proceeded with Commandant Fereira and a small mounted force to the place where the fugitive had been located in a cave about twelve miles from the battlefield. Fereira tried firing into the cave, but shots were returned. Clarke then experimented with a conflagration at the mouth of the cave, but this device likewise proved abortive.

★★★★★★★★★★

> The illustration of the cave in which the fallen chief had taken refuge is from a water-colour sketch that was made at the time by McCalmont's step-sister, Miss Rose Barton (now R.W.S.). The sketch, which was done from a rough drawing of the spot by McCalmont while he was waiting for Sekukuni to emerge, was presented to Sir Garnet Wolseley, and it used to stand on his desk years afterwards in his study at Hampton Court Palace. On the death of the Field-Marshal it was bequeathed back to McCalmont.—C.E.C.

★★★★★★★★★★

A brief siege followed; but the food supply of the occupants of the cave had been cut off, and on the morning of the 2nd of December the fallen potentate yielded at discretion. I had gone out to watch the proceedings and therefore witnessed his surrender as he was carried out on a stretcher, and as some wives and offspring crept out after

SEKUKUNI'S CAVE

him. He was an oldish man, with a grey beard and very frightened eyes, who, when taken, evidently feared the very worst—not without reason, if he imagined that the Swazies were to be let have a go at him—and it cannot be said that in demeanour nor yet in appearance he compared favourably with Ketchwayo, who had remained the king, even after he was run to earth in the Ngome Forest. I found and carried off some of Sekukuni's belongings, and then hurried off to bring the news of his capture to the encampment of the troops near the scene of their victory four days before.

I had the pleasure of taking charge of the ex-monarch on his way from his territories to Pretoria, and was always a little nervous during that trek lest my distinguished prisoner would, somehow, manage to give us the slip, although he, in reality, was much too afraid of falling into the hands of the Swazies to try anything of the sort. He was in an abject funk when his photograph was taken. I used to accommodate him and his wives in a bell-tent during the night, and had a guard sleeping all round the tent, with a brace of sentries on the watch. At the beginning of our journey, we moved along with headquarters; but before we got to the capital they had gone on ahead as the progress of our little caravan was comparatively slow. I wrote on the 12th of December, after getting back there:

> You would have laughed to see Sekukuni coming into Pretoria. He was escorted by 100 dragoons, himself seated on a heap of skins in a mule wagon, the mules of which were hardly able to crawl, surrounded by his wives and daughters—only three spouses left out of, well, I don't know how many.

After this interesting little campaign, which had had the effect of relieving the Transvaal Boers of the one native menace that was left after the destruction of the Zulu power, we settled down for the time being at Pretoria. It was evident that a General Election must take place very soon at home, and I still believed that there might be a chance of my being chosen to stand for the County Antrim. My mother was very anxious that I should become a legislator, and the idea rather attracted me; but my entering the lists obviously must depend upon whether we got home or not before Lord Beaconsfield appealed to the country.

This made one very anxious to have done with South Africa, now that all fighting appeared to be over. There indeed seemed no particular reason for retaining Sir Garnet in the country, and he himself was in great hopes that, now that Sekukuni was disposed of, he would be recalled; but, as it turned out, we were booked for some more months in South Africa.

The cable connecting the Cape with home had recently been completed—during the Zulu War there had been no place in telegraphic communication with the United Kingdom nearer than Madeira—and very shortly after our return from Sekukuni-land to Pretoria the news began to come through of the very severe fighting around Kabul that took place just before Christmas, and of the trying experiences which my old regiment, the 9th Lancers, had undergone in the Chardeh Valley. Had I remained with them I should now have been in command, as all the officers on the list between myself and Cleland in 1870 had disappeared, and Cleland had been very severely wounded in Afghanistan. As it was, I was a long way down on the list of the 7th Hussars, with little prospect of getting command of the regiment until several more years should pass.

Billy Russell had gone away off home immediately after the conclusion of the Sekukuni business. A few days after his disappearance a copy of *The Daily Telegraph*, the journal which he had been representing, came to hand, in which there appeared a long article (written, of course, some weeks previously) that reflected none too pleasantly on things military in our part of the world. It raised something of a storm in Pretoria and in Natal, the local Press finding a good deal to say on the subject.

Sir Garnet declared that it was all my fault because I had on one occasion put a great monkey in the old fellow's bed; but not for a moment would I admit that this *beau geste* of mine could possibly have been at the root of the mischief. It was not the sort of thing that any reasonable being would be disposed to take umbrage at. The storm, of course, blew over after a time, as such storms generally do, and the eminent war correspondent had, as a matter of fact, always manifested a critical turn of mind when descanting upon questions connected with soldiership and military administration.

It had been arranged that Colley was to return to South Africa from being with Lord Lytton in India, and that Brackenbury should take his place out there. On Brackenbury's departure I was for some time employed by the chief as his Military Secretary in addition to my other duties, and this kept me pretty busy until Captain Herbert Stewart joined the staff to take on the job. The government at home had decided that Sir Garnet was to remain until Colley arrived to take his place; but in anticipation of an early departure for home we moved from Pretoria to Natal in the beginning of April. His Excellency, for some reason best known to himself, thought fit on this occasion to ride the first 200 miles of the way, instead of going by post cart, and he rather knocked himself up by this exhibition of activity.

He came in looking more dead than alive, but "I'll ride you for a fiver," he called out to me cheerily the moment that he saw me. The General Election was by this time in full progress at home, and from the returns of the first few days, as cabled out, we learnt that old Dizzy's rule must be at an end, and that the country was going to be let in for a Liberal Government under Gladstone, which was likely to lead to a change in the policy that was at present being followed out in South Africa.

I wrote to my mother from Government House, at Pietermaritzburg, on the 19th of April:

> We are all this morning in great form, as a telegram has arrived, Sir Michael Hicks Beach's last gasp, to say that Sir Garnet may return to England. And the sooner the better, I say. We shall be home a week after you receive this, and indeed would leave this week, but the Empress must be received on Thursday at Durban. (The Empress Eugenie was on her way to Zululand to visit the scene of the Prince Imperial's death.) .. I got Sir G. to give D.F. six months' leave, and last night asked him to take home a set of skins of Sekukuni's as a present for my Aunt M. They are curiously sewn together, and I got them in the cave into which we ran Sekukuni. No doubt they were his own. The one he had on was not nearly so good.

We sailed from Cape Town, after various ceremonies had been gone through at Pietermaritzburg, Durban and there, on the 4th of May, in the *Conway Castle*, and we arrived at Plymouth on the 25th. Except for a day or two on getting back from Constantinople in the summer of 1878, and another day or two on getting back from Cyprus in 1879, I had been absent from the United Kingdom since leaving for Armenia three years before.

Zululand by a Staff Officer

By Arthur FitzRoy Hart-Synnot & Beatrice M. Hart-Synnot

In June 1874, Hart got his company. During the next two years he was employed by the Intelligence Department upon the scheme of defence of England. This was most congenial work to him, as it entailed life in the open air—chiefly surveying in the eastern counties.

In 1877-78 he was Brigade-Major to General Shipley, who commanded the 2nd Brigade at Aldershot. In the autumn of that year Aldershot was on the *qui vive*, for rumours of war with Russia as well as with the Zulus were in the air.

In November, Captain Hart was sent on special service to South Africa. On his arrival at Durban, he was appointed Staff-Officer to Major Graves, who was to command the 2nd Regiment of the Native Contingent. This force was formed from volunteers from the South African Colonies, and from friendly Kaffir tribes, who arrived equipped for war with *assegais* and shields.

The first few weeks were spent in equipping, arming, and organising this force into two battalions, and when this was accomplished, they marched to the Tugela and joined Colonel Pearson's column of invasion, which consisted of some regular troops, the Naval Brigade, and "Graves' Regiment."

The story of this column's hard fight at the engagement near the Inyezane River, on their way to Ekowe, is fully given in one of the following letters.

When, after the retreat to the Tugela, "Graves' Regiment" was completely broken up owing to the desertion of the natives, Hart was appointed Staff-Officer of the Lower Tugela district, and of the Ekowe relief force, with which latter he took part in the action of Gingindhlovu.

After the relief of Ekowe, Lord Chelmsford reorganised his forces, dividing them into three parts—two divisions and a flying column;

and he appointed Captain Hart Brigade-Major to the 2nd Brigade of the 1st Division.

And when Lord Chelmsford had taken Ulundi and reduced Cetywayo's capital to ashes, "the king became a fugitive, and the Chiefs of the districts from the sea to Ondini tendered their submission." Sir Garnet Wolseley, who had just arrived from England, finding that so large a force was now unnecessary, sent some of the troops back to Natal to embark for England, and reorganised the remainder, making two new columns, under Colonels Clarke and Russell, to advance upon Cetywayo from the south and west, while some Swazis, led by an English officer, closed upon him from the north.

Colonel Clarke, who was allowed to appoint his own staff, chose Captain Hart for his chief staff-officer. When Cetywayo was finally captured, and all the Zulu tribes had submitted, except one on the Natal frontier, Clarke's column marched back that way, and after receiving their submission, the war being over, they once more recrossed the Tugela.

Hart was several times mentioned in despatches, and at the end of the war he received a brevet majority and the medal with clasp.

His letters give a full account of the part he took in the campaign, and are in themselves a little history of the war.

On board the *Roman*,
Nov. 1st, 1878.

My dear May,—I embarked on board the *Roman* at Plymouth. The 1st of November was a Friday, and so, in respect of sailors' superstition I suppose, the *Roman* had commenced her voyage the day before from Southampton.

The officers on board are:

> Major Bengough, 77th Regt.
> Captain Buller, Rifle Brigade.
> Captain Cherry, 32nd Regt.
> Major MacGregor, 29th Regt.
> and myself

on "Special Service," and there are also on board for "Transport Service":

> Captain Hon. R. Campbell, Coldstream Guards.
> Captain Essex, 75th Regt.
> Captain Gardner, 14th Hussars.

Captain Barton, 7th Fusiliers.
Captain Huntley, 10th Regt.
Paymaster Bacon.

Captain Barton you will remember very well, as *aide-de-camp* to General Shipley. He received a telegram from General Shipley, just before we embarked, wishing us both goodbye and good times.

Captain MacGregor, you know. Captain Gardner was in my batch at the Staff College, the others are all strangers to me, at least they were nine days ago, for now we know each other very well. Barton and I are very old friends; we were at Fleming's together before we entered the army, when we were both in "Russell's Regiment," in the Ashanti War, and afterwards he was General Shipley's *aide-de-camp*, when I was his Brigade-Major. We have taken a cabin together on board.

Everything on board the *Roman* is excellently managed, and she is, for comfort, a yacht by comparison with those abominable vessels that ply between Liverpool and the Gold Coast.

There are eight civilian first-class passengers. Among them is a Mrs. ———, the fattest woman I have ever seen, fatter than a woman I once saw for a penny, at Charlton fair, twenty years ago; fatter than I ever imagined a human being could be, and live—I expect she is the fattest woman in the world!

Nov. 23rd.—I am hard at work learning the stars of the southern sky. Nightly, stars I have never seen before appear. I am a stranger to the southern sky. The use of this knowledge will be to obtain my exact latitude and longitude, if I should be in remote parts of the country not accurately known.

Nov. 30th.—We reached Algoa Bay (Port Elizabeth) about nine this morning. The first thing was to inquire for news, and all news was very satisfactory. We heard that the Kaffirs have concentrated in Zululand, their own territory, to fight us there, and that the operations of Lord Chelmsford's forces against them are about to commence, so it appears that we arrive in good time. The dreadful idea of my being too late sometimes crossed my mind on the way out. Then again, we got news from England up to the 10th of November, that had been telegraphed to St. Vincent in cypher, for the Cape newspapers; and this news assured us that there was no prospect of war between England and Russia. You can imagine my distress if there were war now with Russia, and I not with the 2nd Brigade! The *Roman* stops a few hours at East London, to pick up some irregular troops for the front, and then we shall be due at Durban on Thursday.

Dec. 7th.—Early this morning we went ashore in a tug-boat. From the landing-place, we had to go a couple of miles by rail to reach Durban. On arrival, there were only orders for me awaiting us. I was appointed Staff-Officer to Major Graves' 3rd Buffs. Major Graves is to command an irregular regiment, composed of 2,000 natives, taken from friendly Kaffir tribes, and he and I will have to organise this force, and take it to the front to fight if there is war. The question of peace or war will remain undecided till the end of a fortnight, after Tuesday the 10th of December.

An ultimatum will be received by Cetywayo, the Zulu Kaffir Chief, on Tuesday the 10th inst., and he will be given a fortnight to agree to all the terms of it. If he refuses, we shall invade Zululand at once. It is not expected that there will be an agreement, and war is looked upon as certain. Cetywayo has been arming for a long time, and has been overbearing and insolent. His capital is Ulundi, and if there is war, Ulundi must be captured. I remain at Durban for the present with Major Graves. Our two thousand natives have been raised, and will be sent to us at an appointed place, near the Zulu frontier, when the equipment is ready. We shall probably form a camp there. You had better address my letters as before, to the care of Lord Chelmsford.

Dec. 8th.—I dined this evening with Commodore Sullivan; he commands on the African station, as far as the navy is concerned.

Dec. 9th,—All the others who came out with me in the *Roman* went off this morning for Pietermaritzburg, the present headquarters, to get orders.

I am very fortunate in my appointment, and very much pleased with it.

Dec. 13th.—I told you in my last that Major Graves is to command one of the irregular regiments. It is called the 2nd Regiment of Natal Native Contingent, and will have two battalions. I have been appointed Staff-Officer, and Major Graves and I are the only two officers of the regular army in the regiment. All the others are volunteers, from various parts of the South African Colonies. Lord Chelmsford has refused the assistance of any more regular troops, probably on account of the Russian question.

The Tugela is the frontier of Zululand and Natal. A naval force of, I believe, nine officers and about a hundred men, has been landed at the mouth of the Tugela, where the principal road from Natal into Zululand crosses by a ford; and they will cover us from the enemy while we are forming on the Nonoti.

I have been at work on the question of arming, equipping, and supplying our force on the Nonoti, and I hope we shall be assembled there in a few days.

You cannot imagine what a strange collection of men the Europeans of our regiment are: we have English, Irish, French, Germans, Danes, Swiss, Dutch, Norwegians, Swedes, Belgians, and besides these Europeans, America is represented. I expect there are some strange personal histories among those men. I dare say by degrees I shall become acquainted with them.

Dec. 16th.—This morning we received by telegram, from headquarters, permission to move to the Nonoti, and encamp there, as soon as we could get our regimental equipment. I found the tents, &c. were not likely to be ready for a long time. I proposed that we should go to the Nonoti with such as we could get, and then make huts to supply the deficiency. This was approved on the morning of the 16th, and I then set to work with all my possible effort to get the equipment. On Thursday the 19th of December I started about noon, by special train from Durban, with the officers, sergeants, and corporals of the regiment, our baggage having already gone on ahead. I thought we should have gone very quietly, but there was a crowd at the station to see us off; Major Graves was not yet able to join us, so I started in charge.

We numbered about two hundred altogether. Railway carriages being few, open trucks were provided chiefly. I got into a carriage, but finding it extremely stuffy, I got out again at once, and took a place in one of the trucks. In this I had plenty of air, a pleasant breeze, and could see the country well. The Nonoti River is about sixty miles from Durban by road, to the place near the mouth of the river where we were to form camp. There is a railway from Durban for sixteen miles in that direction, to a place called Saccharine, and as the highroad between Durban and Saccharine is particularly heavy and bad, it was arranged that the transport bullock wagons should go to Saccharine and meet us there, we going by rail.

The country we passed through was very interesting to me. Most of it was laid out in plantations of sugar-canes, and there were also plantations of tea and coffee. Large tracts of coffee had been abandoned to go wild.

The railway is only opened to the public from Durban to Avoca, half-way to Saccharine, but the metals being laid to Saccharine, the Government allowed us to proceed so far. Avoca is a pretty vale, but does not approach in beauty the original, from which, I suppose, it is named. As we reached Saccharine, it changed from a bright summer day to wet. The bullock wagons, ten in number, were ready, and I set all hands to work to unload the trucks and load the wagons. It was cheerless work doing this in the rain, and the ground soon worked up into deep sticky mud. It was not an easy matter to get my men to do the unloading and loading methodically, especially as there was a strong point of adverse attraction in the form of an inn close by.

However, I got the wagons loaded before daylight failed, though not in the manner exactly that I had wished. Our supplies were somewhat mixed, and we thereby suffered inconveniences on the march, that would have been avoided had all my party entered heartily into the task—that is, as heartily as was possible in the rain and up to the ankles in mud! I had hoped to get on our way a few miles farther before night, but I found this impossible, so I gave the order to bivouac at Saccharine.

The railway authorities gave leave for us to take shelter under a large, half-completed, iron shed, and placed the little station-house at my disposal. No sooner had I given the order to bivouac, than little fires were lighted on the ground, in the open, in all directions. I had rations of preserved meat and groceries to be issued. The rain fortunately ceased, and soon all were merrily preparing an evening meal. Up to this, I could have got through a vast deal more with disciplined British soldiers, but at this stage the British soldier would have been more or less helpless, whereas these men could shift at once for themselves, and I had no need to look after their welfare. At such times the independent colonial life that my men have been accustomed to, perhaps all their lives, saves their commander all trouble and anxiety.

I had better describe what my party consisted of. The regiment consists of two battalions. Major Graves commands the whole regiment just as a general commands a brigade, and I am the Staff-Officer. My duties are like those of a Brigade-Major in the field, but I have besides to direct and superintend the whole work of organisation and equipment. Major Graves and I are the only officers of the regular army, all the others are volunteers for the war; and the sergeants, corporals, &c., are volunteers also.

Major Graves, besides commanding the regiment, is also *comman-*

dant of the 1st Battalion; and one of the volunteer officers named Nettleton is *commandant* of the 2nd Battalion—that is, does the part of Lieut.-Colonel of a battalion, but is called "*Commandant.*" The volunteers in each battalion are:

    10 Captains.
    20 Lieutenants.
    30 Sergeants.
    30 Corporals.
    1 Bugler.
    1 Interpreter.
    1 Adjutant (Lieutenant).
    1 Quartermaster
    1 Sergeant-Major.
    1 Quartermaster-Sergeant.

Total 96

Then there is a doctor for the regiment, so that adding him and myself, we white people number 196 altogether. I had better mention the native chiefs' names, because I may have to speak of them a good deal hereafter. They are:

In 1st Battalion.

Chiefs' Names.	Number of Men.
Delewayo	200
Zipuku	100
Macabo	200
Musi	500
Total	1,000

In 2nd Battalion.

Chiefs' Names.	Number of Men
Umgawe	500
Sotondose	400
Dikwayo	100
Total	1,000

At present only half the full number of natives summoned have joined us, but we expect to receive all in the course of a few days. They were ordered to assemble at the Nonoti by 21st of December, and we were to meet them there.

And now to return to the bivouac. Dr. Mansell and I laid ourselves out on the floor of what will be the ticket office of the railway station, rolled in our blankets, and soon every square foot of space in the station and around, under the verandah, was occupied by bodies in blankets.

It was a dark night, but all seemed in very good spirits, notwithstanding the wet and dirt.

I could hear nothing all round but the croaking of frogs and bursts of laughter as the later arrivals searched for a spot to stretch out upon, and in doing so trod upon, or tumbled over, the earlier sleepers. One man tried for an hour to imitate the croaking of the frogs, and at the end of that time he succeeded tolerably well. This, I imagine, was exclusively entertaining to himself, and I was glad when he fell asleep.

I ordered our march to commence next morning at 4.30, and all were up and ready by that time; but the difficulty of starting the wagons was so great, that it was a quarter to six before the whole was *en route*.

There were ten wagons, each drawn by a span of sixteen or eighteen oxen, but during the night the wheels of the laden wagons sank very much in the soft ground, and it was difficult even with two spans to start them.

When a wagon sticks, part, or the whole of a second span, is hooked on in front, the native drivers get on both sides with whips ready, and at a signal down come the lashes on the oxen, accompanied by the most awful shrieks man ever uttered; you might, if you shut your eyes, imagine your ear at a loophole of hell! These infernal yells are kept up and joined in by every available native, while the oxen, perfectly unexcited thereby, strain with dignity at the rope. Sometimes they fail to move the wagon an inch, and then the process is renewed after a few minutes' rest. Sometimes they get the wagon in motion, and then the whips are at once applied with redoubled force, a sense of justice to the ox being drowned in the current of opinion that the wagon might stick again.

About 10 a.m. we halted near a town called Verulam. It would be called in England a pretty village. We halted here to "outspan." Almost everywhere there is excellent pasture *pro bono publico*, and oxen are never given anything else. At 12.15 p.m. we were *en route* again, and at about 5.30 p.m. we arrived at a beautiful park-like place where we stopped for the night and bivouacked in the open under a clear sky. All the country around was like park, beautiful grass with groups of trees and patches of bush here and there in the same state of nature as it has always been; but no inhabitants, except at intervals of many miles.

I went to have a bathe in a small stream close by, and on chance of finding a duck there, I took my gun with a couple of No. 4 cartridges. To my surprise there were numbers of wild duck, and I killed one flying on the opposite side of the stream, with my first shot. I went back to the bivouac for some more cartridges, but the darkness came on suddenly, as it does here, before I could get them.

Dec. 21st.—This morning we were all ready to march at 4.30, but the oxen delayed us till past six. Last night my horse strayed away, and was lost. He was knee-haltered, which is the invariable practice of the country, and I allowed my horse to be knee-haltered, contrary to my opinion, by the advice of those who have lived in this country all their lives. My invariable practice in camp and bivouac had been to secure my horses by their headropes, close to where I sleep at night, so that during the day I could see they were properly looked after. Diligent search this morning failed to produce my horse, and we started without him. He is a good strong animal that I bought from Major Graves.

All the country we pass through now is the same unending park. Here it was that fifty years ago hunters found countless herds of antelope, elephants, giraffes, zebras, and the lions and leopards that prey upon them. Now the great herds have receded before the colonists, and though there are plenty of antelopes, they are very shy, avoiding the open and frequenting the bush, so that without many guns and many more beaters, it is difficult to shoot them, and a solitary hunter has but a poor chance.

At midday we outspanned on a plateau called Compensation Flat. I suppose the "compensation" is the ever getting there, for the roads to the plateau from both sides are very steep, and as heavy as the plum-duff of my schooldays!

About 3 p.m. we had reached a river called the Umhlali, (pronounced M'plah-lee, with a sort of hiccough at the beginning. Oh! the pronunciation of the Kaffirs!) Well, here we outspanned again, for the oxen, notwithstanding the "compensation "of Compensation Flat, were distressed. The beauty of the river atoned for the spasm produced in speaking of it by its own name.

Then we went on, and an hour before dark I ordered bivouac by the Tete River. It was a bright starlight night, cool and comfortable;

fires were lighted all about, to cook our evening meal, and afterwards we laid out our blankets on a rich meadow on the hillside.

Dec. 22nd.—All were ready to march at 4.30 a.m., except the oxen, and soon it was evident that they had been driven away by neighbouring Kaffirs, probably to prevent them eating their corn in the night. At last, they were found, miles away, and brought back, but it was nearly seven before we commenced our morning march.

Our first breakdown occurred today, but the wagon was repaired properly in about an hour. We crossed the Umooti, a comparatively large river, by a ford, called always a "*drift*" in this country, and about noon outspanned at Stanger. Stanger is the most advanced military depot of supplies on this line of operation.

At Stanger, I was joined by a hundred and forty of Delewayo's natives. They were all armed alike with *assegais* and shields. An *assegai* is a short spear, with a flat, sharp, double-edged blade forming a point at one edge, and a wooden shaft. Some of the native tribes produce excellent steel for their own use, by smelting the ironstone of the country with charcoal. Some *assegais* are made to throw and some to use as a lance. They use them with great dexterity. Their shields are made of hide, with the hair left on, are oval in shape and very tastefully ornamented by, I think, the paler antelope skin, worked on to a dark hide ground.

They wear a little, but sufficient, clothing hanging from the waist. Vanity seems to me to have reached its maximum in the human race amongst the Kaffirs. No coiffure that European lady ever achieved comes up to the elaborate hairdressing of a Kaffir. The time it must have taken to arrange his head I have not yet discovered. His hair is pulled and twisted and toozled, in a marvellous but always becoming manner, whenever he has leisure to attend to it, and then his head is decorated with remarkable care and symmetry with beads of various colours, particularly red, the colour so particularly becoming to black men.

The amount of attention bestowed upon ornamentation of himself is the most apparent characteristic of the Kaffir, and as I have said, I see in him vanity in its intensest form. The Nonoti River is about seven miles from Stanger. I started on ahead of my party to choose the camping ground, and took the hundred and forty natives with me. At 6.15 this afternoon I reached the Nonoti River. The rain, which began as I left Stanger, was now pouring down in torrents. I passed the natives across by the drift, to the opposite side of the river, and made them understand that they were to shift for themselves till next morning.

They at once betook themselves to a bushy clump, lit fires and made shelters for the night. They were very pleased at coming on ahead with me, and of course I knew they would be. I put them across the river to be out of our way till we had formed camp. I chose the ground on the near side of the river, the right bank, for our camp. My party arrived just before dark, drenched; and to make things more comfortless, two wagons stuck fast before they reached the camp, and these wagons contained the personal luggage and the tents. They stuck when close to camp, but darkness came on, and it was therefore impossible to find individual baggage, nor did the men care to carry up tents and pitch them in the dark on the soaking ground.

Under these circumstances, I ordered one of the bales, containing blankets for the natives, to be opened; the wagon conveying them had got into camp, and I distributed blankets to everyone on loan. A few fires were lighted with great difficulty, but the majority of the men being very tired, rolled themselves up in their blankets, head and all, and lay down to sleep in the rain. Dr. Mansell had got the ambulance-wagon up, and had pitched its two tents: one was reserved for any sick, and in the other, Mansell accommodated whom he pleased. I was glad to hear a "bed" had been made there for me. The "bed" was a hospital blanket laid on the wet ground!

I managed to get my lantern off the baggage wagon, and I walked about to see all settled down for the night, before I retired. All at last were rolled up for sleep but one man. I found him standing alone in the rain. He was a Frenchman. He addressed me in piteous tones as *"mon Capitaine."* He was *"trop malade"* to roll up and sleep, he had rheumatism apparently in all parts, *"ici et la"*; his *"baggages n'arrivaient point,"* the water tumbled and *"il ne savait que faire."* I took off my waterproof coat, put it on him, put him in the hospital tent and advised him to *"coucher la"* in the coat.

Then I went to my bed; the others were all fast asleep in the tent, and the little space left for me seemed luxury compared to what I had seen outside! The others had taken off their wet boots, but experience had taught me to keep mine on. In the morning they all felt very cold, while I was warm: and they could not get their boots on again without painful efforts. . . .

Dec. 23rd.—Another wet day, but there were intervals without rain. I got all the wagons unloaded, and enough tents pitched to shelter everyone.

Dec. 24th.—No rain today, and never in my whole life have I ever before so heartily welcomed a dry day. I laid out a great part of our camp today.

Dec. 25th.—Another fine day. The thermometer 90° in my tent, but a cool, refreshing wind blows constantly. I heard this morning that Major Graves had reached Stanger, and had got my lost horse. Major Graves arrived in the afternoon. *Paddy Wack* had been found by a Kaffir, not far from where I lost him.

Dec. 31st.—It is now New Year's Eve. During the past week I have been incessantly at work, forming our two battalions, dividing the equipment, arranging the camp and drilling the 1st Battalion for Major Graves. I am very pleased with our natives. They are the most intelligent blacks, and best black soldiers—so far as I can tell without yet having seen them fight—that I have ever seen. I am sorry that only a tenth of them is to be armed with rifles, that is, only ten men in each company of a hundred; the remainder are to have only their *assegais* and shields. There are not arms enough in the colony, I believe, to arm more. I take out the 1st Battalion to drill every day, and it is astonishing how quickly these natives grasp the idea of the movements I consider it necessary to teach them, and the spirit with which they do them is splendid.

Already they can march well in line, change front, and attack a position. I place the captain in front of the centre of his company at all times; and a lieutenant on each flank; the sergeants and corporals behind the company. My words of command are, of course, understood by all the officers and serjeants and corporals, and then I depend upon them to get the companies into their proper places. This they do by signs and native words they have learnt for the purpose, and they do it very well. My drill to attack a position is this:—I form the battalion in line, in two ranks—the natives always move in two ranks—and I point out the position to be attacked; then I call out to the front, the ten riflemen of each company, and they spread along our front, a sergeant with each ten.

On my giving the order to advance, they run forward twenty yards, halt, and fire two or three rounds. Then they run forward another twenty yards, halt, take up the best cover they can, and fire again: and so, they go on twenty yards at a time. I follow leading the whole line of natives, with their *assegais* and shields. At my signal, the whole line rushes forward after the riflemen, and at my command and signal they all fall flat on the ground. At my signal they rise and rush forward again, and again fall flat, so as to escape the enemy's fire as much as possible: and so, we go, the natives uttering fearful war yells at each rush; then, as we get near the supposed position of the enemy, I let the whole line rush forward upon it pell-mell, and in this way, I hope the *assegais* will come into effective use.

I hope to break the enemy's position up with the riflemen, and then to let the rest close with him in all their savage fury. Major Graves has allowed me to undertake and carry out the drill. A red *pugaree* has been provided for every native, as a distinguishing mark. In the 1st Battalion it is worn over the right shoulder and under the left arm. In the 2nd Battalion it is worn round the head. The 1st Battalion have blue blankets, the 2nd grey. In marching order, the blanket is worn in a roll over the left shoulder, and tied at the ends under the right arm. The native delights in that blue blanket; no matter how hot the day, he loves to carry it; and when he is arrayed in blue blanket and red sash, he is as proud as can be!

This is a lovely spot; a more delightful camping ground could scarcely be conceived. It always reminds me of Ballymoyer demesne, except that the large veteran trees are absent. There are no very large trees here. The Nonoti at this place forms a loop, and our camp is on a little hill in the loop, affording ample and more than ample space. The river flows forward along our left side, then bends round across our front and flows back along our right side, so that there is water everywhere within easy reach. The drinking water is drawn from our left upstream.

We are about two miles from the sea. I have had presents of delicious venison. I have not had time to go out shooting myself, but those who have, have shot antelopes close by. One day, some of our natives hunted an antelope right into our camp. In an instant the whole of our natives were under arms, each with a handful of *assegais* and his shield. I never saw so quick a transformation. The poor beast had no chance; it was surrounded in a few seconds and killed close to my tent. This achievement so excited Delewayo's men, that they instantly after assembled, and, to relieve their excitement, stormed a neighbouring hill with great violence; there was nothing but its steepness to resist them!

Today we heard news that Cetywayo has refused the ultimatum, defied us, and added that he would "Chew us up like beef." So now for war!

On Sunday next we are ordered to cross the frontier, the River Tugela.

Colonel Pearson, 3rd Buffs, will command the column of invasion on this road; and on Sunday he will assemble his column beyond the Tugela. It will consist of regular troops, the Naval Brigade, and "Graves' Regiment."

On the 29th, Lord Chelmsford paid us an official visit. The 1st Battalion formed up to meet him a little way outside the camp, the natives lining the road on both sides in martial array. Lord Chelmsford walked down this avenue of men, and they then followed and marched past him, singing their war songs. He was very much pleased with the progress of the 1st Battalion.

The Zulu Campaign

Ekowe, Zululand, Jan. 24, 1879.

My dear May,—I am now about thirty miles beyond the Tugela, in Zululand, with Colonel Pearson's column of invasion, called No. 1 Column.

We are obliged to put all lights out every evening at eight o'clock, so I cannot write at night as I used to do in the Ashanti War; and I consequently find it very difficult to write you an account of our proceedings.

On the 11th January we marched from the Singwasi to the Tugela, and encamped on the Natal bank. The 99th Regiment arrived from England, followed us and encamped there also. There we joined Colonel Pearson, who had already with him the "Buffs," a naval brigade of about a hundred sailors, landed from one of H.M. ships, with two small rifled field-guns (seven-pounders) and a gatling-gun; a few Marines, a few of the Royal Artillery with two small field-guns to be taken on with us, and some large field-guns to be left in a fort that had been built on a hill on the Natal bank.

Commanding the passage of the Tugela one company of Royal Engineers, and further, some irregular cavalry, about 200 I think, and some irregular pioneers. The whole of Colonel Pearson's column numbers about 4000 fighting men.

On 12th of January, Sunday, at daybreak, the crossing of the Tugela commenced. Long-continued rains had put an end to the ford for the time, and a deep and rapid stream, 270 yards wide, flowed where in dry weather one can walk across.

A steel hawser had been stretched over the river by the Naval Brigade, and a ferry-boat, large enough to take the heaviest laden wagon, had been built, and this boat, or raft, was dragged backwards and forwards from bank to bank by ropes pulled sometimes by our natives, sometimes by bullocks, the boat being all the while attached to the steel hawser. The operation of crossing in this manner was necessarily tedious, but I dare say it was the most expeditious manner, since any bridge able to stand the force of the current would have to be made of a size and strength that I think would have required more time than was occupied by ferrying across.

From the 12th to the 18th of January, the process of crossing continued all day, and as much as possible all night. The heavy wagons and oxen were the most difficult part. Several attempts to make the oxen swim the river were made, and many thus went across, but so many turned back, and so many allowed themselves to be carried unreasonable distances downstream, that it was found to be shorter work to ship them over on the raft.

On the 18th of January, part of Colonel Pearson's column advanced from the Tugela, upon the road leading to Ulundi, the Zulu king's capital.

This first division of the column consisted of some of the irregular cavalry, four companies of the "Buffs," the Royal Artillery, and Engineers, part of the Native Pioneers, the Naval Brigade, and 1st Battalion of Major Graves' Regiment, less two companies left at the fort on the Tugela. Major Graves and I both went with the 1st Battalion. This advanced column was not allowed to take more baggage than absolutely necessary, nevertheless it required about thirty wagons, for we had to carry fifteen days' supply of provisions, meat excepted, our meat carrying itself on its own legs!

We encamped for the night on the Inyoni River. No signs of the enemy had been observed, but we took every precaution, carefully guarding our flanks and rear against surprise. On arrival in camp, wagons are collected on the best defensive ground, the oxen turned out to graze, but all collected before dark, and the alarm post of every part of the force assigned. Before sunset we all take up our positions of defence for practice, and at 3 a.m., just two hours before daylight, we silently occupy these alarm posts, and there remain under arms till daybreak.

This is done because the Zulus are apt to attack at such a time, and it is considered essential to our safety to be able to receive them in the darkness. This we do every night, and it is the most harassing duty we have. At 3 a.m. one is in one's deepest sleep, and to turn out then, as often as not in the rain, and remain on the *qui vive* for nearly two hours, is equally obnoxious to white man and black. A curious sound composed of a thousand coughs, yawns, and sneezes unrestrained, satisfies the commander that his camp is awake, and may, for all we know, have stopped the Zulu in his advance!

On 19th January we advanced to the Umsundusi River, and encamped just beyond it.

Early this morning the remainder of Colonel Pearson's column left the Tugela; it consisted of some of the irregular cavalry and pioneers, five companies of the 99th, the two guns of the Naval Brigade, and the 2nd Battalion of Major Graves' Regiment, less two companies left in garrison on the Tugela. With this second part of the column came the remainder of the baggage—about eighty wagons. In the afternoon this division joined us at the Umsundusi, but all could not cross the river before dark.

So far, the weather had been rainy, and consequently comfortless and unhealthy for us, unable to avoid everlasting wet feet. I suppose constant exercise has done much to keep me continually in good health under the circumstances.

The Zulu country is like Natal: unending park, groups of trees and wooded ravines, with the richest pasturage in the world growing all over the open ground, except near the numerous Kaffir *kraals* where Indian corn, sugarcane, pumpkin, kidney beans, &c., are grown. I suppose everything in the vegetable kingdom would grow here luxuriantly. The surface of the country is very hilly, but the hills are not very large and they are too steep to be called undulations. Beautiful and delicious streams of water abound, and the atmosphere is so clear that you are able to see clearly to distances far beyond what is possible in any part of Europe; so much so, that what appears two or three miles off to an English vision, is nine or ten miles off.

We remained all the 20th on the Umsundusi to gather up the tail of the wagon column. Our whole column, when on the line of march, is several miles long from the head to the tail. On the 21st we advanced again, and encamped about three miles beyond the Amatikulu River.

On Wednesday, 22nd January, we advanced again, and in the course of that day we found the Zulus, in a very formidable position, across our road and on either side. No sooner did our attack commence, than they at once came down upon the flanks of our column, and endeavoured to surround us, while they engaged us warmly in front. A hot engagement lasting several hours took place, and ended in our gaining the heights in front and repelling the flank attacks. I am obliged to defer a description of this engagement till my next letter, as I have been too often interrupted by various duties to have time to describe it in this. . . .

Lower Drift, R. Tugela, Jan. 30, 1879.

My dear May,—The news of the Zulu victory and terrible British disaster will reach England by this mail, and you will be anxious for news of me. I briefly mentioned at the close of my last letter that we, Colonel Pearson's column, had gained a victory over the Zulus on 22nd of January, after several hours' hard fighting, and next day reached Ekowe and began making a fort there. That same 22nd of January, many miles away on our left, beyond sight, reach or hearing of us, the Zulus also attacked the rear of Lord Chelmsford's column, with terrible success. He had gone forward with part of the column to attack the Zulus in front, but they cleverly avoided him there, and came upon the after part of the column in overwhelming numbers, killing seven companies of the 24th Regiment to a man, capturing the guns, sacking the baggage, and inflicting losses, not yet fully notified, upon the irregular troops.

News of a British defeat reached us at Ekowe, on 26th or 27th, in very vague terms; and on 28th came a message from Lord Chelmsford, without any news of his disaster, telling Colonel Pearson that the whole Zulu Army was marching against Ekowe, and directing him to take any steps he thought best for the safety of his force, but, if possible, not to abandon the left bank of the Tugela. Colonel Pearson decided to hold his ground, complete his fort as speedily as possible and stand a siege; but as he would not be able to feed all the force for any length of time, he ordered Major Graves' Regiment to retreat to the Tugela, leaving all our baggage at Ekowe, and to cut our way through the enemy if intercepted.

We started about 1 p.m. on the 28th of January, and reached the Tugela, thirty miles distant, about 2 o'clock at night without having met any resistance. The ford here is fortified on both banks of the river. Lord Chelmsford is, I believe, coming here with his column, and a powerful force is to be assembled as soon as possible, to relieve Ekowe and break the Zulu Army up. Experience has been gained, which I hope will ensure our success.

I had a remarkable escape in the fight on the 22nd. I was driving back some Zulu scouts with the leading company of the advanced guard, before the action began, when a mass of Zulus suddenly rose from concealment on our left, and opened a heavy fire upon us, killing six out of the nine white men who were with me. I must keep the details for a future letter.

Feb. 1th.—I had not time in my last to give you any details of the fight on 22nd January, in which I took part with Colonel Pearson's column. There were two hard fights that day, at places far apart, and while Colonel Pearson's column was engaged, and gaining victory on the road to Ekowe, we had no idea that many miles away, on our left, Lord Chelmsford was suffering a disaster. Nor did we hear anything of it till several days after, and then in such meagre terms, that we thought the Native Contingent there had suffered alone and lost their leader, Colonel Durnford. It was not until I reached the Tugela with our Native Contingent, on the night of the 28th, that I heard what had happened. I will go back to the 22nd January.

On the morning of Wednesday, 22nd of January, we started early from our encampment, which I think I told you was about three miles beyond the Amatikulu River, and purposed to reach Ekowe (pronounced Etch-ow'-ah) in that day's march. A slight change had been made in the order of march that I have already sent: a company of Graves' Regiment of Native Contingent was put at the head of the column, and marched from a quarter to half a mile ahead, as advanced part of the advanced guard, and two other companies marched one on either side, at from a quarter to half a mile from the road, to search the country and guard against surprise.

I undertook the direction of these three companies, a duty which I liked much. Each company consisted of a hundred natives; and its white men were a captain, two lieutenants, three sergeants, and three corporals. All the white men had rifles, and about ten men in each company had rifles; the remaining natives having only *assegais* and shields. Bear those facts in mind as you read this narrative. We had marched a few miles; and I had proceeded about half a mile beyond a small river called the Inyezane, with the leading company, when Colonel Pearson decided to halt there for breakfast, and to outspan the oxen to graze. We had not been molested by the enemy, but we had seen for the first time, today, Zulu scouts watching us from the tops of distant hills.

Colonel Pearson himself rode to the head of the column and gave the order to halt for breakfast, and noticing the scouts, that I had already reported to him, still watching from the heights, about three-quarters of a mile ahead, he said at the same time, "Hart, go and make a raid upon those fellows." I immediately took on the company of our Native Contingent that had been leading the way. We were then in the river valley. In front, at about three-quarters of a mile off, a steep hill rose on the right-hand side of the road and another steep hill on the left of the road, while the road itself rose gradually upon a third and less elevated hill between the other two, and was within effective musketry range of their summits.

The whole country was covered with rich grass, with groups of trees standing, park-like, here and there, and thick bush at the bottoms of the ravines, or "*kloofs*" as they are called, between the hills. The hill on the right of the road was the highest of all, and one or two scouts stood there at first, but disappeared before I advanced; but on the spur that ran towards me from the base of that hill, several scouts remained, and did not seem disposed to retire. I accordingly turned off the road to my right with the company, and advanced towards this spur. The Zulus then retired, and on reaching the spur I could see them running away beyond a second spur of the same hill that lay behind.

A small ravine lay between the spur we stood on and that beyond, and I ordered the company to cross and pursue. We all advanced together. The *kloof* was, as usual, full of bush, and there was also a marsh, but there was no difficulty in crossing. I found a track through the marsh by which I crossed easily on horseback, and soon we were all advancing on the further side, my men opening fire upon the flying scouts. Suddenly a mass of Zulus appeared on the hilltop on our left, and opened a fire of musketry upon us at a distance of about 400 yards. I saw at once that we had almost fallen into a trap, and I instantly gave the order "Retire."

At the same moment the Zulus poured down the hill by hundreds at the top of their speed, with a tremendous shout, while others above kept up the fire over the heads of those descending the hill. The *kloof* was not far behind us, and we reached it, as far as I could perceive, without any loss, although the bullets whistled amongst us and struck the earth all about us as we went. There only remained to cross the *kloof* and we should be safe. I was at the end of the company next the enemy—the end next the hill—and I even had to ride some little way towards the Zulus, to reach the track by which I was certain my horse could cross.

So, it seemed to me that as I had got safely over the *kloof*, all the others, who were further from the enemy, must necessarily have done so too, and it was not till the close of the general engagement which followed that I found that one of the lieutenants, two sergeants, and two corporals were killed in the *kloof*, evidently with *assegais*. I have never been able to make out how this occurred, although I have questioned all who I thought might be able to throw any light on the matter. I have not been able to find anyone who saw any of them killed.

Their bodies lay among the not very dense bush in the *kloof*, and they all appeared to have met their death by *assegais*. Their rifles and ammunition were gone. Whether they were overtaken in the *kloof*, or whether Zulus were concealed in the *kloof*, and only appeared upon our retreating, I cannot determine. It has been suggested that they were murdered by our own natives, but this idea I see the strongest grounds for rejecting at once.

On passing the spur beyond, where we had first seen the Zulu scouts, I met Colonel Pearson, who had ridden forward at the sound of the firing. I told him that the enemy was coming on in force, and that he would require regular troops to the front at once, as the enemy would in a few minutes be on top of the spur in front of us—the spur I have just mentioned, and which formed a long ridge with patches of bush on the top. Some men of the "Buffs" were already close up, and they formed front in the direction I pointed to. Hardly were they in position, when puffs of smoke along the ridge and the sharp crack of bullets striking the wood about us showed that the enemy had reached the ridge.

From the summit of the high hill above—the hill on the right of the road—a ploughing fire was opened upon us, but the range was now too great for it to be effective at this spot. That high hill is called Majia's Hill, after a chief named Majia, whose *kraals* are situated about it. It was on Majia's Hill that the scouts appeared before my advance, it was Majia's Hill that poured down the fire that obliged my party to retreat, and Majia's Hill formed, as you shall hear, the key of a most formidable position, occupied by several thousand of Cetywayo's best soldiers, bent upon destroying Colonel Pearson's column.

The soldiers of the "Buffs" replied at once to the fire from the ridge; a gun was brought up and some rockets; and then a second gun and a gatling. Masses of Zulus could now be seen about a mile off, marching towards the rear of our column, along our right flank. Upon these masses the guns were directed, and shell after shell burst in their midst; while the rockets also were sent amongst them. But for all this they made, later on, a most determined attack upon our baggage train, endeavouring to surround our column. While the first few shells and rockets were being fired, I ordered the company of our Native Contingent, that had been with me on the raid, to rally near the gun.

The enemy had now begun to fire upon us from a *kraal* that stood close by the road, about half-way up the hill I have already described to you; the road passes between the two high hills, Majia's on the right and another on the left. This fire was coming into the backs of our troops who were engaged near the gun. I accordingly marched the company I had rallied together, with another company of the natives who had been on the advanced guard, against the *kraal*; but the courage of our natives utterly failed, they crouched down under any cover they could find, and after fruitless efforts to make them advance, I called upon the white men of the two companies to go with me without them.

We advanced steadily against the *kraal* by the main road, the officers, except myself, dismounted; and the little party used their rifles well, and did as I directed, halting to fire, and advancing again when I gave the word. Thus, we approached the *kraal*. It was a small *kraal*, but it occupied a very advantageous position; the enemy covered by it could fire a quarter of a mile down the road; and the road up to it, and the ground about it, was under the fire also both of Majia's Hill and the hill on the other side of the road. As we approached, the enemy retreated from the *kraal*, except a few men who remained almost until we reached it.

Not one of our party was killed or wounded in taking the *kraal*; but several dead bodies of the enemy there showed that our fire had been more effective. I at once set the *kraal* on fire, and as the flames shot high into the air, in consuming the huts, we gave a loud cheer all together, and I trusted that flames and cheer would as much dispirit the enemy as they would exhilarate our men. The Zulus, who had retired from the *kraal*, now made a stand, a few hundred yards farther back, upon the road, the ground still rising towards them. I ordered my party to advance again, but found they had not a round of ammunition left.

I knew that our ammunition reserve was a long way off, so fearing that there might be a difficulty, I rode back myself to where Colonel Pearson was still engaged with the guns and the "Buffs," in the place I have before described, and I got leave to take ammunition from the first supply, no matter to whom it might belong. I thus got a supply at once, and got some of our natives who were crouching about to carry it, but so great was their dread of the fire upon us as we went, that it was only by pointing my revolver at their heads, and threatening to shoot them on the spot, that I could manage to get them up to the *kraal* with their loads. On my way back to get this ammunition, I met part of the Naval Brigade and some of the "Buffs" coming up to the *kraal*—then in flames. I was therefore not a little surprised to read in Colonel Pearson's report, when I saw it long after, that the *kraal* had been taken by the Naval Brigade!

AA. Valley of the Inyezane River.
B. Majia's Hill.
C. Kloof where five white men of our raiding party were killed.
D. Position taken by Colonel Pearson, with two guns, gatling, rockets, and part of the " Buffs " and Naval Brigade.
EE. Spur occupied in force by the Zulus.
F. Kraal stormed by white men of the 2nd Regt. N.N.C.
GG. Route by which Majia's Hill was stormed.
H. Heights from which the Zulus fired upon left flank of our attack.

When my party had replenished their ammunition pouches, some minutes were spent by ourselves, the sailors and the "Buffs," in replying to the enemy's fire, directed upon us from in front, from right and from left. I tried to push my party on, but found the enemy's number so great, that we could make no impression on them. So I went to Colonel Parnell, who commanded the detachment of the "Buffs" at the *kraal*, and told him that my men would go on and charge up the heights, if he would support with the "Buffs"; for without them, we had not rifles enough to put down the enemy's fire—in fact I had only about eight men with me; they were fighting with great coolness and courage; but from such a handful, a good lead was all that could be expected.

We had commenced the attack in this direction, and I was anxious we should not lose the lead. Colonel Parnell's answer was, "Very well, go on." So once more my party advanced. One of the sergeants—the remaining sergeant of that unfortunate company that had commenced the battle today—was here badly wounded in the leg, and died a few days after. As we advanced, the enemy began to show signs of fear, and his ranks on the hilltop thinned very perceptibly. I urged my men to their utmost speed, but it was severe work for them, on foot, breasting the hill. The sailors and detachment of the "Buffs" followed them up.

A very fortunate circumstance now favoured us. I had seen the value of it to us some time before. Whereas the high hill on our left was separated from us by a deep and difficult ravine, Majia's Hill was joined to the hill on which our road lay by a neck of land, so that Majia's Hill could be reached without crossing a valley—without, in fact, descending at all—by following this neck of land; and so, I led along. The summit of Majia's Hill was now before me, about 200 yards off, and the enemy, though still firing upon us from it, were now reduced to a small group, who held their ground.

My little party plodded steadily on; they were now but half a dozen white men, and so perseveringly had they clambered up the steep ascent, that the "Buffs" and the Naval Brigade were now, at least, fifty yards behind us. Two hundred yards more, and the position would be ours. I urged my men to their utmost speed, and charged forward on horseback at the group of Zulus on the summit. They fled—all but one man. He stood leaning forward, watching me intently, his left hand on his knee, and his rifle ready in his right. I could see glistening on his head the black ring that signifies in Zululand a married man.

The Zulu monarch forbids men to marry till they are forty years old, because he cherishes a large and well-organised army, and considers that the attractions of wife and *kraal* extinguish the martial spirit of his warriors. Here before me was a remarkable exception to that idea. I was rapidly approaching him, he was now only a hundred yards distant, and in a few moments, I should use my revolver, but just then he dropped quickly on one knee, took very deliberate aim at me for a couple of seconds, and fired. He seemed scarcely to believe he could have missed his prize, for he waited to take one eager look at me, as his smoke cleared away, and then seeing me still coming on, he bolted away and disappeared.

Directly afterwards I was on the summit, and saw hundreds of Zulus crowding down the opposite side of the hill in full retreat. I fired my revolver into the crowd, and looked round for my men to open fire, but it is one thing to ride up a hill and another to walk up! It was some minutes before they reached me. Then up came the "Buffs" and the men of the Naval Brigade. We stood on the key of the enemy's position. We commanded the whole country round. This the Zulus knew, and they retreated from all quarters, then from our position we opened a heavy fire upon them in all directions.

They swarmed below us, some crowding as fast as they could run across the open country, others darting from tree to tree in the *kloof* below, and many walking along under our fire, apparently with the utmost indifference, but probably quite out of breath. So rapid had been our advance and so unexpected our capture of Majia's Hill, that we had surprised all these masses of men before they could get out of range. Here I stood upon the very hill where the men were posted who early in the day had so nearly entrapped my company of raiders.

Far away, towards the tail of our long column of wagons, we could see the 99th Regiment advancing across the low ground of the Inyezane River valley, in fighting order, towards Majia's Hill. It struck me that they thought the hill still in possession of the enemy, so I suggested a British cheer, to undeceive them. We all gave three hearty cheers, they were understood at once, and we saw the 99th withdraw.

The engagement was now quite over, the Zulus had dispersed, and we prepared to resume our march. The Zulus, with their usual tactics, had endeavoured to surround us, but they had been successfully kept back by the rear-guard. Another lieutenant of "Graves' Regiment" was killed, shot through the head, in the attack upon the rear of our column; so that Major Graves' Regiment lost by this engagement seven of our white men, including the sergeant who died afterwards.

Our casualties were extraordinarily small, considering the thousands of bullets fired at us from advantageous positions. The only other white men killed were two privates of the "Buffs"; four of our natives only were killed; and sixteen white men wounded. Colonel Pearson's and Colonel Parnell's horses were both shot under them. The position chosen by the Zulus was remarkably strong; my description of it will, I dare say, make that clear. It is by far the strongest position between the Tugela and Ekowe. We know now that Cetywayo sent there several thousand of his best troops, and ordered them to destroy Colonel Pearson's column.

The Zulus took up their position excellently, and were so well concealed, although in such numbers, that we were unaware of the presence of any force until we were actually engaged. We have since learned that their plan was not to attack us until the column was between the two high hills, but that in consequence of my raid, the engagement was brought on prematurely, and their plan spoilt.

How fortunate then was that raid! It cost five good lives, but perhaps it saved the column from a disaster—or at least from a repulse. The Zulus fought well, showing judgment and courage quite equal to their enemy, but although they outnumbered us greatly, they could not hold their ground against our artillery and superior rifles. We had the best rifles in the world; they, for the most part, merely muskets, weapons of the past; so that while we reckoned our losses by units, they must have reckoned theirs by hundreds.

Our own natives I found utterly useless in battle—but I will speak of them in my next letter.

We dug a large grave by the roadside, and buried all our killed white men therein together. Our chief interpreter, a clergyman, read the burial service.

Meanwhile, the head of the column had proceeded on again. We did not reach Ekowe that day, but bivouacked for the night, well prepared against attack.

Next morning, Thursday, the 23rd of January, we proceeded, and soon reached Ekowe, and at once began to make a fortified post there, to form the first depot of supply in Zululand, preparatory to our further advance....

Lower Drift, Tugela River,
Natal-Zululand Frontier,
March 8, 1879.

Ekowe was merely a little Norwegian missionary station a short time ago, but now it has become a place of renown in South Africa, if not in England too, by this time. My time at Ekowe was principally spent in fortifying the post, and I had already made our natives expert at entrenching. My plan of entrenching ground with them was simpler far than the military regulation one of marking out the lines of the trench with white tape. I dispensed with the tape, and made the natives all hold hands, and stretch out thus in a string at arm's length. Then I walked along the string of men, and put them exactly on the ground where the entrenchment was to be dug. Next, I had a pickaxe and shovel put by other men at the feet of each man in the string, and then, but not till then, I let the men leave go hands, whereupon they would commence to dig where they stood, each excavating a bit of trench from where he stood, to his neighbour on his right.

I had thus entrenched the most exposed parts of the position at Ekowe, while the Engineers, with the regular soldiers, were making a substantial fort within. This fort was well in progress; and I was proceeding to entrench the less exposed parts of the position, when, about noon on 28th January, Colonel Pearson received a message from Lord Chelmsford, briefly telling him to expect the whole of the Zulu Army down upon him; to take any steps he thought best for the safety of his force; and if he retired, to endeavour to his utmost to hold the left (Zulu) bank of the Tugela.

That was all—not a word about the disaster at Isandhlwana, so we were still quite ignorant of its occurrence, and had only heard a rumour that Colonel Durnford had been killed and his native contingent defeated; but at the same time, rumour said that Lord Chelmsford had next day gained a tremendous victory. His present message was dated several days back, so the Zulus might be upon us at any moment, perhaps twenty or thirty thousand strong.

There was no time to be lost. Colonel Pearson called the commanding officers together, and it was decided to hold the post, but that, as the place would probably be invested by the enemy for many weeks, the whole of the irregular cavalry and Native Contingent (*i.e.* the two battalions of "Graves' Regiment") should at once retire to the Tugela, to enable the provisions at the post to hold out long enough; and they were to endeavour to cut their way through the enemy, should he be found to have intercepted them, as was not improbable, between Ekowe and the Tugela.

I was called in then, from work at the defences, and was allowed to give Colonel Pearson my opinion. I read Lord Chelmsford's message. It was evident that he had received at least a serious check, for his message made no allusion to any possibility of his being able to assist Colonel Pearson; and his mention of the Tugela, and desire that the passage of that river should be held, showed me that there was no hope of reinforcement of Ekowe.

I advised Colonel Pearson to take the opposite course. I recommended him to destroy all his stores, except such ammunition as could be easily conveyed, and to retire at once on the Tugela, while there was a possibility of doing so; and I gave the following reasons:—

1. Because the position was naturally weak, being commanded at effective musketry range by hills that the enemy could occupy; while the artificial defences required at least a day more to complete them in the simplest form.

2. Because the water supply was outside the defences, under fire of ground accessible to the enemy, and within his power to reach and poison.

3. Because there was nothing of material importance in the post to render its defence desirable; neither town, wounded, women and children or garrison artillery to suffer by the evacuation of the post.

4. Because if the Zulus acted wisely, the post could not be relieved without severe sacrifices of our troops; so that a present retreat to the Tugela and subsequent advance again in great force, would probably in the end gain a greater moral and material advantage over the enemy, while it would certainly secure us from reverses in battle.

However, Colonel Pearson adhered to the decision to hold the post; and I at once prepared the Native Contingent to march. We left all our kit at Ekowe, only taking what we could carry on our persons or horses, and this was principally ammunition, for we expected a fight on the way.

My plan, which Major Graves approved, was that, as we knew the natives could not be depended on in battle, but would go just where they thought safest, we should not depend upon them, but that all the white men should march together—both battalions—and the natives follow by companies. The officers mounted to ride first, the white men on foot to follow immediately after; and the pace to be regulated by the powers of the latter, the mounted officers to lend horses, by turns, to those on foot who might break down.

If we met the enemy, we were to keep together, attack vigorously, and endeavour to force our way through towards the Tugela.

About 12.30 that afternoon of 28th of January we started. I said goodbye to Colonel Pearson, and added that my greatest hope was that my advice would prove to be bad advice. It is now 8th of March and I can still hope this. Our latest news of him is dated the 24th of February, and he had not been attacked, so his defences must be most formidable now, perhaps impregnable. The Zulus have invested the place, but they are evidently too wise to attack it now. He has ample provisions to the end of March, and before then we shall have forces enough assembled here to expect to relieve him. *If* we can do this successfully, without the loss of too many lives, then it will be well that Ekowe was not evacuated. There remains, therefore, only one "If."

The beginning of our march was intensely hot on foot, but pleasant riding. As we approached Majia's Hill, I noticed our natives eagerly gathering the leaves of a shrub and stuffing them into their nostrils. This was in prospect of the stench from the battlefield, and I was glad to follow their example. The leaves chosen had a very pleasant smell.

We halted when we had passed the Inyezane River, to draw in stragglers; and I then took the sketch. We pressed on our march, and as night came on it became cool and refreshing. There was good starlight, so it was not difficult to keep the track. We passed, after dark, safely through the Amatakulu Bush and crossed the Amatakulu River into open country again, a long, weary, and anxious march.

Our natives, as I expected, did just as they thought best for their personal safety—two thousand of them—sometimes they ran far ahead of us, sometimes they followed behind, sometimes they kept as close to us as possible.

Once across the Amatakulu I felt sure we were safe. We had seen nothing of the enemy, and I was sure now that we should not; and that if he was following us up, our pace was too rapid for him to overtake us before the Tugela.

Thus, relieved of my chief anxiety, sleep came over me, and from time to time I slept soundly as I rode; and I slept without relaxing hold of my reins or of my carbine, which I carried in my right hand—facts which surprised me and surprise me still. The wakings from these naps were not pleasant. Everything within sight, in the starlight, assumed weird and hobgoblin shapes of the most unaccountable and fantastic form—the combined effect, I suppose, of fatigue and care upon the brain. It always took several seconds of staring and eye-rubbing to dispel each. Only once in my life before have I seen these phantasmagoria: it was in Ashanti, as I was being carried at night, in a hammock, after a long and anxious day's work.

At last, this weary march of thirty miles approached the end. It was two hours past midnight when we reached Fort Tenedos, as it is called, after the crew of H.M.S. *Tenedos*, who made it, the fort which covers the passage or drift of the Tugela here on the Zulu side.

We unsaddled our horses and let them loose, and lay down on the dewy ground outside the fort. We had no kit, so we had no preparations to make for our repose; saddles made pillows, and that was all. I fell at once into a sound and refreshing sleep, "*Sleep that knits up the ravell'd sleeve of care.*"

Next day our natives deserted. They said the Zulus were going to enter Natal, and that their wives and children and cattle would be captured in their absence; so, they laid down all Government property that had been issued to them, and departed without leave to their *kraals*. Thus, up to 13th of February there was a complete collapse of "Graves' Regiment."

On 12th of February, Lord Chelmsford came here; he appointed me Staff-Officer of the Lower Tugela district, which extends five-and-twenty miles from this. Colonel Law, who commanded the Artillery, he made at the same time *Commandant* of the district, during the absence of Colonel Pearson (the real *commandant*) at Ekowe.

The 2nd Regiment of Natal Native Contingent was ordered to reassemble at once, and has done so; but the two battalions are in future to be quite separate, and will not therefore require a staff-officer. Major Graves has been called back to his civil employment at Durban, and Captain Barton, whom you know, has been appointed to command his battalion. There is much to be done up here in the front; and I have been hard at work, principally fortifying this place and organising with Colonel Law, the relief of Ekowe. He is to command the relieving force, and I go as Staff-Officer. We shall take 1,000 regular soldiers, Nettleton's battalion of natives, and Barton's if ready. We shall leave no stone unturned to ensure our success.

Lower Drift, Tugela River,
Natal-Zululand Frontier,
March 21, 1879.

My dear May,—From the 29th January, when I had retired here from Ekowe with the Native Contingent, till 12th of February, when Lord Chelmsford arrived here, there was a lull.

The road to Ekowe was intercepted by the enemy, and all communication with the garrison cut off. The natives of Major Graves' regiment had gone to their homes; and we, with the white men here, encamped on the Natal bank of the river, awaiting orders for the future.

Nothing could have gratified me more than my new appointment. Our plans have been changed more than once. At first, we were going to try and open communication with a force of 600 regular soldiers; taking no baggage, and carrying our own supplies of ammunition, and food enough for four days. Then Lord Chelmsford promised to reinforce our expedition up to 1,000 men, soldiers and sailors; and we had decided upon the 13th of March to advance. But before that time, we received news of the prompt despatch of troops from England; and as Ekowe was well provisioned.

Lord Chelmsford decided that we should wait for them, and decided wisely, I think, for there would have been no necessity to risk the defeat of our force by overwhelming numbers. We have since heard that the Zulus were aware of our intention, and had placed 20,000 of their soldiers to meet us—that information may or may not be accurate.

The 57th and 91st Regiments and the 3rd Battalion of the 60th Rifles are now marching here from Durban, their landing-place; and these, with the troops already here and our Native Contingent, will give us a force able, we may confidently expect, to defeat any army Cetywayo can send against us.

Colonel Law and I are at work unceasingly, all day. The organisation of supplies and transport is the great difficulty; and it is greater here, where the enemy may come from all sides at once, than it is in European warfare. To protect a long train of wagons in this war is a serious matter. Our train of wagons for this approaching movement is no less than four miles long! How to protect such a string of wagons was the question.

My plan, which the general has approved, is, never to let the train get more than two miles long, and to manage that in this way: when the head of the column has advanced about two miles, it will halt upon an advantageous place, and remain halted until the tail of the train has drawn up to it and the wagons all reassembled. Then the head will move on again another two miles, and halt as before. The rate of advance will be slow in this manner—it will not average more than a mile an hour—but it will probably make our convoy secure, and remove the great weakness that is inseparable from a long line of impedimenta, I have no doubt we can securely guard a length of two miles.

All attention now is concentrated on this coming movement, and it may produce the decisive battle of the war. On the other hand, the Zulus may perhaps decline combat and retire to fight their decisive engagement nearer to the king's *kraal* (Ulundi). We shall take every precaution against surprise.

From time to time, we have managed to pass native messengers between this and Ekowe, and their adventures *en route* have generally been most hazardous. We reward them liberally. But the most successful means of communication has been by flashing the sun upon Ekowe with a looking-glass. This has been so far perfected within the last few days, that now we hold conversation with Ekowe all day when the sun shines. We signal from a hilltop in about two miles in advance of this.

From the hilltop Ekowe can be distinguished with a telescope, sixteen miles distant, in a straight line.

It is done in this way. A frame with two wires crossing in the centre is set up, and behind it a looking-glass fixed upon a stand by a screw, as well as vertically upon its own hinges. Then a little hole is scraped in the mercury, at the centre of the looking-glass, and the stand is arranged so that on looking through the hole in the mercury, the cross-wires and Ekowe are in one line. Then the glass is moved, so that the sun is reflected on the cross-wires, and we are sure then that it is reflected on Ekowe.

One man keeps altering the glass as the sun moves, so as to keep it reflected on the cross-wires; and another, by passing a screen across in front, makes long and short flashes, by which letters of the alphabet are made, as in the telegraph code. They do the same at Ekowe. We use only a small bedroom looking-glass, and theirs must be a very small one, yet their flashes when well directed are very brilliant.

They have made sorties and attacked the enemy, and are now engaged in making a road towards us, which will be a short-cut saving three miles.

The Zulus have never ventured to attack their fort, but they hang about and capture their cattle from time to time. They have also attacked the working parties at the new road, but not with effect. The Zulus at first came down upon the new road when the working parties retired for the night, and tried to destroy the work, but the garrison left torpedoes behind and blew them up. All this was, amongst other things, telegraphed by flashes. I went out to the signal station last Sunday, and just as I arrived came the sad message that Captain Williams of the "Buffs" died on the 13th. He was in the 41st Regiment at Aldershot, in my brigade. How melancholy after all this waiting, and when relief was drawing so near.

They are all right as to provisions at Ekowe. They have had some sickness; but besides Captain Williams, only three or four deaths—private soldiers.

All luxuries in our baggage that we left behind have been seized and sold by auction. Pickles fetched 12*s*. a bottle, tobacco 30*s*. a pound, and penny boxes of matches sold freely for 4*s*. 6*d*. each!

It is a great thing now, that we can signal to Ekowe and tell them exactly when we start. They can assist much if the enemy gives battle.

I shall be glad to recover my kit again. I managed to buy a second shirt and a second pair of socks here; but I should like a change of clothes in wet weather. I hate getting up in the morning and putting on wet clothes to begin the day in. Happily, we generally have sun enough to dry everything.

The socks I bought here from a travelling salesman are of unique manufacture; they have been cut out of some stocking-looking material and then sewn together; the large seams on the inside are comfortless in walking.

However, here, one is almost always in the saddle. Before long I shall have all I want. I brought my "housewife" from Ekowe, for it is always useful; and I find that if I go several days without repairing my only suit, it is in a bad way, too ventilating all over; and if I neglect to repair it for a few days the rags have set in! Imagine my feelings under these conditions at finding that my housewife had been stolen. I can now only tie myself together with string. It is something to know that I have a ball of string: in this country without railways, the difficulty of getting anything is great.

I am much grieved at the death of Colonel Home: the whole army and perhaps the nation suffers a loss. Besides this, I have lost in him one of my best friends.

In Bivouac, Gingindhlovu, Zululand,
April 2, 1879.

My dear May,—All is well. We, the relieving force for Ekowe, have got to a day's march of the place. Zulus attacked us fiercely this morning, completely surrounding us, and rushing up almost to our bayonets.

We successfully repulsed them, and then chased them a mile or two.

We were formed in square, cattle in the centre, wagons enclosing cattle; and troops outside the wagons, behind a simple entrenchment in a square.

We lost only one officer and about five men killed; and have about thirty wounded. We have counted four hundred and seventy-one dead Zulus round our square within a thousand yards of us.

My best charger was killed, shot through the body.

We hope to reach and relieve Ekowe tomorrow. The garrison of Ekowe signal to us by looking-glass sun flashes from distant hills, from whence they must have seen our fight with telescopes, as their first message was "We congratulate you." This was after the fight, no sun before. The officer killed was Lieutenant Johnson, 99th Regiment....

Entrenched at Gingindhlovu, Zululand,
April 17, 1879.

My dear May,—I had only time to give you a hasty account of the progress of our column to the relief of Ekowe and a summary of our fight here on the 2nd of April. I shall now be able to recount what has happened more fully.

From the 13th of February, when Lord Chelmsford appointed me Staff-Officer of the Lower Tugela district, under Colonel Law, to the end of February, we were quite on the defensive, preparing to resist an invasion of Natal; and my time was chiefly occupied in strengthening and increasing the fortifications on the Natal bank of the Tugela at the Lower Drift. A strong redoubt had been built on the Zulu bank there, but it was expected that the Zulu Army would cross higher up the river and attack our depot of stores on the Natal side.

In this work, I was much assisted by a young lieutenant in the 99th named Alexander. I heard he had been through a course of field fortification and was a good officer, so I put him in charge of the working parties, to carry out the works I traced. This he did most industriously and exceedingly well; and so, I was glad to discover that he was a son of your friend Lady Louisa Alexander.

The Zulus did not enter Natal. When they could have done so they did not; and when they would have done so, heavy rains swelled the Tugela and they could not.

From the beginning of March, Colonel Law and I were deeply occupied in preparing a force for the relief of Ekowe. We found great difficulty in passing a messenger to Ekowe. Only natives could possibly evade the Zulus between us and the place; we offered good rewards, there were many attempts and many failures—our messengers coming back after perilous adventures and hairbreadth escapes. At last, for some time, no natives would attempt it, even for a reward of five head of cattle apiece. Let me interrupt myself here just to speak of the value of cattle to a native. He has to buy his wife, and her price is cattle.

Every Zulu girl is the property of her father, or of her eldest brother if the father is dead. Every daughter born is a treasure because she is worth more or less cattle. A suitor must pay for his wife ten or fifteen head of cattle, according to her estimated beauty; and he may have as many wives as he can pay for. If he is a very poor man he may have to put up with a widow; for widows are almost as little esteemed by Zulus as by Sam Weller's father: one indifferent cow is considered ample payment for any widow. The rules of marriage are very strictly guarded; and so, you will see that a native who is not born in possession of herds must be provident and work for years more or less, to earn the price of the wife of his choice; and when he refuses a reward of five head of cattle to make a journey of thirty miles, something very grave must lie in the way.

At length a messenger was got through to Ekowe and back. He travelled by night only, keeping off the road and going from copse to copse as opportunity offered; we had not then established signals by the looking-glass.

All was ready; and Colonel Law and I were to start with 1,000 men, he in command and I as Staff-Officer. Happily for us and for all concerned, that movement did not come off. Before the 13th the news of the coming reinforcements was received from England, and Lord Chelmsford stayed the relief of Ekowe. Colonel Law and I knew our expedition would be a perilous one, and we expected to fight a hard, perhaps a desperate battle, but it was not until long after, not until the relief of Ekowe, that we learnt that our force must have been annihilated, swallowed by the numbers Cetywayo prepared to meet us.

The Zulus, we know now, had learnt our intention, and for days before the 13th Colonel Pearson and his garrison saw streaming past Ekowe, beyond the range of his guns, day by day, thousands and tens of thousands of Zulus in military array, all moving towards the formidable position of the Inyezane, that lies between the Tugela and Ekowe. What would they not have given to warn us of this! You can imagine, perhaps, what they felt then, and what they felt afterwards when they heard we had remained.

And now, from that time up to the 28th of March, Colonel Law and I worked harder than ever to prepare all that was required for the greater force that was to relieve Ekowe. Three complete British regiments were to be added, besides several hundred sailors and marines, and further, the reassembled natives that formerly made "Graves' Regiment," 2,000 in number; and this time all, or nearly all, armed with breech-loaders.

And so, the relieving force finally amounted to 3,400 white men, with two guns, two Gatlings (*mitrailleuses*), and four rocket tubes.

All the preparations Lord Chelmsford left to Colonel Law and me; and we did our best to carry out well the trust placed in us. It was not a light or simple task to assemble the carts and wagons required to convey the equipment and supplies, and to determine the best equipment for the object in view, and then how best to dispose of it; to organise a transport of several miles in length, out of civilian materials; and lastly, to put all across the Tugela by the ferry, in order on the Zulu bank.

On the 28th of March all was ready. Lord Chelmsford moved his headquarters to the Tugela some days before, and prepared to take command of the force himself.

From that time Colonel Law and I were daily in conversation with him. At such times I am well conscious of the advantage of having always worked hard at the study and practice of my profession. Otherwise, one would feel as he who cannot swim feels in five feet of water, a dismal sense of loss of weight, and with it desire to take a step lacking the force required to plant the foot.

Lord Chelmsford's plan was to proceed with the whole force for Ekowe, taking with us a month's supply of provisions; to give battle where the enemy might present himself in our path, and having defeated him, to withdraw the whole garrison of Ekowe replacing it by one regiment, some natives, and the month's supply of provisions.

I suggested to him not to attempt to take that long train of supplies to Ekowe, but to entrench it in a strong position, before reaching the difficult Inyezane country, and leaving a sufficient guard with it, strongly fortified, to proceed with the rest of the fighting men, unhampered by baggage train, onwards for Ekowe; and having overpowered the Zulus wherever they might oppose us, to withdraw the garrison of Ekowe altogether, and abandon the place, with the intention of forming a post at the Inyezane instead. This plan Lord Chelmsford at first approved and decided upon, but next day he returned to his own original plan. He was, I believe, disinclined to abandon even temporarily, to the enemy, any ground we had gained.

On the evening of the 28th of March, Colonel Law and I crossed the Tugela and bivouacked with the relieving force; we had no tents. Heavy rain began to fall and poured down all night, drenching us thoroughly. I wrote out the orders for the march to commence next morning; and I wrote in pencil, while a man held out a waterproof coat over my head and paper in the rain. Then I went round and read the dripping orders myself to the dripping commanding officers, for I doubted if they could read them. All this time I hoped the rain was wetting the Zulu powder.

At daylight on the 29th of March we started, and soon the sun came out and dried us. That night we assembled and bivouacked by the Inyoni River, ten miles from the Tugela. We took every precaution, forming a *laager* with our wagons and an entrenchment outside. A *laager* is a Dutch contrivance; it is an enclosure formed by jamming the wagons close together; the cattle are put inside, and the defenders are sometimes inside the wagons, sometimes behind an entrenchment outside.

Lord Chelmsford now came up and took command, and so Colonel Crealock, his military secretary, became the senior Staff-Officer of the force, and I, with the General's two *aides-de-camp*, Captain Buller and Captain Molyneux, were the others. Hitherto I had been the only Staff-Officer.

This was our force:

Seamen and Marines of H.M. ships *Shah*, *Tenedos*, and *Boadicea*	640
2 Companies of the "Buffs"	140
5 " " 99th Regt.	430
The 57th Regiment	640
" 3rd Batt. of the 60th Rifles	540
" 91st Highlanders	850
" 4th Batt. of Native Contingent (Barton's)	800
" 5th Batt. of Native Contingent	1200
" Native Scouts	150
" Mounted Troops	230
Total fighting men.	5,620

And there were besides, our commissariat, transport, and medical men, drivers, &c., and 136 vehicles, *viz*. 44 carts, drawn by four mules or six oxen, and 94 wagons drawn each by from sixteen to eighteen oxen. This train, if stretched out and without gaps, would extend over four miles of road.

At daylight on the morning of the 30th of March we advanced again and formed our *laager* for the night on the near bank, the right bank of the Amatakulu River. We had thus gone only between four and five miles this day, but as we could not have got the whole force across the Amatakulu and entrenched it before dark, the general wisely waited in a strong position on the near side of the river. I worked hard with the natives all the afternoon and evening, and by moonlight some way into the night, improving the approaches to the ford on both sides of the water.

The water at the drift was about thirty yards wide and waist deep, with a round, even, gravelly bottom. I widened the road of approach at both sides of the stream and smoothed it; reeds grew in abundance close by, and I had them laid across the road, so that next day our wagons moved easily up the steep ascent from the ford, the wheels not sinking in at all.

The whole of Monday, the 31st of March, was occupied in crossing the Amatakulu, and we made our *laager* for the night about a mile and a half beyond.

On Tuesday, the 1st of April, we advanced to the locality where I am now writing, Gingindhlovu, seven miles from the Amatakulu, and there formed *laager* as usual.

Our *laager* was nearly a square of about a hundred and fifty yards a side, formed by the wagons drawn close together. Inside this were the cattle. Outside was a square entrenchment, leaving a space about twenty yards wide between the wagons and the entrenchment. In this space were the troops and the guns and rocket tubes, all in assigned places.

The entrenchment was in its first stage; that is, it was merely a little trench two feet and a half wide and a foot and a half deep, the earth heaped up in front, to give as much cover as possible. Such a trench is quickly made—a regiment can dig cover of this kind for itself in half an hour, and it shelters one rank of men kneeling, very well. As time admits, it can be developed and made more and more effective to any extent. Every soldier entrenches, or should entrench his post, beginning, if time presses, with the first simple trench I have described.

It has great advantages. It gives much cover from the view and fire of the enemy, and it makes the ground the soldier is to hold and fixes him there when under a heavy fire; without it, he might otherwise retire to seek cover. Furthermore, it is no hindrance whatever to his advancing at any moment, for he can step forward out of it.

About six o'clock on Wednesday morning, the 2nd of April, a shout ran round our entrenchment, "Stand to your arms!" The bugles sounded the "Alarm" and everyone bounded in to his place. Directly afterwards shots were fired by our outposts and we saw them retiring upon the entrenchments. Soon they were all inside with us. Close by me was one of our natives, his eyes fixed with the look of a hawk, while with one hand he pointed towards the Inyezane valley and said to me, "*Impi*," that is "Army." I looked there and saw what might have been easily mistaken for a streak of bush, bordering a stream and disappearing back into the distance miles away. But it was not bush; a few instants of observation showed that it was in motion: it was a stream of black men rapidly approaching our position from our left front; it was a Zulu Army!

When the head of the stream arrived at about a mile from our entrenchment, it split into two streams and began winding round our left, towards our rear; and the other passed across our front and then circled round our right, meeting the head of the other black stream in our rear. Thus, they surrounded us. Then began the most splendid piece of skirmishing eye ever beheld. No whites ever did, or ever could skirmish in the magnificent perfection of the Zulus, unencumbered by much clothing, in the prime of life and as brave as it is possible for any men to be, they bounded forward towards us from all sides, rushing from cover to cover, gliding like snakes through the grass, and turning to account every bush, every mound, every particularly high patch of grass between us and them, and firing upon us, always from concealment.

If total concealment were possible, we should not have seen a Zulu till he reached our trench, but it was not possible, and we could see them as they bounded from one point of concealment to another, always approaching. When a Zulu fires from concealment he instantly throws himself flat, to escape the shots fired to where his smoke has disclosed his place.

On they came. At one part they were about two hundred yards off, at another they had closed up to forty yards. Our soldiers fixed bayonets. However, they were not to be required to use them, for the deadly fire that combed the grass as it were all round us had killed every Zulu within several hundred yards. One hour had passed, and their fire evidently was rapidly diminishing, although there was no failing in the numbers still crowding up from the Inyezane valley.

At this sign of failing, we gave three tremendous cheers. Those cheers echoed through the valley and were heard far away; and they were received as a sign of victory, as I have seen them received by Africans before, at Abrakrampa, at Ordahsu, and on Majia's Hill.

And now our two thousand natives rushed out of our entrenchments, our mounted troops went too; and after one vigorous effort of the Zulus to stop the sortie, by wheeling up and firing into the right flank of the advancing troops, they turned and fled.

But their bravest men had not breath to run away, and they perished. Let me draw a veil over that part of the scene. Chivalry ends when pursuit begins; but the dire necessities of war oblige that a defeated army shall also be dispersed, so that it shall never fight again; it is called consummating the victory.

We had had a short but hard fight of an hour and a half. One of the first few shots fired killed my best horse, the one I rode on the 22nd of January. I was not on his back at the time.

All the bodies within a thousand yards of us were ordered to be buried at once, and they numbered 471. Such fine fellows—herculean limbs and the high intelligent forehead of European races. But the British public's notion of Zulus is its one notion of all black races, and that notion is the savage described by Defoe in Robinson Crusoe.

On Thursday, the 3rd of April, Lord Chelmsford found the ground towards Ekowe so swampy, that he could not take on the wagons of supply, and so he once more decided to abandon Ekowe. We entrenched our wagons strongly here, and advanced to Ekowe with the 57th, 60th, and 91st Regiments, and some mounted troops, leaving the rest to guard our entrenchment. We met with no opposition on the way, and reached Ekowe after dark. Next day the whole of the old garrison evacuated the place and started for the Tugela. We remained there during the 4th, and on the 5th of April abandoned the place, and marched back to Gingindhlovu, reaching this place on the 6th. . . .

> Fort Chelmsford, Inyezane River, Zululand,
> May 2, 1879.

My dear May,—After the relief of Ekowe, Lord Chelmsford reorganised his forces and divided them into three parts, called 1st Division, 2nd Division, and Wood's Flying Column. General Crealock was given command of the 1st Division, and General Newdegate that of 2nd Division. These generals have just arrived from England. Each division has two brigades of three regiments each. The 1st Division, to which I belong, is made up of the troops that have been operating from the Tugela. Its 1st Brigade is commanded by Colonel Pearson, now promoted to be a Brigadier-General; and its three regiments are the "Buffs," 88th, and 99th. The 1st Brigade is now at the Tugela. The 2nd Brigade is commanded by Colonel Pemberton, 60th Rifles, and its regiments are the 60th Rifles (3rd Batt.), the 57th, and the 91st Highlanders.

The 2nd Brigade is now here about twenty-five miles in front of the Tugela, and holds the most advanced position. Great was my joy when, after the relief of Ekowe, Lord Chelmsford told me I was to be Brigade-Major to this brigade. I have mentioned all the regiments of the 1st Division, because this division will be the force operating from the Tugela in the renewal of the campaign, and it will be convenient to you to know this when reading the papers. Besides these regiments we have the Native Contingent, to which I began by being Staff-Officer, only instead of being "Graves' Regiment," they form two battalions called the 4th and 5th Battalions of Natal Contingent. Captain Barton, 7th Fusiliers, commands the 4th, and Nettelton, a good volunteer officer, experienced in the Colony, commands the 5th. These natives are here now; and we have also with us some irregular cavalry and about 400 sailors and marines attached to the brigade. So that altogether we have about 3,000 white men and 2,000 natives here under arms.

Gingindhlovu, where I last wrote from, was a very bad station, owing to the bad water supply. We drank entirely from a marsh and there was a good deal of sickness and some deaths from dysentery. We have no filters. Colonel Pemberton had to be sent back to the base hospital behind the Tugela, suffering severely from dysentery, so Colonel Clarke, 57th Regiment, commands the 2nd Brigade for the time. I expect Colonel Pemberton will recover, as he has such courage about it. Those who fear soon die. Colonel Pemberton sent for me one day; he was very bad, and spoke with difficulty; he said:

> Mind, Hart, if we are attacked, I am going to get up and command my own battalion. I shall not deprive Colonel Clarke of the chief command. I have no right to do that when I am on the sick list, but I shall command my own battalion.

At last, we got leave to advance, and on the 24th of April, Colonel Clarke and I with half our force moved on four miles to the Inyezane, and took up a strong position that Colonel Clarke and I had examined and chosen some time before. Next day the rest of our force joined us, and here we all are.

This is the same river that flows by Majia's Hill, where the fight was on 22nd of January, only we are much nearer the mouth of the river and only about five miles from the sea. We have water enough, though the river is but a small one; and we are on a high and healthy spot.

A fort and depot for provisions is to be established here, preparatory to our further advance, and we have been ordered by General Crealock to call it Fort Chelmsford.

We have no Engineers with us, so I am building the fort, and this together with all my other duties keeps me hard at work all day. The digging is very good exercise for the men and helps to keep them healthy.

On the 27th I went with a body of irregular cavalry about nine miles in advance of this, to the next river—the Emlalazi—to make a reconnaissance of its mouth, with a view to its fitness for landing supplies there when we advance. This would be a great saving in time and labour over the tedious wagon traffic. A low line of sand dunes, covered with thick bush, lay between the beach and the country, then a marshy tract, and then high hills rose at about a mile from the shore. We approached by these hills, and then, taking due military precautions, passed the marsh, crossed the bush on the sand dunes—only about two hundred yards wide, but very dense—and reached the beach, fine firm sand. I examined the mouth of the river; and as no signs of Zulus appeared, enjoyed a good bathe in the sea, the surf being only moderately heavy.

We then began to retire, but Lieutenant Startin of the navy, who had come with us, was a little behindhand in dressing after his bathe, and while we were hurrying him on, two shots were fired at him from the bush on the opposite side of the river, about two hundred yards off, and one of the bullets struck the sand very close to him. I never saw a man finish dressing more quickly! but he did finish, and retired without leaving one article behind! We fired a shot back at the spot the smoke came from, and there were no more. When we had reascended the heights, we saw a few small parties of Zulus, one of which went to examine our tracks in the sand and the others remained watching us from the farther side of the river.

May 23rd.—I enjoy my work here very much, while those who are behind, at the Tugela, find life rather dull. This is still the most advanced post; and the delay, now, to our march onwards, is necessary to accumulate sufficient supplies here for the whole division, when we go forward to attack the king's position. We have ammunition enough, and supplies of food only are required. Twice a week we receive a large convoy of about a hundred wagons, each carrying three or four thousand pounds weight, of chiefly food. This has been going on ever since we have been here, yet much more is required.

The stock of provisions certainly grows, but the rapid shoot that it makes on the arrival of a convoy, shrinks alarmingly before the arrival of the next! It reminds me of the progress of the snail, who got three feet up a wall by day and slipped back two in the night!

We have sent back 1,000 of our natives for the present, half to the Tugela and half of them to Fort Crealock, on the Amatikulu; so that our force here is not much over 4,000 men, but how they do eat! A large herd of oxen is driven up to us, and in a very short time we have eaten it all up. Perhaps it will interest you to hear what our rations are. Each officer and white man is given daily, without any charge of payment:

1¼ lbs. of fresh meat, or 1 lb. preserved meat.
1½ " bread, or 1 lb. biscuit,
Third oz. coffee.
Sixth " tea.
2 ozs. sugar.
½ oz. salt.
Thirty-sixth oz. pepper.

½ lb. to 1 lb. of fresh vegetables, if there are any, or ¼ lb. rice, or ½ lb. of peas or beans, or 1 oz. of preserved vegetables. Whenever we are under arms before daybreak, we get an extra ration of a third oz. of coffee, ½ oz. of sugar, and ¼ lb. of biscuit. As we here always get under arms every morning an hour before daybreak, and await attack till it is light, we get this extra every day. When there are no fresh vegetables, an ounce of lime juice and ½ oz. of sugar with it is issued to each. I think I have only tasted fresh vegetables about half a dozen times in the field—usually pumpkin, or sweet potato, looted from the Zulu gardens.

I think our rations are very liberal and they are excellent in quality. But withal, a ration of tough ox requires good and experienced cooking to be chewable! Also, I find it well to draw several days' supply of such items as tea and pepper, as the whole of a ration was liable to adhere to the Commissariat-scales, when inverted over my receptacle!

The tea is very good and the coffee splendid. The latter is grown in Natal, and so we get it very fresh and with a full and delicious flavour. I never enjoy it so much as after that early morning turn out.

Oh! how I hate that hour before daylight. The turning out in the chill and wet, in cold blood, to be ready for the enemy who never comes with the dawn. Often then do I repeat to myself the Ancient Mariner's exclamation:

> *Oh! Sleep it is a gentle thing,*
> *Beloved from Pole to Pole.*

Indeed, it is; and add thereto on my own account:

> *And waking is a hateful thing,*
> *Abhorred with all my soul.*

The precaution is wise, because the Zulus *might* come. But he enjoys the gentle thing Sleep, as much as other people do, and he detests cold. He wraps himself up in his blanket, head and all, and gets up a high temperature within the blanket, where, if he may, he will await the sun.

And during the whole campaign, there has never been but one attack at daybreak—the attack that produced the disaster at the Intombe River. You will have seen the details of the annihilation of the convoy there, in the papers.

As I told you, there being no Engineers here, the construction of Fort Chelmsford was left to me; and I was very glad to undertake it. The fort is now finished, as far as its defences go, and has been finished for many days; but I am still hard at work putting up sheds for the garrison inside, and store sheds. The natives give me most valuable assistance in the matter. I was given no instructions or conditions in building this fort, and this I was very glad of. It was left entirely to me.

Our troops are entrenched on a commanding hill, near the Inyezane; and on the summit of this hill, within the entrenchments, I have built Fort Chelmsford, calculated for a garrison of 300 men, which, I think, is as much as we ought to allow to hold this position, when we advance. A certain quantity of our stores will be inside and the rest outside in sheds, which I have so placed, that they give no cover for the enemy and are within effective fire from the fort, so that they cannot be approached without heavy losses. All round the fort, inside, I have put up sheds close to the parapet, the roofs lifted high enough for the garrison to fire between roof and parapet. Under these sheds, the future garrison will sleep on the ground that they will stand up upon to fight, in case of attack.

Water will always be kept stored in barrels, never allowed to be empty.

In the middle of the fort, I have sunk a mine, eleven feet deep; and already three galleries diverging from the bottom are making good progress. The ammunition will be stored there. All is very successful, and everyone is well satisfied with the fort.

The general has not paid us a visit yet. He is at the Tugela with the 1st Brigade. I speak of General Crealock.

Since I last wrote to you, he ordered us to make a reconnaissance of a particular spot on the Emlalazi River, with a view to our forces eventually crossing there. This is the next river, eight or nine miles in front of us—the river, the mouth of which I have already told you about when we explored it. He ordered the reconnaissance to be made by our irregular cavalry, and that I and a Lieut. Sherrard, R.E., who was sent up, should go with it. We were to cross the river at the drift mentioned, and explore the opposite side.

This reconnaissance we undertook on the 16th of May. We found the drift from the description, but it was tidal and not then fordable. Hardly had the advanced cavalry scouts reached the river bank, than the Zulus began to gather in small clusters on the opposite hilltops. There was a hill on our side of the drift, about three hundred yards from the river, where we formed up our main body. At about three hundred yards beyond the river and opposite, was a little circular hill, of about the same height. In a few minutes, some five hundred Zulus, who had collected on a hill a mile off, started at a run towards us, very cleverly got the little hill I speak of between them and us, and soon, as we expected, reached its summit, keeping covered by the long grass there, but just showing their heads now and then. We had already dismounted our men, sent the horses back a little way to get cover, and were in line ready for them.

They opened fire first, and we of course returned it. A few of their bullets struck the ground amongst us, but the rest all whistled overhead.

Sherrard and I made our observations, and an eye sketch of the position, while our men kept the Zulus occupied; and after about twenty minutes we had noted all that was necessary, except that we could not measure the width and depth of the water, the Zulus outnumbering us too much; nor could we have crossed the drift, even if fordable. However, we made an estimate of it, that I expect will be pretty accurate.

We had under 200 men only with us. The Emlalazi is evidently now considered by the Zulus the line of demarcation between us.

While this was going on two messengers from Cetywayo were at Fort Chelmsford, asking for peace. They were by no means humble. They said the king had told them to say he had lost a great many men in the war, and so had we, and therefore it would be well to stop now. "And so had we," mark that! Right well he knows it!

This request for peace reminds me of the Ashantis' similar, but most humble, petition just before the Battle of Amoaful.

There are those though, of weight, who think Cetywayo means peace. We shall see.

Emlalazi River, Zululand,
June 25, 1879.

My dear May,—We are established on the next river to the In-yezane, eight or nine miles beyond it, and at the very drift that I have told you we reconnoitred on the 16th of May.

From the time that I posted No, 15 to you, up to the 21st of June, when I started with our main body for the Emlalazi, my time was chiefly occupied in strengthening Fort Chelmsford and in building huts to store our heaps of provisions in. Large parties of soldiers and natives worked at this daily, under my directions; some going out with wagons to fetch timber from distant woods, some gathering reeds for thatch on the river bank, some digging, some building, and others cutting raw ox-hides into strips for lashing the logs together, and tying the rafters.

We had no nails and no cord, nor could we get any, so I had the hides of the cattle we eat cut up, and though the smell was severe, for there was not time to wait to dry the hides, one day's sun generally purified the lashings, and as they shrunk in drying, they bound the timber together like iron bands.

Our natives cut up the hides; they do it very quickly and cleverly, making a whole hide into one continuous strip, by cutting a band about an inch wide, round and round the edge of the hide, till it is entirely used up.

We were all very glad when the order to move on arrived, for, besides the desire to progress with the war, our situation was not a healthy one—it was the reverse. Fever and dysentery attacked us; and for some weeks we sent every week to Natal from forty to sixty and sometimes more men invalided.

I have enjoyed continuously excellent health—I may say, bounding health; it is a circumstance for thankfulness, not for boasting, for when these maladies are in the air, or the water, or wherever it may be that they arise, no one can say he will not be stricken.

There was, unfortunately, to the prevailing windward of us, a large extent of low wet country. I rode across this ground one day, in the course of duty, and recognised therein, at once, the normal smell of the Gold Coast—concentrated essence of malarious emanations—a smell that alarmed me when I first met it some years ago, but that I grew familiar with, and even took kindly to, when I found there was nothing else to breathe! No doubt much mischief was blown from this low tract up to our fort on the hilltop.

But there were also two other very probable causes of sickness: one our numbers, for congregation is in itself a source of disease, and the other our water.

The Inyezane is a small stream, and now in the winter, the dry season, it almost ceases to flow and the water taken from the pools is not good. Added to this, a considerable number of dead Zulus had long been in the river, upstream of us, some as near as a mile. Whether they were thrown in to poison the water, or whether, as our natives say, they were wounded men retreating from Gingindhlovu, drowned in trying to cross the river when it was swollen, I do not know.

You will perhaps remember my telling you in the Ashanti war, that when the Ashantis retired from Brokamp, they rendered undrinkable every source of water along the bush path behind them, by throwing in dead bodies, and even killed their own men to supply bodies enough—for some distance the bodies were all Fantis; then they were Ashantis.

I don't know whether this is a Zulu practice, nor am I going to make any inquiries that might set the suggestion afloat. The bodies in the Inyezane were almost reduced to skeletons when we found them.

In the bullet pouch, on the belt of one of them, was found a letter from Colonel Pearson to Lord Chelmsford, written at Ekowe and sent by a native messenger. He must have been killed, poor fellow.

The natives who took, or attempted to take, messages between the Tugela and Ekowe, were always volunteers for the purpose. Brave fellows indeed were they who, without a single eye to applaud, without the stimulus of any excitement, without any prospect of decoration to incite ambition, undertook to make their way in the cold, dark night through the Zulu host. Sometimes quite successful, sometimes sorely chased, sometimes "missing."

The letter was still quite legible throughout. Probably the skeleton on which it was found was that of the Zulu who had killed the messenger.

At first, Colonel Pearson used to send his letters rolled up in the inside of a reed, but later, they were more securely hidden, thus: the iron plate was unscrewed off the foot of the messenger's rifle, then a hole was bored into the butt, at the part that was covered with the metal plate, the letter was put in the hole and the plate screwed on again. When two messengers went together, each had a copy of the letter thus hidden in the butt of his rifle.

We got the noxious remains out of our drinking water! But the Inyezane at best is not large enough for men to drink by thousands.

At Fort Chelmsford we received several important messages from Cetywayo. But I have omitted to tell you that before we left Gingindhlovu, as long ago as the 21st of April, an important Zulu chief, named Umagwendu, joined us. He is a half-brother of the king's; the same father, but different mothers. He had been against his brother's policy of continuing the war. Cetywayo suspected disloyalty and sent him this message:

> Are we not brothers? Had we not both the same father? Come to me, and if we are to die, let us die together.

Umagwendu, however, went the other way. It happened thus:

Some of our natives, foraging one day in the neighbourhood, took prisoners several women and children, and brought them to our camp. Another of our natives immediately recognised among the women his mother-in-law. This man had fled from Cetywayo's power into Natal, and taken a wife without the king's leave. The wife was safe in Natal, and here was the mother.

From his mother-in-law, this native learnt that Umagwendu wanted to join us, but feared we should kill him. I suppose that as he held an important command in that terrible fight at Isandhlwana, he thought we might retaliate on him. However, some of the prisoners were sent to tell Umagwendu that he might come, without hurt.

The first reply was that Zulu soldiers sent by the king, were watching his movements, and that he could not move without a certainty of their cutting him off.

At last, having walked hard all through the night with three or four of his wives and some twenty or thirty attendants carrying babies and baggage, he arrived at our outposts, and his party there laid down their arms; Umagwendu himself depositing a first-rate Martini breechloading carbine, equal to the best we possess.

He is very heavy and unattractive, apart from the circumstances that he has a dreadful squint. He led the way into our camp, followed by two of his chief men, and then came the wives. These dames were exceedingly substantial. They wore short kilted skirts, and their shoulders were wrapped in shawls of brilliant stripes. After the custom of all Zulu women when they marry, they shave their hair off from their foreheads to the crown of the head. The remaining portion was worked up into an elaborate bunch and coloured red by a preparation of red clay.

The deportment of these ladies was peculiar; they bent themselves at the waist till their heads were little above the waist, and remained staring at the ground in this attitude, with a solemn expression, for about a quarter of an hour, while I arranged quarters for the whole party.

This was bowing down with their faces to the earth, in salutation, only instead of doing the bow again and again as the patriarchs of Genesis did, they made them all into one. I thought the pain of straightening themselves again after being thus cramped for a quarter of an hour must have been acute.

All that I could offer Umagwendu for the accommodation of himself and party was the underneath part of a wagon. We had no tents. All our men slept on the open ground. And this wagon was the best accommodation we had to offer. There was no hood to the wagon, so I got a tarpaulin pulled over it, so as to hang to the ground on three sides and on the other if desired.

I then told Umagwendu he had better put the ladies and babies under the wagon, and that as for himself and the others, they could sleep under sky or cloud, as we did. He did not appear to like his quarters at all, but I left him to make the best of it; and soon they filled up all the basement story of the wagon. Umagwendu himself took a place there, the retainers formed a half circle in front of the entrance, a fire was lighted in the middle, meat began to frizzle, all the babies began to sing together, and the whole party were quite happy.

To keep off inquisitive people, I ordered a boundary-line formed of boxes of ammunition to be laid round the party. These boxes of ammunition were conveniently close, so I took them. Umagwendu at once showed evident signs of alarm. He knew what those boxes were, for he had captured hundreds upon hundreds of them at Isandhlwana, and I imagine he thought we were going to blow the party up. So, I sent the interpreter to tell him they were put there to keep our own people from crowding round him as they had done. His answer was, "Thank you; they were worse than the flies in summer."

The Zulus make remarkably good similes in their conversation.

When, after the disaster of Isandhlwana, our troops once more began to advance across the Tugela in force, one of our Zulus watching the bodies of men going over the river, said to another, "The Zulus kicked the white ant-heap, and see, the ants come swarming out."

Shakespeare would have been pleased to hear that speech.

Next day, we sent off Umagwendu and his people to Natal. He said that his other wives and all the rest of his people and his cattle had been cut off by the Zulu soldiers, and were killed by this time as a matter of course; and he asked leave to join us and fight to avenge them.

As Cetywayo has circulated a false report, to intimidate the disloyal, to the effect that we tortured Umagwendu brutally, cut off his ears and so forth, his request has been granted, and he is now here in the front to show himself to any Zulu messengers who arrive.

From Umagwendu, I learnt that no prisoners were taken at Isandhlwana—all died fighting.

Several petitions for peace were sent by the king to us, at Fort Chelmsford, but they were not very satisfactory.

On the 6th of June, three of the principal chiefs arrived with such a message. One of them, I was very glad to find, was Mabilwane, who commanded in the engagement at Inyezane. I much wished to ask him some questions, and when business was over I did so.

He said he had heard of those white men being killed in the *kloof*; that there were Zulus concealed in the *kloof*, but he could not say whether the white men were killed by them, or by those that rushed down from Majia's Hill at us. No men, he said, had come forward to say they had done it.

He saw me ride up Majia's Hill on what he called "the great red horse," though he was not near enough to recognise the rider. And when I asked him why so many men ran away when I reached the top, he said:

"Because when the men who were behind saw a horseman appear on the summit, they could not imagine that he could have got there unless a great number came too; and they at once raised a cry, 'Here they all come,' and then there was a panic and a flight."

On the 18th and 19th, General Crealock joined us on the Inyezane. The "Buffs" and a force of the navy had come up.

On the 20th we sent forward an advanced party of one regiment, the 91st, some guns, and the Engineers to repair the road.

On the 21st, the main body followed. Rain had made the roads so heavy, that we had to *laager* for the night on the way; and on the 22nd we reached the Emlalazi.

All Zulus had retreated, and no resistance was made to our bridging the river. General Crealock, on arrival at Fort Chelmsford, received me very warmly. I had never met him before. He expressed the greatest satisfaction with the fort, and was well pleased and satisfied with all Colonel Clarke's force had done.

This is a much nicer locality than that we have left. We have not a good enough supply of water for so many men, but then we go on again, probably in a day or two.

The river is tidal, as we are only about two miles from the sea, so it does not afford us drink. It is a small stream, only about twenty yards wide.

We are busy now daily, working at the road near the bridge, to make it firm enough for our wagons. And the Engineers are making a small redoubt on the top of the hill on the opposite bank, the hill the Zulus fired from, to be called Fort Napoleon, after the late ill-fated prince.

We have left a small garrison at Fort Chelmsford and shall leave another in Fort Napoleon.

Emlalazi Plain, near Point Durnford landing-place,
July 3, 1879.

My dear May,—We are now encamped close to the seashore, between the Emlalazi and the Umhlatuzi Rivers, about five miles in advance of the Emlalazi.

The whole of my brigade (the 2nd) is here, also the "Buffs" and some detachments of the other regiments of the 1st Brigade, irregular cavalry and the artillery of the 1st Division.

General Crealock is here too, so the whole of our division is assembled at this place, except part of the 1st Brigade that is either in garrison at the forts on the road behind us or following us up.

Sir Garnet Wolseley is a little way off the shore, on board H.M.S. *Shah*, which cast anchor there yesterday morning. Sir Garnet could not land yesterday owing to the surf, but is expected to do so this morning.

Two steamers with provisions are lying at anchor close by. They arrived on Monday, and part of their cargoes has already been landed.

The object now is to form a base of supply here, and thus avoid the long, difficult and severe process of transit by wagons from Durban to the front. I have used the word road, I dare say, frequently in my letters, but I must tell you that a road in this country and in Natal is merely the wagon track upon the natural surface of the ground. In places it is hard, and the wagons run easily enough, but more often the wheels follow deep ruts already made, or, in making a new track, cut several inches deep into the fresh turf. In wet weather progress is scarcely possible, sometimes it is quite impossible.

The surface of the country is a succession of innumerable hills and valleys, small and steep; the road bends about in all directions, to follow the least difficult course, but cannot avoid constant ascents and descents. The sufferings of the oxen *en route* are dreadful to contemplate. At very difficult places the wagons are double-spanned, as it is called; that is, two spans or from twenty-eight to thirty-two oxen are attached to one wagon, several whips are worked with cruel severity, the usual yelling is kept up, and occasionally men push behind at the same time with all their might. For all this I have seen a wagon fail to move. Then the oxen are given a few minutes' rest, and the effort is made again. Now and then a wagon sinks up to the axles in a soft place; then it has to be off-loaded, drawn out empty and reloaded.

You will not be very much surprised after this, when I tell you that on our first day's move forward from the Emlalazi we made only three miles' progress.

The wretched ox has a very bad time of it. In England there are humane laws, which would forbid half the degree of severity an ox here receives as his daily meed, and lookers-on in England would prevent it.... The necessities of war also press heavily upon the Natal ox. Besides his labour and torture, he now gets indifferently fed. It is midwinter and the grass is dry and distasteful to him, except here and there when it was burnt at the proper time of autumn and is now succeeded by a rich green crop.

The advanced guard of our division left Fort Napoleon on Thursday, the 26th of June, and next day the main body, with which I was, followed.

Next day we proceeded, and joined the advanced guard here, after sunset; forming our entrenchment by moonlight.

We had descended from the top of a high hill, on which our *laager* was formed, and entered a meadow plain stretching away for many miles to the front, and separated on our right hand from the sea by a range of wooded sand-hills bordering the beach.

Numerous short palm-trees grew in the plain, and huge clusters of their fruit hung down within reach. This fruit was the size of a medlar and the same colour, with a polish on the skin, but the interior was almost entirely occupied by the kernel. The pulp is very sweet, but very poor eating.

On Monday, the 30th of June, the ships arrived and anchored off the shore.

I have not had time to have a bathe yet, but hope to have a dip tomorrow.

Although it is midwinter, I must remind you that the temperature is about the same as the English midsummer, but a little warmer in the middle of the day, and colder in the middle of the night. I don't know, I am sure, why it is winter, for the trees remain in leaf, and there are flowers and butterflies all about, just as they were in December.

Night has come, and Sir Garnet has not been able to get on shore. I trust he will do so tomorrow. Lord Chelmsford and Colonel Wood from the north must be close upon Ulundi, if not actually there, and it is time we were there too, and the war ended.

The surf here is small compared to the surf at Cape Coast Castle; but they have not got here, either the splendid surf-boats or the clever Fantis to work them. The Zulus hate the sea, and there is not, I believe, a canoe or a fisherman in the whole nation!

July 9th.—At the close of my last letter, I just mentioned that the ships of provisions and the *Shah*, with Sir Garnet on board, had all gone on the morning of the 4th, landing being impracticable owing to the surf.

The *Shah* steamed straight away for Durban, but the ships merely stood out to sea until the wind fell; and in a day or two afterwards returned and began putting their cargoes on shore. This is done by what they call here "surf-boats," but the term "boat" is not satisfactory; barge would be more fitting, for they are one-masted, decked vessels, about the size of, and having a general resemblance to, a Thames barge. They are cleverly worked in this way. A strong hawser is fastened at one end on the beach, and the other end is anchored several hundred yards out to sea.

The loaded surf-boat leaves the ship and picks up the hawser, as far out as possible. The hawser is then passed lengthways over the boat, through a fork at the bows and a fork at the stern. The rudder is removed, and the surf-boat is then ready to move backwards to the beach along the hawser, and has a flat bottom for repose upright when aground.

The process by which the boat is moved along the hawser is very ingenious. Two "stoppers," as they are called, are put on the hawser. A stopper is simply a hitch made with a small rope upon the hawser, one end of the rope being fast to the boat and the other in a man's hand on board. When the man pulls the rope, the hitch tightens, and will not slip along the hawser, so the boat is stopped; when he relaxes his hold, the boat is released again.

One stopper prevents the boat going forwards and the other prevents it going backwards. When a roller comes in, the stoppers are relaxed at the moment it reaches the boat, and the boat is then carried by the roller some distance towards the shore. The moment the roller leaves the boat, the stopper is applied which prevents the boat slipping back upon the reflex of the wave; for, you know, there is always a surging to and fro of the waves.

The next roller is treated in the same way, and so the boat progresses, bit by bit, till it passes through the surf and strikes stern upon the beach.

The cargo is passed out by hand, and the boat got out to sea again by the contrary process simply.

The sight is very fine, for all this is done in very troubled waters; the huge boat being one moment hidden completely from view, and the next almost pitched out of the sea.

Such is the Indian Ocean on it most tranquil days. Yet it is calm compared to the Atlantic, upon the western coast.

On Saturday, the 5th of July, General Crealock sent forward a column to seize Ondini, Cetywayo's old *kraal*, since converted into a military *kraal*, the headquarters of one of the Zulu regiments.

The organisation of the Zulu Army by regiments, each having a muster-place, when they mobilise for war, is done with a system and method that is quite on a par with European powers.

Our force consisted of our irregular cavalry, supported by a battalion (the 91st), a gun, a Gatling, and 500 natives, under Colonel Clarke.

He was to *laager* his force for the night at the Umhlatuzi River, while the cavalry pushed on, and next day to follow up in support of the cavalry.

We, Colonel Clarke's party, started from this about 4 p.m., but got so bogged on the way, that we were overtaken by the darkness, and had to halt till 7.30, when the moon was up and we could see our way.

We reached the heights overlooking the Umhlatuzi, distant nine miles from this, and formed *laager* there.

I was very tired, having been in the saddle all day, on various duties; and had just rolled up in my blanket, and sunk into a comfortable sleep, when the general, with the cavalry, passed through our position on the way forward.

The general said he wanted me to go on with him; so, I had to saddle up and go on again.

Our guide took us four miles out of the way, so it was two o'clock at night when we reached the Empangeni mission-station; which was in ruins, having been destroyed by the Zulus.

This spot was seven miles from Colonel Clarke's *laager*, but we had been eleven.

The general now changed his mind, said the cavalry should go on to Ondini, and that he would go back to Colonel Clarke, and return with his force to camp.

I was so tired, that I had frequently slept soundly as I rode.

The prospect of starting for another seven miles was not cheering; still less so a march back. I was right glad, then, when the general said he would wait at Empangeni for two hours.

I immediately stuck my sword deep into the ground, tied my horse to the handle, and lay down in the long, silky meadow grass, when I got shelter from the cold night wind, and at the end of two hours' deep sleep, woke punctually, quite refreshed.

The cavalry marched for Ondini. The general, his staff, and I, with a cavalry escort, took the direct road to Colonel Clarke's *laager*.

I trotted on ahead with the message to Colonel Clarke, not to advance.

Colonel Clarke met me as I approached, with a warm shaking of the hand and much expression of joy, for he had expected me some hours before, and at last feared I must have been killed on the way back.

While breakfast was cooking, I enjoyed a bathe in the Umhlatuzi; the water was shallow and quite clear, so I had no fear of crocodiles.

Then we proceeded back to this camp. On our way we heard our guns firing a salute, which was in honour of Lord Chelmsford's seizure of Ulundi. The news of his victory had just arrived.

On Monday, the 7th of July, Sir Garnet Wolseley arrived here, with Colonel Brackenbury (his military secretary) and Captain Maurice, and two men, *aides-de-camp*, that I don't know. Colonel Russell is following up.

Lord Gifford, who has been with us—his regiment, the 57th, being one of my brigade—has joined Sir Garnet in his old position as *aide-de-camp*.

The cavalry returned from Ondini on the evening of the 7th; they found it evacuated, but it had been occupied recently. It was a very large *kraal*, 350 yards in diameter, and containing 640 huts. They burnt it.

I paid my respects to Sir Garnet on the 8th and was received very cordially. We have had several days of heavy rain, quite unusual at this winter season: the result is, we are shut in upon our plain by impassable marshes that have formed. So, it is well we have communication by sea.

Working parties are hard at work all day making roads over the marshes, and the unloading on the beach still goes on.

We shall probably know soon what effect the capture of Ulundi will have upon the war.

The Zulus are surrendering here by hundreds, laying down their arms. They are splendid fellows; it is always a pleasure to look at them. By surrendering, they and their families are protected; and they save their cattle, but are obliged to sell some to us.

There is a remarkable *hauteur* in their manner as they surrender, as if they would say, "We are down now, but we have hit you as hard as you have hit us."

Ondini (Ulundi), Zululand,
Aug. 13, 1879.

My dear May,—You will see by the heading of this letter that I have left Port Durnford and am at the Capital. In all English maps it is called Ulundi, and therefore this name has been taken up by the British forces, but no such place or name is known to Zulus, or to white residents in Zululand. Ondini is the proper name and spelling of this now famous place.

I told you of Sir Garnet's arrival at Port Durnford. Soon after, he made great changes in our army.

So large a force was no longer necessary. Lord Chelmsford had reached Ondini. And the Zulus commanded by Cetywayo himself, or at least acting under his gaze, had made but a half-hearted resistance of half an hour, and then fled, abandoning the most venerated place in their land, the king's chief *kraal*.

Ondini was burnt. The king became a fugitive, and the chiefs of the districts from the sea to Ondini tendered their submission to Sir Garnet.

A much smaller force would therefore do to finish the campaign by overpowering such troops as Cetywayo could rally, and subduing the districts beyond Ondini.

Sir Garnet accordingly broke up our existing organisation. Most of the generals and their staffs returned to Natal, to embark for England, and part of the army was ordered to follow.

Sir Garnet then formed two new columns: one under Colonel Clarke, to advance upon Cetywayo from the south; the other under Colonel Russell (my chief in Ashanti), to advance upon him from the west. At the same time the Swazis, a neighbouring people hostile to the Zulus, led by an English officer, and strengthened by a contingent of white irregular cavalry, were to descend upon the king from the north.

Oham, the king's first cousin, a great chief in Zululia, had long ago joined the British side, and now at the fitting time he had been sent to his people in the north of the country, to raise them in arms against Cetywayo.

And thus, on all sides but one, the Zulu king is being hemmed in. On that remaining side are the Lebombo Mountains, a range over which there is only one pass, and beyond the pass deadly climate and tribes that hate the Zulu.

I have made a sketch-map, which I enclose; it will show you the present situation more clearly than it can be described. I have noted on it the position and strength of our forces, and the roads we use for communication and supply. I have also marked all our fortified posts used either to secure the roads or to protect depots of provisions.

You will see the road to Ekowe by which I first advanced under Colonel Pearson's command, and the coast road to Port Durnford by which I afterwards advanced under General Crealock. Notice, then, the road from Port Durnford to Ondini by St. Paul's—that is the road by which Colonel Clarke's column has moved. The column was made up of:

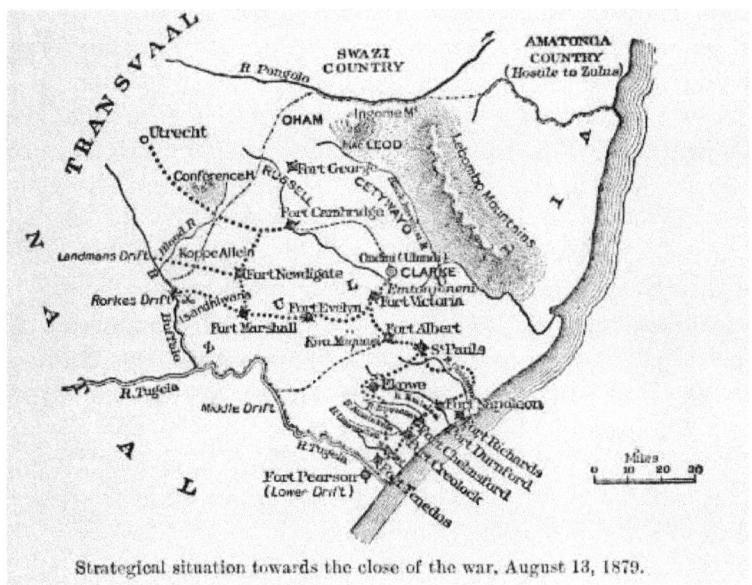

Strategical situation towards the close of the war, August 13, 1879.

The 57th Regiment.
3rd Batt. 60th Rifles.
5 Companies 80th Regiment.
Barton's Battalion of Native Contingent.
100 Native Scouts.
350 Irregular Cavalry.
2 Guns.
4 Gatlings.
150 Engineers and Native Pioneers.

There were at first over a hundred wagons for baggage and provisions, and at St. Paul's the number of wagons was more than doubled, each wagon drawn by from sixteen to eighteen oxen. Then there was our Field Hospital, composed of several wagons and ambulances some fifty regimental pack-mules carrying ammunition, and about thirty carts with reserve ammunition, entrenching tools, &c.

We take two hundred rounds of ammunition for each soldier; he carries seventy himself; two mules follow every company with thirty rounds more for him, and the carts following with the baggage carry the remaining hundred.

Sir Garnet told Colonel Clarke that he might choose his own staff. Colonel Clarke offered me the post of principal Staff-Officer; and I need not tell you that I joyfully accepted his good offer.

On Thursday, the 24th of July, we started from Port Durnford for Ondini, Sir Garnet Wolseley had gone back to Natal, and said he would join us at Emtonjaneni, by the Rorke's Drift road, on the 6th of August. He also told Colonel Clarke that, though he should accompany his column, he did not intend to interfere with him in the command. He has kept his word, for excepting the necessary general directions, he has left Colonel Clarke quite alone.

Sir Garnet Wolseley knows that this is the best way, when you have chosen a good man, to get plenty of good work done by him.

The weather was very pleasant, like English midsummer. The country, too, was exceedingly pretty. On our left hand was a range of hills, with rocky precipices; and elsewhere the country was the same continuous park that I have described before.

By the streams were thousands of those large white lilies, esteemed in England for their beauty, but here they possess besides, a faint but delicious perfume, and this in midwinter.

We had no expectation of attack, but we ran no risks, and entrenched our camp every night.

It was pleasant camping, for fresh ground here is always nice.

St. Paul's, an English mission-station, is on a plateau which rises very abruptly from the Umlilatwzi valley, to about 1,000 feet; and so, the ascent to St. Paul's—called the Inkwenkwe Hill—is very steep; and though only three and a half miles long, it took us a day to surmount the plateau, double-spanning each of our wagons and hauling with drag-ropes at the steepest parts.

On the 30th of July we reached St. Paul's. Here was one of our military posts. We halted a day, to make some alterations in our transport, and proceeded now upon the plateau.

The country on the plateau was not inviting. There were no trees, not even a bush, nothing but grass, and it was chilly even in the sun.

We were obliged to carry with us several days' supply of firewood, for cooking; and serve it out stingily, at the rate of one pound weight per man a day. Water too was scarce, and it had to be sought far down the plateau sides.

On Sunday, the 3rd of August, we reached Kwa Magwasa, which was our foremost military post, called Fort Albert, Colonel Thynne of the Guards was in command there.

Here there was an English mission-station, belonging to Mr. Robertson, who accompanied Colonel Pearson's column to Ekowe at the beginning of the war. The Zulus had destroyed it, as they had St. Paul's, but the flowers in the garden were blooming luxuriantly amidst the ruins....

We proceeded next day. In the evening rain began, and we were obliged to halt all the following day, the roads being unfit for the wagons owing to the wet.

On the 6th we proceeded, and joined a convoy which had been sent up to us with supplies by the Fort Evelyn road. It was escorted by detachments of the King's Dragoon Guards and the 24th and 58th Regiments.

Major Marter was with the first, and my old Ashanti friend, Bromhead, with the 24th.

Next day was our last on the plateau, and we descended at Emtonjaneni to the valley of the White Imvelosi. The last part of the plateau was a dreary sight. Lord Chelmsford's force had encamped there; and the ground for miles was strewn with the skeletons of horses and oxen and the yet imperfectly decayed bodies of oxen, that had been left sick, to recover or perish. A horrible stench clung to the plateau, and flocks of vultures and crows careered about.

We were right glad to get down into the wholesome and pleasant valley. Here we were again in the warmth of English summer, with plenty of wood and water.

Colonel Clarke and I rode on ahead to choose a camping-ground; for we were to halt a day to build a fort and establish a military station there, to be called Fort Victoria.

We chose a very pleasant place, and there was then no sign of the approaching storm.

The grass was full of partridge and quail, and a large partridge about half as big again as the usual size, that they call here a pheasant, but it certainly is not a pheasant. There were also hares and some small antelopes.

Soon the column came up; camp was pitched, and the men spreading about, of course, started those hares and antelopes that were foolish enough to have remained. The most exciting chases then resulted; the hare or antelope bounding in all directions, amidst the shouts of the men, and everywhere finding retreat cut off, till at last someone became the slayer or the capturer.

A beautiful antelope called a springbok was thus caught alive. It would be impossible to exaggerate the beauty and elegance of this creature.

Sir Garnet joined us in the afternoon. Towards evening a strong wind and rain set in; the storm increased towards night, so I prepared for wreck by packing up everything in my tent except my bed; and I then turned in, and drew my waterproof-sheet over me, for the rain was blown with such violence that it showered through the canvas.

I had fixed all the tent-pegs most firmly beforehand. The storm was raging as I fell asleep, but the tent was bearing it well.

After some hours, I was awakened by being slapped violently and severely about the head. I started up. The tent was tottering and flapping furiously; the ropes had slipped and many pegs had drawn. In another minute it would be down. The canvas, shaken by the wind, inflicted grievous boxes in the ear or nose as the case might be. I bounded out with the mallet and, assisted by some soldiers, secured the tent just in time, and it weathered the remainder of the storm.

In the moonlight, I could see that many tents were blown down and the occupants had taken shelter elsewhere.

I thought the officer in the next tent to mine was smothered under his, and was glad to feel it was only a box. He had fled!

My horses, poor creatures, with their eyes shut, their noses between their knees and their tails in the teeth of the wind, stood in the gloom, like iron statues.

Meanwhile, I had got very wet, and when I got back into my tent, I found my blankets wet. But every conception depends upon comparison. I could conceive only comfort and luxury in rolling up in those wet blankets after my experience outside the tent. To be out of the wind, to be sheltered from the downpour, to lie in only a moderate shower—it was too delightful. I was soon asleep again.

Next day the wind had abated, but the rain continued all day.

We heard that Sir Garnet's tent had been the first to blow down in the night. His staff went quickly to the rescue and soon put it up again.

None stirred out during the day who could avoid it. The following day, the 9th of August, the sun rose upon a perfectly blue sky, and a match could be lighted in the open air. The day was beautiful, but what a scene of death lay around. Four hundred and fifty-two of our oxen lay dead in the camp, killed by that storm!

The 9th of August was passed in making Fort Victoria, drying clothes, and burying oxen.

On the 10th we advanced to the White Imvelosi River, and encamped on the bank in a lovely spot—meadow grass, mimosa trees, and beautiful specimens of crystalline rock all about, aloes in flower, and birds of brilliant plumage.

Next day, Monday the 11th, a very different scene. We crossed the White Imvelosi and marched to Ondini—an undulating grassy plain, bounded by a circle of fine hills; scarcely a tree or bush; burnt *kraals*, and here and there human skeletons, the remains of Lord Chelmsford's conflict.

The cavalry, after a careful search yesterday, found hidden a few miles off, the British guns, captured by the Zulus at Isandhlwana.

Ulundi,
Aug. 31st.

. . . Cetywayo is captured. And on Tuesday next, the 2nd of September, I march with Clarke's column for Natal. On arrival at Durban, I shall embark at once for England, as far as I know.

I have been hard at work surveying Ulundi and the neighbourhood. It seems to be one of my functions in war to survey. It has not been part of my regular duty in this campaign, as in Ashanti. However, Sir Garnet wished me to survey Ulundi, and I was very glad to make the survey of this interesting place.

The weather has been delightful ever since we have been here, so the work has been very pleasant, albeit the frequency with which I have come suddenly upon human skeletons in the grass has been forbidding—especially as I have been quite alone. When one is not alone, the light of one's companion's presence dispels all the gloom of horrors, just as the arrival of a lamp spoils a ghost story!

There is nothing so dead and harmless as a skeleton, yet when you contemplate them in solitude, they appear to possess a life of their own, especially when there are many together. Some look angry, some threatening, some foolish, some astonished, and those that are on their faces seem to be asleep.

These skeletons were Zulus, killed in Lord Chelmsford's fight on the 4th of July.

On arrival here, search was made for the remains of the Hon. W. Drummond, a young man not in the army but attached to Lord Chelmsford's staff on account of his knowledge of the country. He was missing after the action, and so assumed to be killed, for Zulus never take prisoners. We heard from certain Zulus who had submitted to us, that after the action he had ridden forward amongst the retreating enemy, who, of course, killed him at once. They indicated about where this happened, and after a long search his remains were found, and identified by some of his hair remaining, but principally by the boots with spurs. His bones alone remained besides, and they were duly interred by our chaplain.

The body of Captain Wyatt-Edgell, 17th Lancers, which had been buried, was exhumed and put in a coffin made by the engineers, and lined with tin from our empty provision cases, to be brought to England.

While all this was going on with the dead, it fell to my lot to be more useful and to bring back a body alive, that was supposed to be dead. A private soldier of the 60th Rifles was in hospital here with fever and became delirious, a common result of this fever. In his delirium he managed to escape from the hospital tent one morning and disappeared. The most diligent search was made for him all day—even the streams were examined—but he could not be found. He was absent all night, and when next morning he was still lost it was considered from the state of health he was in that he must be dead somewhere, and attention was then directed to find the body.

In the course of my surveying, I found the man wandering in the bushes. His delirium appeared to have passed, for he seemed to be heading towards camp; and he gave me his name correctly when I asked him, and told me who I was when I asked him if he knew me, but he gave me an altogether absurd explanation of what he had been about. He was very weak, so I put him on my horse and led him to camp, much to the surprise of his comrades.

Let me correct a mistake in my last letter. I told you this place is called by Zulus Ondini. I should have said Undi. Ondini is a locative case of Undi, and means of, from, to, or at Undi. This locative case is a peculiarity of the Zulu language. So that if you ask a Zulu coming this way where he is going, he will say, "Ondini," meaning to Undi. And by "Ondini" he would express that he was a native of, or was living at, or coming from Undi. Undi, I find, is an abbreviated form of Ulundi, which has long been disused and is now quite unknown as a name in the country, though it is used in our maps, and by ourselves in consequence.

After a long hunt the king has been taken, and if it had not been that his own people disclosed his whereabouts, there is no saying how long the hunt might have been prolonged.

There is one general feeling of relief and gratification at his capture.

He was taken on the 28th instant by Major Marter (King's Dragoon Guards). I believe it is decided that the credit of the capture is due to Lord Gifford.

Gifford, who was the most pertinacious of all the pursuers, having several times nearly caught the king, at last marked him down at a certain *kraal*.

This *kraal* was separated from Gilford's party by an open expanse, but there were wooded heights beyond the *kraal*.

He decided to wait till dark to approach, lest the king, whose lookouts would discover him, should get the alarm in time to escape into the wood. But Gifford sent the information of where the king was to another party. This information, it appears, fell into the hands of Major Marter, who with his party was on the wooded side, not knowing in the least where the king was. He at once closed on the *kraal* and made the capture.

With Major Marter, was my interpreter, Mr. Oftebro, who knew the king well personally.

Cetywayo's first expression was surprise at his being caught at that side. He did not think horses could pass on those hills.

Then he requested that he might be shot at once. Later on, he became in very good spirits, Mr. Oftebro tells me, and made jokes at Marter's expense.

For instance, alluding to the strong guard Marter kept upon him, he said to Mr. Oftebro:—

"I am just going out of the hut for a minute, but before I go out, tell your master to put a 'Company' (using the English word) here, and a 'Company' there, and a 'Company' there" (pointing with his finger all round).

And then he laughed at the precautions he thus burlesqued.

Another time, he told Mr. Oftebro that when the cavalry were very inconveniently close in pursuit of him, he happened to have eight horses, so he gave some of these to some boys, and told them to ride away across the open to a certain bush and there dismount and escape. This they did. The ruse took splendidly, and away went Major Barrow and his horsemen as hard as they could go, while the king moved leisurely to another *kraal* in the opposite direction. Cetywayo laughed a good deal as he told the story.

I don't know how I have omitted to introduce Mr. Oftebro to you before in my letters. He is a young man of twenty, the son of a Norwegian missionary, to whom the celebrated Etyowe (spelt Ekowe in the map) belongs. He was born in Zululand, went to school in Norway, but has been most of his life in Zululand. He speaks the language like a native, and very good English. He knows Zululand well, and Cetywayo intimately. He has been my constant companion from the time I prepared the column for the relief of Ekowe with Colonel Law. He lives with me in my tent, and is to me an unfailing fund of Zulu information.

All the spelling of places and persons I mention are on his authority, and he can always give me the reason why a name should be so spelt.

The Zulu language has been carefully reduced to grammar. The letters have their particular sounds; and so, a word can only properly be spelt in one way.

It is a most pleasant language to the ear, and excepting certain clicks which occur occasionally it sounds rather like Spanish.

The king arrived here today. He declined to ride or drive, and walked into camp at a slow and dignified pace, looking a monarch all over although a prisoner.

He is the finest Zulu I have seen—very tall, of herculean build, splendidly made, stout without being corpulent, and remarkably handsome!

Cetywayo is king by right of descent, but he might well have been chosen from the whole nation, after the manner of Saul, for his superior body, without reference to his virtue.

Three men, who were taken with the king, attempted to escape by a rush on the way here; one did escape, but the other two were shot dead by the escort.

The escort, entering the camp, was composed of parts of various corps that had been on the chase. In front marched some of the King's Dragoon Guards, then some of Barton's natives, then some of the 60th Rifles, then the king, then more of our men.

The king wore at his waist the leopard skin, which is reserved exclusively for royalty; and, thrown over his shoulders, a red shawl with broad green stripes, of those bright colours which are so becoming to blacks. On his head was simply the black ring which all married Zulus wear. Cetywayo is married; he is in fact very much married, and I don't know that the number of his wives has ever been estimated even by himself!

At two o'clock this afternoon he was despatched to Natal. He went in an ambulance wagon drawn by eight mules, with an escort of irregular cavalry, taking with him a few servants and a selection of wives. He goes to Pietermaritzburg first.

All the Zulu tribes have now submitted, except one near the Natal frontier, so Clarke's column marches back that way, and we shall either receive or force the submission of these. We fully expect they will submit on our approach, and we do not at all imagine we shall have any fighting.

Our road to Natal for this purpose will be by the "Middle Drift" of the Tugela.

The state of my clothing has long called loudly for peace. I will not say much about it, because I know this gives rise to laughter, whereas it is more properly a subject for tears. Every device that engineering can suggest has been applied inside my garments to keep them together, but they are in that state in which engineers pronounce a bridge or house unsafe. They may fall into ruin at any moment by any sudden and injudicious movement on my part, such as a gesticulation of joy at the prospect of returning home.

I had to dine with Wolseley with one knee out in the open air! A new knee had been put in, but it had been taken from that which remained, and the rent was made worse. Well, it was that he said to me, "Come as you are."

I could push my finger through my flannel shirt, but I don't. It is immaterial whether I put my socks on through the toe or through the ankle, they are equally open both ways. My staff patrol-jacket had loops of braid, which have now come in useful to tie it together—the hooks and eyes being no more.

Sept. 1st.—Today, which curiously happens to be Cetywayo's coronation day—the day that six years ago he was crowned at Ulundi by the British Government—Sir Garnet Wolseley received the principal chiefs of the land, and divided Zululand into several parts, announcing that Cetywayo should never reign again.

The several divisions of the country are to be ruled each by a chief, who was named by Sir Garnet, and these chiefs are to be independent of each other. They themselves, or representatives for them, signed the terms of peace.

Sept. 2nd.—We crossed, or rather recrossed, the White Imvelosi today on the homeward march, and encamped for the night on the opposite bank.

Sir Garnet inspected the column when we were formed up ready to start; we marched past, and then he took leave of us most warmly. He goes to the Transvaal to settle matters up that way, escorted by five companies of the 80th Regiment, some dragoons and artillery.

Today, for the first time since I entered Zululand, I had leisure to go out shooting. What a change in the state of things! No more anxiety for the safety of the camp, no scouting for the enemy, no necessity to entrench, no preparations to receive attack. A comfortable encampment, with plenty of room, and only ordinary precautions.

I came upon a flock of guinea-fowl and killed three with two shots. I found them very large, almost small turkeys.

Sept. 3rd.—We started at 2.30 this morning by moonlight and reached our camping-ground near Fort Victoria. Here it was that we had the severe storm. We encamped on fresh ground beyond the position of the 452 dead oxen.

This also is a beautiful place, always park, but here and there craggy hills and deep precipitous ravines most picturesque to behold.

Mr. Oftebro and I dined on one of the guinea-fowls. It was delicious, quite equal to pheasant, and more than two hungry men could eat. . . .

> On the Zulu bank of the Tugela,
> Middle Drift,
> Sept. 18, 1879.

My dear May,—The war is over. All the chiefs of this, the last conquered region of Zululand, have submitted to us. We are on the banks of the Tugela. Part of the column crossed over and encamped on the Natal side this morning, and the last of the column with its headquarters will evacuate Zululand this afternoon.

What a long time it has taken to subdue the Zulus, and what a capital resistance they have made, without artillery, without horses, without telegraph, without a single written order or message!

I crossed the frontier with the first troops that invaded Zululand from the Tugela on the 13th of January; I recross it today with the last of our army eight months afterwards.

The march from Ulundi has been most pleasant. The weather has been delicious, and the country passed through very beautiful. We left Ulundi on the 2nd of September; we have marched every day but one, when we waited to receive certain submissions, and we arrived here yesterday. The distance from Ulundi by the route we have followed is a hundred and fifty miles.

It is not a regular wagon road, so we have had in some places to make a road for our wagons. In some places the hills were so steep that we could neither drive over nor round them, so we had to cut a road along the steep side wide enough for our vehicles. With great care we had only one accident—by bad driving—the mess-wagon of the 57th Regiment ran off the cutting and rolled over and over down the hill, to the great grief of the officers and the contents.

We all thoroughly enjoyed our return march. No sooner had we started than the Zulu chiefs sent in their submission, and began to arrive at our camp even before the appointed time.

Instead of finding the country desolate, we now found the natives living fearlessly with their families and herds in their *kraals*, which are dotted all over the country; and so confident were they of the white man's fair-play that they came at once to headquarters with a complaint in the case of any misbehaviour of our people, and I am glad to say such misbehaviour was limited to a few—a very few—petty thefts and one or two compulsory sales of articles of curiosity.

The Zulus were so sharp in identifying the offenders, that nearly all their grievances were redressed. As an instance I will mention the following:

Two Zulus came to my tent. They told me that a white man had asked them to sell him a wooden milk-pail and a pillow (let me just observe that a Zulu pillow is a piece of wood carved for ornament and curved at the top to fit the head—I suppose their woolly heads find this soft enough). Well, they declined to sell them; whereupon, they said, the white man threw down a shilling and walked off with the pail and pillow. They remonstrated and went with him, but he threatened to shoot them; they then watched him from a far distance, and noted the tent he entered.

Now it is by no means an easy thing to distinguish a particular tent in a large camp, but these men, when I sent our military police with them, at once walked to the tent and pointed it out. Their property was discovered inside. The offender was one of our wagon conductors. I censured him for the want of fair-play he had shown, and pointed out the discredit such acts might throw upon negotiations with the conquered. He admitted the truth of the Zulus' story, and I ordered the articles to be given back. The loss of his shilling, I told him, he must bear himself; for the Zulus had refused to touch it, and one of our natives passing at the time accordingly picked it up, as rejected by both parties, and had appropriated it—to him it represented the wages of a day and a half.

The presence of the native families and cattle was a guarantee that there would be no treachery on our line of march. Zulus have no reason to wish to attack us, for the terms of peace are manifestly for the benefit of all Zulus excepting a few great men, whose greatness departs with the fall of Cetywayo. Thus, our march back has been most enjoyable. Our camps have been pitched in the pleasantest instead of the strongest places, and those who liked, have been able to wander about shooting and fishing in perfect security. This change, after many months on the *qui vive* in contact with the enemy, after months of hard work by day and nights passed in boots and accoutrements, is enjoyed by all.

We reached Entumeni on the 12th of September, and started next day along the unknown road to the Middle Drift. Every day we encamped in some delightful spot—rich grass underfoot, pleasant woods in the *kloofs*, and cheerful brooks of water.

It is now spring, and a fresh variety of wild flowers are springing up in bloom. The *kloofs* or ravines are warmer than the hill-tops, and there the vegetable world is finest. It is nothing by comparison with the luxuriant wild growth of Fanti-land and Ashanti, but it is very fine for all that. A small stream generally trickles through the *kloof*, and in that stream grow fragrant lilies, while beautiful ferns spread along the banks. Most conspicuous among these is the tree fern. These tree ferns are of all sizes, from a few inches up to ten or twelve feet, and are, I think, the prettiest plants I have ever seen. The stems are straight and clean up to the top, where the young leaves in a ring uncoil, erect and then bend over gracefully in a circle of immense, magnificent fronds.

The streams are full of fish. I have only once had time to go out fishing, and my tackle was a mule-driver's whip with a hook attached to the lash. Yet with grasshoppers for bait, I caught fish as fast as I could catch grasshoppers to bait my hook. The fish were all the same kind, quite new to me, not bad eating, and something like grey mullet in appearance; in weight from a quarter of a pound to a pound. The water also abounded with crabs, about the size of my hand, and I continually caught them too.

We have crossed the Tugela and are now encamped on the Natal side. The last patrol is just about to evacuate what was the enemy's country, and tomorrow morning we shall proceed for Durban by Greytown and Pietermaritzburg.

Goodbye, Zululia, we shall *perhaps* never meet again; but you will as surely be British territory hereafter as Tuesday follows Monday! . . .

The 91st Argyllshire Highlanders in the Zulu War
By G. L. J. Goff

On the 11th of February news was received in England of the great disaster in Zululand at Isandlhwana, where the camp of part of the troops under command of Lord Chelmsford was surprised by the Zulus, and the force nearly annihilated. This intelligence caused the Government to decide on sending out reinforcements at once, and among the battalions of infantry selected was the 91st, who were ordered to prepare for embarkation in the s.s. *Pretoria*, one of the steamers belonging to the Union Company, on the 19th of the month.

In order to bring the 91st up to the required strength, volunteers were received from the following regiments—*viz*. 2/5th, 1/8th, 1/10th, 2/19th, 2/20th, 32nd, 36th, 41st, 55th, 84th, and 108th, the total number required being 374 men. The last party of volunteers to arrive only joined on the 17th. On the morning of the 18th, H.R.H. the Duke of Cambridge inspected the regiment in field-service order, after which they marched past in fours the volunteers from other regiments, being dressed in their own uniform, gave the battalion a mixed appearance.

After the men were dismissed, the commander-in-chief addressed the officers, congratulating them on the compliment which had been paid to the regiment, in its having been selected for this service, and expressing confidence that they and all ranks would sustain the reputation the regiment had always borne. The battalion was on this occasion under command of Major A. C. Bruce, Lieutenant-Colonel Kirk having been compelled to put himself on the sick list, from a cancerous tumour in the right foot, from which he had been suffering for some months previously, and which resulted shortly afterwards in amputation of the leg above the knee.

He was thus obliged with deep reluctance to relinquish, when almost within his grasp, this opportunity to proceed in command of his regiment on active service. In this heavy blow to his prospects as a soldier, Colonel Kirk met with the deepest and most sincere sympathy from all his brother officers and comrades in the 91st.

On the morning of the 19th, the 91st, consisting of thirty officers and 906 men, left Aldershot by special trains for Southampton, being played down to the station from the Permanent Barracks by the 41st Regiment. The trains arrived at the docks at about 11.30 a.m. and the men were paraded on the quay facing the transport.

The s.s. *Pretoria*, Captain George Larmer, which was the newest of the Union Company's Cape fleet, had only arrived home eight days previously, and in that short space of time had discharged her homeward-bound cargo, been docked and fitted with a new propeller, and had all the necessary alterations made to convert her into a transport ship. The main deck aft, with the sleeping berths, remained in its usual state for the use of the officers and transport officials. The fore main deck, usually occupied with cabin and state room for second-class passengers, was entirely stripped of its fittings, and with the orlop deck, fore and aft, ordinarily used for goods, was appropriated and fitted up for troops.

The embarkation commenced at twenty minutes to twelve, and was completed by twenty-five minutes to one, the whole regiment having been safely housed on board in five minutes less than an hour. At five minutes past one, the last gangway was hauled ashore, and the *Pretoria* steamed slowly off, amid the cheers of an enormous crowd who had forced their way into the docks to bid the regiment Godspeed. The transport anchored in Southampton Water, off Netley, and, after a final inspection, sailed in the evening about seven o'clock for her destination.

The names of the officers who sailed with the regiment were as follows:—Major A. C. Bruce (in command), Major W. P. Gurney; Captains G. Stevenson, J. Rogers, W. S. Mills, G. O'Sullivan, J. Boulderson, W. Prevost; Lieutenants H. Fallowfield, W. R. Craufurd, D. MacDonald, A. Tottenham, F. Cookson, G. Robbins, D. Fowler, G. Goff, G. Collings, H. Johnston; Second-Lieutenants T. Fraser, C. Richardson; Lieutenant and Adjutant J. St. Clair; Quarter-Master J. Gillies, and Paymaster W. Caudwell.

The voyage to the Cape was uneventful. Madeira was reached on the 24th, where the ship remained about six hours to coal; from there on, there was a fair-weather passage to Cape Town, which was

EMBARKATION OF REGIMENT AT SOUTHAMPTON.

sighted mid-day on the 12th of March. The *Pretoria* only stopped for twenty-four hours to coal and provision, and arrived outside Durban on Sunday the 16th. The officer commanding, with the adjutant, went ashore to report arrival and receive orders, which latter were, that the regiment should disembark the next day. The disembarkation began early the next morning, but owing to the heavy swell, and the consequent difficulty in getting the tugs which were to convey the men over the bar alongside, there were still two companies left on board in the evening.

However, the next day everybody had arrived in the camp, which was situated close to the centre of the town, on some waste ground. During the voyage the men who had joined from other regiments as volunteers had been dressed in 91st clothes, and the kits of the whole battalion had been thoroughly inspected and weeded in order that each man should go into the field with a kit in thoroughly serviceable condition, consisting of one serge coat, two pairs of trews, two pairs of boots, three pairs of socks, two towels, and one hold-all. The remaining articles were packed in waterproof bags to be left at Durban.

With the exception of the 57th Regiment, which had arrived from Ceylon two days previously to the 91st, the regiment was the first of the reinforcements to reach Natal.

The day after arrival, the Scotchmen of Durban formed a deputation to present an address to the regiment, which was presented by Mr. Jameson, a merchant of that town, and was as follows:—

"To Major Bruce, commanding 91st Highlanders.

"Sir,—The undersigned Scotchmen, residents of Durban, beg to tender you and your officers, non-commissioned officers, and men, a very hearty welcome to the colony. It affords us the utmost gratification to see among us, for the first time in our history as a colony, the tartans of our Highland soldiers, and to hear the familiar accents of our countrymen once more, reviving as they do associations of our native land, which we cherish as our most precious heritage. Our little colony yields to none of Her Majesty's dependencies in loyalty to our Queen, and we welcome therefore at all times her uniform; but on this auspicious occasion we feel justified in doing more in extending to our countrymen of your regiment a particularly hearty greeting, which we beg you will convey in our name to all ranks. We are confident that if your services are brought into requisition in the field, the traditions of the 91st will be gallantly sustained by the officers and men under your command, and that in Zululand, another laurel will be added to your colours."

Attached were the signatures of over seventy of the leading Scotchmen of Durban.

Major Bruce, in a few words, thanked the deputation for their address and the compliment they had paid to the regiment.

Before commencing the account of the movements of the 91st during the Zulu War, it will be interesting to give a short history of the nation and the state of affairs which brought about the war.

About 1820 a Zulu king called Chaka conquered all the surrounding tribes, and converted their chiefs into his own vassals. Chaka was the grandson of Dingiswayo, who was the first Zulu to raise regiments and make a standing army. He is supposed to have copied his system from the white troops which he had seen; he had also noticed there were no women with the white troops, so he came to the conclusion they were not allowed to marry, and framed his military laws accordingly.

The reigning Zulu chieftains, for their subsequent safety, always made it their custom to slay their male children, but the mother of Chaka, just before giving him birth, went into hiding with another tribe, where she left her child, and so preserved its life. Neither Chaka nor the Zulus forgot this act of motherly solicitude, and when his mother died, general mourning was ordered, and numbers of people, to show their grief at the loss of such a good mother, slew their cows which had young calves, so that the latter might suffer, and thus, in company with the nation, feel how terrible it was to be bereaved of a mother.

When Chaka became king, he greatly developed the military system of his grandfather, and, as already stated, subjugated the neighbouring tribes. Although Chaka ruled his people with unmitigated severity, every Zulu speaks of him with pride, especially with reference to his military prowess. Among his other military reforms, he introduced the short or stabbing *assegai* instead of the long-handled ones that had been used formerly as missiles. This was to make his men come to close quarters with their enemy. Chaka was assassinated by his brother Dingaan about the year 1830, who became king in his place.

The new monarch was a most cruel man, as he murdered all his brothers except Panda. His treacherous slaughter of the Boers under Retief is a matter of history. On that occasion he received the party, who had come with the object of entering into a treaty, most hospitably, and then invited them into his *kraal*, making them leave their arms outside, as it was explained to them that that was the etiquette; directly he got them inside, he butchered the lot. The result of this dastardly deed was that the Boers invaded Zululand, but without success. Shortly after this, Panda, who was the brother he had thought not worthwhile to murder while he was getting rid of the rest, revolted and joined the Boers, and succeeded in driving Dingaan out of the country. He fled to Swaziland, where the inhabitants put him to death.

Panda now became king. This was in the year 1840. His reign was not marked with so much bloodshed as his predecessor's, but nevertheless the country was continually fighting over who was to be his successor. The Natal Government eventually induced Panda to name Cetywayo his successor, so on Panda's death, in 1872, the Government sent Mr. Shepstone with an escort of Natal volunteers to install Cetywayo as king.

At this ceremony, which was conducted without the usual scenes of bloodshed, the following articles were agreed to:—

> That the amicable relations existing in the time of Panda between the Zulus and the Natal Government should continue, and should be strengthened if possible; that the indiscriminate shedding of blood should cease; that for minor offences fines should be instituted; that no Zulu should be condemned to death without a fair trial; that he should have the right of appeal to the king.

Mr. Shepstone also tried to bring about the abolition of witch doctors, but this he was unable to add to the agreement, as the people believed in them too strongly.

Cetywayo worked hard at developing the military system of Chaka. Every male from the age of sixteen to that of seventy was a soldier. No one was allowed to marry without permission, and this was generally granted to a whole regiment at a time, when they reached the age of forty. Consequently, there were married and unmarried regiments. The former wore a ring of black resin round their heads, which distinguished them from the unmarried, who wore no ring.

Before the war of 1870 broke out there were about thirty-three regiments, nineteen of whom were married. They differed greatly in numerical strength. As a corps got old, its numbers diminished, for the vacancies were not filled up.

The men were armed with *assegais* and *knobkerries*, while a certain number had guns; but opinions as to how many there were who had

Cetywayo

them are so diverse that it is impossible to do more than guess. There were probably some 8,000 or 9,000 guns in the country. Each man carried a shield made of bullock's hide, slashed down the centre, with a long stick run through.

There is no doubt that, a long time previous to the outbreak of the war, the attitude of the Zulus had become very threatening. It is said that the young regiments were clamouring to "wash their spears," one of the traditional qualifications for matrimony, and Cetywayo was looking about to give them an opportunity.

In 1878 a Zulu *impi* (army), composed of some 3,000 men, made a demonstration on the Natal border, along the left bank of the Lower Tugela. This was done under the pretence of hunting. It nevertheless alarmed the white inhabitants of Natal, who felt that there was nothing to prevent the Zulu king from marching 30,000 men over the border and sacking Durban in twenty-four hours. Under these circumstances, it was decided to station troops along the border.

In December a meeting was held between the commissioners of the Natal Government and Indunas respecting the Zulu king. The former consisted of Colonel Forester Walker, C.B., Scots Guards, and Messrs. J. Shepstone, Brownlie, and Fynn. The Natal Government representatives presented an ultimatum, which demanded fines for raids and outrages committed by Zulus, also insisted that promises made by Cetywayo at his coronation should be carried out, and further demanded that the Zulu Army should be disbanded; that a British resident should be appointed, and should live in the Zulu country, and be a medium of communication between the two governments; and also that the missionaries should be respected and allowed to return to their places, from which they had been driven out by the Zulus. No notice being taken of this ultimatum, a force advanced into Zululand, under command of Lord Chelmsford, in five columns, during the second week of January, 1879. The columns were stationed as follows:—

No 1, commanded by Colonel Pearson, was encamped at Lower Tugela Drift, and numbered nearly 4,000 men; its base was Durban and its advanced depot was at Stanger.

No 2 column, under command of Lieutenant-Colonel Durnford, R.E., was stationed at Middle Drift, with Pietermaritzburg as its base and Grey Town for its advanced depot; it was composed of about 3,500 men.

No. 3 column, commanded by Colonel Glynn, C.B., was at Rorke's Drift, with Pietermaritzburg as its base and Ladysmith as its advanced

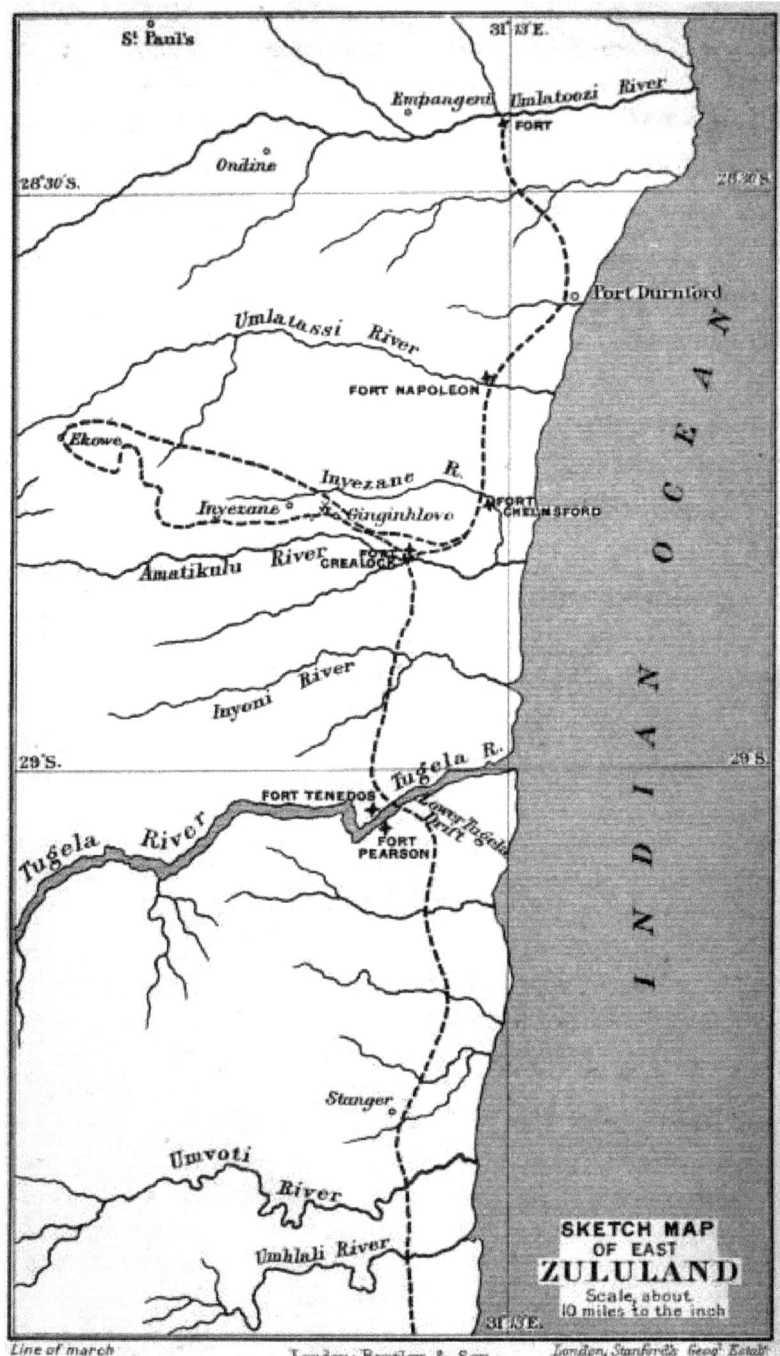

men, was witnessed by a large number of townspeople at the railway station at Durban, where three special trains were provided, to convey them to Saccharine, which at that time was as far as the railway was laid. The last detachment arrived at Saccharine by 2 o'clock in the afternoon, and a little after 4 o'clock the 91st started to march to the front. A halt for the night was made on the north bank of the Verulam River.

The Naval Brigade of H.M.S. *Boadicea*, numbering about 250 men, under command of Lieutenant Carr, R.N., accompanied the regiment on its march to the Tugela from this place. The following night a place called Victoria was reached, and owing to the heat an early start was made the next morning. The night of the 21st was spent on the banks of the Umtati River, when heavy rains fell, causing a halt next day to get things cleaned up.

The march was resumed on Sunday, the 23rd, and the Tugela River was reached on the 25th, and was crossed in a pont, the regiment encamping near the 57th Regiment, which had arrived the previous day. Two companies of the 3rd Buffs and five companies of the 99th Regiment, formed into one battalion, were also encamped on the enemy's side of the river. On the 26th Lord Chelmsford inspected the regiment, and made a speech to the men.

The force collected at this place to move up to the relief of Ekowe was divided into two divisions. The first division, under Colonel Law, R.A., was composed of the 91st, and of the battalion made up of the Buffs and 99th, the Naval Brigades of the *Shah* and *Tenedos*, who had with them two 9-pounders, two 24-pounder rocket-tubes, and a gatling gun, the mounted infantry under Major Barrow, and one battalion of Natal Native Contingent.

The second division, under Colonel Pemberton of the 3/60th Rifles, was composed of the 57th Regiment, 3/60th Rifles, Naval Brigade of the Boadicea, and a portion of the marines of the *Shah* and *Boadicea*, with one gatling gun and two 24-pounder rocket-tubes, and one battalion Natal Native Contingent; the whole force being under the immediate command of Lord Chelmsford. The orders were to proceed without tents, and in the lightest possible marching order, men to carry seventy rounds of ammunition, and thirty rounds per man to be carried on pack-mules, two of which mules followed in rear of each company, with 1,500 rounds in canvas waterproof bags.

Camp was struck on the 28th, and spare baggage and camp equipment were stacked in some tents protected by Forts Pearson and Tene

FORT PEARSON, LOWER TUGELA DRIFT (FROM ZULULAND BANK OF RIVER).

depot; it numbered about 4,500 men.

No. 4 column, under command of Colonel Wood, V.C., C.B., was stationed at Conference Hill, on the Blood River, with Utrecht as its base, and numbered about 3,000 men.

No. 5 column was commanded by Colonel Rowlands, V.C., C.B., and was ordered to watch Secocoeni, and for that purpose was left at Luneberg. This column numbered about 1,500 men.

Lord Chelmsford, therefore, had a force of about 16,000 men under his command. More than half, however, were natives.

Immediately after entering the Zulu country, skirmishes with the enemy occurred; but it was on the 22nd of January that the small camp at Isandhlwana, composed of some 900 men, exclusive of natives, who ran away after the first shot, were cut to pieces by a large army of Zulus.

The details of this terrible disaster, the cutting to pieces of the 24th Regiment, and the gallant defence of Rorke's Drift, are well known and need not be retold here. It was this disaster, as before mentioned, that caused the 91st and many other regiments to find themselves so quickly brought to South Africa.

Zulu War—April to September, 1879

We will now proceed with the history of the regiment's march up country.

The weather during the two days which the 91st spent at Durban was wretched, and gave them an idea of how it could pour in Natal. Before leaving for the front, the band was broken up and the men told off to act as hospital-bearers and orderlies, under the orders of Surgeon-Major Edge, who had accompanied the regiment in the Pretoria, and was placed in medical charge on arrival in Natal. The boys, seventeen in number, were left in camp under Bandmaster Kelly, with a sufficiency of musical instruments for their instruction. Nine pipers and a small corps of drums and fifes accompanied the regiment into the field.

The 91st left Durban on the 19th for the front, to form part of a column with which Lord Chelmsford determined to start as soon as possible, for the purpose of relieving the force under Colonel Pearson, then shut up in Ekowe, whose provisions were nearly exhausted, and who was surrounded by a body of Zulus variously estimated at from 12,000 to 20,000 strong. The departure of the regiment, which mustered twenty-three officers and 832 non-commissioned officers and

RELIEF FORCE CROSSING A RIVER.

men, was witnessed by a large number of townspeople at the railway station at Durban, where three special trains were provided, to convey them to Saccharine, which at that time was as far as the railway was laid. The last detachment arrived at Saccharine by 2 o'clock in the afternoon, and a little after 4 o'clock the 91st started to march to the front. A halt for the night was made on the north bank of the Verulam River.

The Naval Brigade of H.M.S. *Boadicea*, numbering about 250 men, under command of Lieutenant Carr, R.N., accompanied the regiment on its march to the Tugela from this place. The following night a place called Victoria was reached, and owing to the heat an early start was made the next morning. The night of the 21st was spent on the banks of the Umtati River, when heavy rains fell, causing a halt next day to get things cleaned up.

The march was resumed on Sunday, the 23rd, and the Tugela River was reached on the 25th, and was crossed in a pont, the regiment encamping near the 57th Regiment, which had arrived the previous day. Two companies of the 3rd Buffs and five companies of the 99th Regiment, formed into one battalion, were also encamped on the enemy's side of the river. On the 26th Lord Chelmsford inspected the regiment, and made a speech to the men.

The force collected at this place to move up to the relief of Ekowe was divided into two divisions. The first division, under Colonel Law, R.A., was composed of the 91st, and of the battalion made up of the Buffs and 99th, the Naval Brigades of the *Shah* and *Tenedos*, who had with them two 9-pounders, two 24-pounder rocket-tubes, and a gatling gun, the mounted infantry under Major Barrow, and one battalion of Natal Native Contingent.

The second division, under Colonel Pemberton of the 3/60th Rifles, was composed of the 57th Regiment, 3/60th Rifles, Naval Brigade of the *Boadicea*, and a portion of the marines of the *Shah* and *Boadicea*, with one Gatling gun and two 24-pounder rocket-tubes, and one battalion Natal Native Contingent; the whole force being under the immediate command of Lord Chelmsford. The orders were to proceed without tents, and in the lightest possible marching order, men to carry seventy rounds of ammunition, and thirty rounds per man to be carried on pack-mules, two of which mules followed in rear of each company, with 1,500 rounds in canvas waterproof bags.

Camp was struck on the 28th, and spare baggage and camp equipment were stacked in some tents protected by Forts Pearson and Tenedos, while twenty weakly men were ordered to be left behind to form a guard.

The troops had a very bad time of it during the following night, as it rained like it knows how to do in Zululand, and having no tents, and in fact nothing but a waterproof sheet per man to cover them, the ingenuity of each man was exercised as to how he should keep himself comparatively dry; as a matter of fact, it was impossible to manage this last detail, and in consequence a most miserable night was spent.

The following morning, at 6 a.m., the 91st started as advanced-guard to the force. Progress was very slow, continued halts having to be made to allow the great number of waggons to keep together, which was no easy matter to arrange, in consequence of the heavy state of the track after the recent rains. The waggons numbered 122, and occupied nearly two miles in length when on the move.

In the afternoon an entrenched *laager* was formed on the banks of the Inyoni River.

A South African *laager* consists of an enclosure formed by waggons placed closely together; at some distance outside them the shelter trench is dug; the defenders occupy the space between the trench and the waggons, and the area enclosed by the waggons contains the cattle.

The next morning the troops stood to their arms an hour before daybreak. This plan was adopted throughout the campaign, as the idea was that the hour just before daybreak was the one at which the Zulus generally attacked. The march was resumed in the same order as the previous day, and by the afternoon the banks of the Amatikulu River were reached, and another entrenched *laager* was formed. On Monday, the 31st, the river was crossed; this was a very long and wet operation, as the river was high, reaching over the men's waists, necessitating their carrying their ammunition on their shoulders.

It took all day to get the waggons over, so that the *laager* formed in the evening was only a mile and a half from the one used the previous night. Major Bruce here received a telegram addressed to Captain Chater, from H.R.H. the Princess Louise, which ran as follows:—

> Convey to the 91st my regrets at not seeing them before their departure, also the interest I take in their welfare, wishing them every success, with God-speed and a safe return.

The following day the 91st formed the rearguard, and the enemy was seen for the first time. The *laager* in the evening was formed at Ginginhlovo. The day had been oppressively hot, and after the trenches had been dug, a heavy thunderstorm came on, which nearly filled them. A most miserable night was passed by everyone, as there was not a dry spot to lie down on, and all the ground had got into such a fearfully dirty state, that even walking was difficult.

When morning broke it was found that the country was too heavy to move the waggons; the Zulus also were observed to be advancing in considerable numbers from the direction of a hill beyond the Inyezane. The camp, which was square in shape, having sides about 130 yards long, had its waggons in the centre; the 60th were in line on the front face, the 57th on the right, and the 91st on rear face, except two companies of the latter, which together with the Buffs and 99th detachment held the left face; two gatlings and two nine-pounders were distributed at the corners, in charge of the Naval Brigade. Behind the 91st was a battalion of the Natal Native Contingent.

A little before six o'clock native scouts, which had as usual gone out to scour the country at daybreak, were seen to be falling back, firing while doing so, and directly after, large columns of the enemy were observed coming down the Inyezane hills, and also from the Amatikulu bush. When they had come within range, the gatling and nine-pounders opened fire, as also did the rockets, the first attack being made on the front of the *laager*, which was met by a heavy fire from the 60th. The Zulus then continued their usual mode of attack, which is to advance in the shape of a pair of horns, so as to envelope their opponents, and then finally rush them in rear.

The shining of bayonets in the rear face appears to have led them to believe that the Native Contingent was there, and that the weakest point in the camp would probably be found in that direction; and a most determined attack was accordingly made there on the 91st, which lasted about twenty minutes, when the Zulus wavered and then fled, leaving many of their number within a few spaces of the trenches. When it was noticed that they were breaking, the mounted troops, under Major Barrow, together with the Native Contingent, were sent in pursuit, and terrible execution they did. By half-past seven the engagement was over.

The 91st's loss was one man killed, Private Marshall; while eight were wounded, namely, Sergeant D. McIntyre, dangerously, in the left eye (he died at Stanger, on the 15th); Private Stantidge, flesh wound in the thigh; Private Richards, penetrating wound in the leg; Privates O'Brien and Mallie, wound in their heads; Private Hanlon, wound in abdomen; Private Sutton, wound in left arm; Private Gillespie, slight wound on side of head. The adjutant, Lieutenant St. Clair, had a narrow escape, a bullet having gone through his helmet, within an inch of his head.

The total casualty of the force was, one officer and four men killed, while five officers and thirty-nine men were wounded. The strength of the regiment present at this action was twenty-two officers and 801 non-commissioned officers and men. The colours were in charge of Second-Lieutenants Fraser and C. F. Richardson.

The enemy's loss on this occasion has been variously estimated, but it must have been considerable, as nearly 500 bodies were counted within a radius of 400 yards of the *laager*, and the route taken by the flying enemy was strewn with corpses cut down by the mounted infantry and Native Contingent.

The remainder of the day was employed in burying the dead and altering the *laager* to suit the reduced garrison which was to be left while a flying column made for Ekowe. The evening passed off quietly without any signs of an enemy.

The morning after the action, a flying column, composed of six companies of the 57th, 60th, and 91st, with about 100 of the Naval Brigade, John Dunn's scouts, and some mounted men, started early, with the object of reaching Ekowe in one day's march, the 91st forming the rear-guard.

Colonel Pearson, who was in command at Ekowe, and had been regularly communicated with by means of the heliograph, received orders to hold his force in readiness to evacuate his fort the day after the arrival of the relieving force. The garrison at Ekowe had been a witness of the action of the 2nd of April, as the fort stands on hills which overlook the plain over which Lord Chelmsford's column had marched, and the battlefield was at the foot of the hill. The march of the relieving column commenced at daybreak, and at half-past six the rear-guard had moved off. When the sun had got up, the day became excessively hot, and the march, especially for the rearguard, was most tedious, numerous halts having to be made to allow the waggons to be got through the marshy places on the road.

To show how the column straggled, the advance-guard, which was formed by the 60th, arrived at Ekowe at half-past six, while the rear-guard did not arrive until midnight. The 91st only got their dinners at 1 o'clock in the morning. The men on this occasion marched splendidly, when it is taken into consideration that they had been seventeen hours and a half on the move, yet when they passed the fort, headed

91ST A.H. INSIDE THE SQUARE AT GINGINHLOVO

by their pipers, there was not one man out of the ranks.

Ekowe had before the war been a Norwegian mission station, under charge of the Rev. Oftebro, and consisted of a church; a long building containing several rooms, one of which was used as a school; and a third building, which was the residence of the missionary. The two latter were thatched with reeds, while the church was roofed with corrugated iron. The station stood on an extensive plateau, about 2,000 feet above the sea, and was commanded on every side except the south by low hills distant about a quarter of a mile. The surrounding hills were destitute of trees, but were covered by long rank grass and overgrown vegetation.

If it had not been for the hurry in which the fort was made, owing to the disastrous news of Isandhlwana, a better position would have been taken up, but there was no time to do anything, and as the buildings, etc., were on the spot, the best was made of the position. A big parapet was made with various traverses, the ditch outside being ten feet deep and fifteen feet wide at the top, with stakes running along the bottom. The garrison was composed of nearly 1,400 white and 450 native men.

The next day, the 4th of April, it was decided to rest the relieving force, while those relieved marched out on their way to the Tugela, which they reached eventually without seeing any signs of the enemy.

The flying column left Ekowe on the 5th, and only marched about six miles, the road taken being different to that which they had come up by. The following morning an unfortunate accident happened, which was caused by a picquet of the 91st, under command of Captain Prevost, who, thinking they saw Zulus creeping in the bushes in front of them, fired, which raised an alarm in the camp and made the scouts and picquets run in. They were fired on by the 60th trench party, who mistook them for the enemy in the darkness. Fifteen were wounded in this unfortunate business.

The march was resumed at 9 o'clock, and the *laager* at Ginginhlovo was reached in the afternoon; but it was found to have become very unpleasant, owing to the frightful smell from the number of dead buried in its vicinity. So, a new *laager* was formed about two miles from the old camp, on a piece of rising ground. The camp was again moved the following day, to a place which was considered to answer the purpose better. The Buffs and the 99th detachments proceeded to the Tugela to join their regiments, and the force in the new camp consisted of the 57th, 60th, 91st, and a portion of the Naval Brigade, with a regiment of Native Contingent and some mounted men, the whole under command of Lieutenant-Colonel Clarke of the 57th Regiment, who received the local rank of brigadier-general.

The entrenchments round the new camp were made of larger dimensions than those of the *laagers* on the march up country, the position being further strengthened with abattis. The daily routine was as follows:—Trenches manned at 4 a.m. until daylight, men standing with fixed bayonets in perfect silence.

At daylight, leave trenches; wood and water parties sent out; after breakfast, company inspections; during the forenoon one or two companies marched to adjacent stream to bathe; after dinner brigade or regimental drill, or bivouac outside the camp, in order that the ground should be thoroughly cleaned; at 7.30 p.m. man trenches, first post sounded; lie down at 7.45, each company in rear of its own alarm post; lights out at 8. One company of each regiment was on trench duty every night, and stood in the trenches all night, one company on picquet covering the front.

On the 18th a convoy arrived from Tugela, bringing up men's kits and officers' light baggage. The kit of the latter, since they had left the Tugela, had been limited to ten pounds weight. Tents, however, were not provided, and owing to the heavy rains and general unhealthiness of the plains on the coast, sickness became prevalent. On the 23rd Second-Lieutenants Dickson, Wyllie, and Lane-Fox joined the regiment on appointment, bringing with them two sergeants, one corporal, and four privates from the hospital on the Lower Tugela.

After being seventeen days in the Ginginhlovo camp, it was decided to evacuate it and advance to a new position about four miles off on the Inyezane River, where a fort was commenced (afterwards called Fort Chelmsford). The construction of another fort was also commenced in the beginning of May, on the Amatikulu River, on the line of communication about half-way to Tugela. This was named Fort Crealock.

The troops at this time were employed on convoy duty, each convoy being escorted by one British regiment, a battalion of natives, two guns R.A., and a few mounted scouts. The three regiments, under command of Brigadier-General Clarke, took it in turns to furnish the escort. 1379. Sickness was now rapidly increasing. On the 5th of May the empty convoy on its return to the Lower Tugela took 150 sick from various corps, including Captain Mills and Lieutenants Tottenham and Goff of the 91st. The nature of the sickness was generally

PORT DURNFORD (FROM THE ANCHORAGE).

fever and dysentery.

On the 10th of May the regiment was moved to Fort Crealock to garrison it, and also complete the earthworks. The troops then, which were under command of Major Bruce, were composed of the regiment, half a company of Royal Engineers, two guns R.A., sixteen mounted men, and a battalion of Native Contingent. The regiment remained here a month, during which the officers in their spare time made expeditions in the vicinity to shoot what game they could find. There was, however, very little to shoot, except an occasional bustard or duck. This was probably owing to the number of Kaffir dogs which were to be found prowling about the deserted *kraals*, which must have found it very hard to get a living now that their owners had left their habitations.

In June, Lieutenant Cookson was attached to the Mounted Infantry under Major Barrow, and served with them during the rest of the war. On the 15th of June the 91st moved forward with the force under command of General Crealock. No enemy was met with, but every precaution was taken against surprise. On the 27th the Umlatazi River was crossed, and the next day Port Durnford was reached. Here it had been arranged a fresh landing-place should be opened, as the naval authorities had ascertained that it could be effected, and accordingly the general in command proposed to make the place a fresh base of operations where a depot would be formed for supplies.

During this month Major Bruce was promoted to the rank of lieutenant-colonel, *vice* Lieutenant-Colonel Kirk, who was placed on half-pay, and appointed to the Intelligence Department.

During the first week in June the Prince Imperial Louis Napoleon lost his life, which sad event cast a gloom over the whole of the troops in Zululand. His remains were at once sent down to Durban to be embarked on board H.M.S. *Boadicea*, for conveyance to England. The band used at Durban on this occasion was one which had been collected and trained by Mr. Kelly, bandmaster of the 91st, and was principally composed of boys of the regiment left behind at Durban.

On the 2nd of July Sir Garnet Wolseley arrived in H.M.S. *Shah*, at Port Durnford, but owing to the bad weather he could hold no communication with the shore. The next day, accompanied by his staff, he tried to land in a lighter; the surf was running rapidly, and although a good effort was made, the tow-line breaking, he failed to make the land, and had to return to the *Shah*, which immediately started on its return to Durban, where Sir Garnet landed, and proceeded by road to

EMBARKATION OF CETYWAYO AT PORT DURNFORD.

the front, arriving at Port Durnford on the 7th.

On the 24th the 91st changed its quarters to a post on the Umhlatoosi River, which was established to assist in maintaining the line of communication between Port Durnford, St. Paul's, and Ulundi; 200 of Nettleton's Native Contingent, and some mounted volunteers, forming part of the garrison.

On the 27th Captain Mills's company proceeded to Fort Napoleon, which lay between Fort Chelmsford and Port Durnford, with the object of holding a post to maintain communication.

Shortly after Captain Craufurd's company made a small fort with the same object, afterwards known as Fort Inverary, as a half-way post to St. Paul's. At the same time Captain Stevenson's and O'Sullivan's companies were sent down to garrison the fort at Port Durnford, which was the headquarters of Lieutenant-Colonel Hale, R.E., who had been appointed assistant-adjutant and quarter-master-general on the lines of communication and base, Lieutenant Goff being appointed his staff officer.

On the 17th of August a party of mounted men was ordered to proceed, under command of Captain Yeatman Biggs, R.A., in the direction of St. Lucia Bay, in pursuit of Cetywayo, the Zulu king, who was supposed to be in hiding in that part of the country. Captain O'Sullivan and Lieutenants MacDonald and Goff accompanied this party, which was composed of some ten officers and fifty mounted men, together with about 100 Native Contingent, under Commandant Nettleton. This party were out about a fortnight, traversing a large extent of wild country seldom before visited by white men. The road taken was along the coast to St. Lucia Bay.

Nothing being heard of the fugitive, Captain Yeatman Biggs decided to make for the junction of the Black and the White Umvoloosi River, and if no news was heard on the way, to go direct to Ulundi, which was eventually done. During the ride it was noticed that there was no game to be seen except a few guinea-fowl, and one or two antelope; this was accounted for by the fact that the Zulus had shot or driven away all the larger sorts of animals since they had got guns. At Ulundi news arrived at the same time as the expedition that Cetywayo had been captured by Major Marter, of the King's Dragoon Guards, and he was brought in the following day.

Captain O'Sullivan and the officers of the 91st only remained at Ulundi a few hours, when they proceeded to Port Durnford. Another officer of the 91st (Lieutenant Cookson), who was attached to the

Mounted Infantry, was also out for several days in pursuit of the king. Cetywayo and the women who were with him were sent, directly after their arrival at Ulundi, to Port Durnford, at which place they arrived under a strong escort on the 5th of September, and were at once taken down to the sea-shore to be embarked on the s.s. *Natal* for Cape Town.

The guard on the beach was composed of Captain Stevenson's company of the 91st, and an escort was sent with Cetywayo on board, of a sergeant (Keene) and six men of the regiment, who afterwards gave a graphic account of the abject state of the deposed monarch when he first felt the effects of the very choppy sea which he encountered in the surf boat taking him out to the steamer. He was accompanied by three female attendants, who seemed to feel more comfortable than he did, and who were apparently vastly amused at the discomfiture of their royal master. The story is that his escort, who were all men picked on account of their being good sailors, were themselves nearly as unhappy as their prisoners.

The capture of the king was the termination of the war, and on the 13th of September orders were received for the regiment to proceed to Durban; the headquarters left the next day, followed by the other detached companies. Nothing of importance happened on the return march, and Verulam, the terminus of the railway from Durban, was reached on the 22nd of the month. There they remained until the 28th. Orders had in the meantime arrived that a detachment of three companies should go to Mauritius and one to St. Helena, while headquarters were to proceed to Cape Town. The Mauritius detachment was composed of F, G, and H companies, under command of Major Gurney, and the company selected for St. Helena was that of Captain Mills.

The headquarters and remaining companies, on arrival at Durban, were embarked on the 30th on the s.s. *City of Venice*, and were composed of sixteen officers and 588 non-commissioned officers and men. The transport sailed the next day, and anchored in Table Bay, after a rough passage, on Sunday, the 5th of October. The following day the regiment was disembarked, and went into the main barracks at Cape Town, with the exception of the B and D companies, who were sent on to Wynberg to be encamped, there being no room for them in Cape Town, as part pf the barracks was occupied by a detachment of the 88th Regiment.

In November, 1879, Lieutenant-Colonel Bruce was appointed a

"Companion of the Bath."

The detachment of three companies who were detailed for Mauritius, embarked at Durban on board H.M.S. *Crocodile*, on the 8th of October, and arrived at Port Louis on the 15th. The transport also had on board the 88th Regiment, and 17th Lancers for India. The names of the officers who landed with the detachment at Mauritius were as follows:—Major W. Gurney (in command), Lieutenants MacDonald, Robbins, Fraser, and Wilson; and with them were 250 non-commissioned officers and men.

On the 27th of January Major W. P. Gurney died of fever, contracted in the field during the Zulu campaign. He was buried with full military honours at Bease Bassin. A tablet to his memory was erected in Stirling Church by his brother officers, as a token of their esteem and respect.

The population of Mauritius, in 1880, numbered about 370,000, composed principally of coloured people of mixed race, of which the imported Indian *coolies* brought over to work the sugar plantations were the most numerous. The influx of these people, who imported their diseases, spread fever over the island, and in 1867, when the great outbreak of fever occurred, the number of deaths was enormous, the troops themselves losing a great number. This fever, which is called "Mauritius fever," attacks every one living on the low land, and as the barracks are situated in the unhealthy part, the 91st suffered considerably, which necessitated frequent drafts being sent up to the Cureppe in the hills for change of air.

On the 22nd of April, 1881, the Zulu War medals were presented to those of this detachment who had served in Zululand.

Nothing of any public interest happened to these companies during the remainder of their stay on the island; they simply spent their time in passing through hospital and sanatorium, so that when they arrived at Cape Town, under command of Major Robley, to rejoin headquarters, on the 26th of May, 1881, they presented a most sickly appearance, and the non-commissioned officers and men had to be kept off duty for a month after their arrival.

The detachment which had gone to St. Helena under command of Captain Mills in January, 1880, remained at that out-of-the-way spot twenty-two months, when they were relieved by another company from the regiment. During their stay there the island was visited by the ex-Empress Eugene, who landed to pay a visit to the place where Napoleon I.'s body had so long lain. She was then on her way out to visit the spot where the Prince Imperial had met his death. On landing she was received by a guard of honour, composed of the detachment of the 91st.

In March, 1881, Sir Frederick Roberts, G.C.B., touched at St. Helena on his way out to the Transvaal, to take command of the troops in succession to General Colley, so the opportunity was taken to get him to present the officers and men with the South African War Medal, which had just arrived to be distributed to those who had taken part in the Zulu War.

At the end of 1880 the Transvaal War broke out. The regiment itself was not engaged in it, but Captain Cameron, who had joined the 91st from the 71st Light Infantry, was employed at Maritzburg on the staff until the termination of the war. On the 29th of December Captain Craufurd and Lieutenant Goff were ordered to proceed to Natal with 100 picked men of the 91st, in H.M.S. *Boadicea*, as convoy to the guns she was to land to proceed to the front. This move, however, was countermanded the day they were to embark. Lieutenant Goff was ordered, in February, to Natal, in charge of 300 horses and mules, which were sent to the front. He was employed at Durban and Maritzburg for some time, returning to Cape Town in April.

The medals for the Zulu War were presented to the headquarters of the battalion in March, by Lieutenant-General the Hon. Leicester Smyth, C.B., on which occasion the lieutenant-general addressed the battalion as follows:—

> I am grateful to Colonel Bruce for the pleasure he has given me in asking me to present these medals—honourable emblems of hardships undergone, valour displayed, and victory won; and I wish the recipients one and all many happy years to wear them. I am the more pleased at being here today, for a long time ago, how long I hardly like to say, I had the honour of campaigning in this country with the 91st Regiment, and then had many opportunities of witnessing and appreciating their gallant deeds; and as the 91st fought in those days of old, and as those to whom I have now given their medals fought in more recent times, so, I feel sure, will the 91st Highlanders of the present day, should they be called upon, in stubbornly upholding the great tradition of their regiment, and do their duty to their queen and country.

Soon after the regiment got settled down in its new quarters in

Cape Town, it was decided to start a pack of fox-hounds, to hunt jackals in the country near the town. There had been hounds before this, during the stay of the 24th Regiment, but all remnants of the pack had disappeared, so drafts were sent for from England, and after a short time, mainly owing to the energy of Captain Cookson, a very fair lot of hounds were got together, and hunting commenced in the spring months. The jackal was to be found within a short distance of Rondebosch and Wynberg, and the flats, as the waste ground is called there, were at this time left quite undisturbed, and only had a few very thin sheep grazing on them; sport therefore was fairly good.

Expeditions were also made by officers to shoot antelopes, but the sport within easy distance of Cape Town was indifferent.

On the 1st of June a general order of that date directed that "South Africa" should henceforth be borne on the Regimental Colours.

The 1st of July brought in the new scheme, in which the regiment lost its number, and, being incorporated with the gallant 93rd, became known as the "Princess Louise's Argyll and Sutherland Highlanders," becoming the 1st battalion of this new amalgamation.

Surgical Experiences in Zululand
By D. Blair Brown

INTRODUCTION

In South Africa our army certainly found foemen worthy of its steel. Though the same amount of glory has not been attributed to the work done there as in some other wars, still the practical experience gained by every branch of the service is such that, systems thought complete having been found wanting, the whole military fabric has undergone revision of an almost revolutionary nature.

Into these changes it is not now my purpose to enter. I shall keep solely to the surgery of the war.

Late in 1878 I sailed for Natal in medical charge of the headquarter companies of the 99th Regiment. War was not proclaimed against the Zulus, but it was thought that the Government would soon do so. By the date of our arrival in Durban war was certain, and our troops were marching on to the Zulu frontier. On disembarking, a telegram was waiting me from the Surgeon-General, directing that I was to proceed at once by post-cart to join the headquarter column. Several days' continuous rain brought the roads into so soft a condition as to prevent any such vehicle proceeding.

The railway then only went as far as Pine Town—10 miles—and I had over 150 to travel. But for this, as events turned out, I should have been in the camp of Isandhlwana on the day of the disaster that happened there. I got to Helpmakaar on the morning of the 21st January 1879, and on the 22nd I accompanied three companies of infantry—chiefly 24th Regiment—on their way to join the main body.

As we neared Rorke's Drift we were met by fugitives who had escaped from the camp of Isandhlwana, who told us the terrible story of its capture. We thereupon returned to Helpmakaar and formed a fort, which was occupied until troops from England arrived as reinforcements. The gallant defence of Rorke's Drift was about to commence when we were turning on the road to go back: had we arrived a little earlier, we should have been sharers in the action. As it was, we wearily toiled up the hill, saw the flames bursting from the buildings, and reached our camp by midnight. In four days afterwards the wounded from Rorke's Drift arrived at Helpmakaar, so that I had the treatment of them. Contracting the prevailing fever of the place, I was sent to Ladysmith. There I afterwards organised and administered the base hospital.

When the new divisions were formed on the arrival of the reinforcements, I was appointed to the medical charge of the staff and departments of the 2nd division under the command of Major-General Newdigate, C.B., and of which Brigade-Surgeon Semple was principal medical officer. In this position I had considerable work to do for both my military and medical chiefs. There were few arrangements made connected with the medical organisation in the field, and no case of surgical interest occurred that did not come under my notice or care.

During the advance on Ulundi, I saw all the killed and wounded, the result of the various skirmishes; and being in the centre of the square formed by our troops during the decisive battle, nearly every case, I may say, passed under my observation. I afterwards remained in Zululand several weeks, and saw numerous Zulus who had been wounded by our men.

I shall never forget my first visit into the wards. An opportunity to test my surgical skill on a fair scale, which I had longed for during my military career, was now presented to me.

The following pages may therefore be taken as a summary of my surgical experience in the field.

To avoid repetition when detailing the cases, the dates of the various engagements in which the men received their injuries is here given:—

Isandhlwana and Rorke's Drift, 22nd January 1879.
Ulundi, 5th July 1879.

Nature of the Weapons and Balls used by the Zulus.

Bravery is a very different thing in the present day to what it was in time of hand-spikes and bows and arrows. The Zulu's real weapon is the *assegai*, a species of instrument holding a position midway between those just mentioned, and is of two sorts, one a short-handled, broad-bladed instrument used for close encounter, and which is never parted with, and the other long-handled and small-bladed, beautifully balanced for throwing in the manner of a dart. The guns possessed by the Zulus were chiefly our old pattern ones, with the Tower mark upon them of 1847 and about that date. After the disasters they became possessed of immense numbers of our modern rifles and ammunition.

However, with very few exceptions, they were unacquainted with their use. In many instances Martini-Henry bullets were found in the cow-hide pouches around their waists, cut in two and separated from their usual cartridge combinations, the powder being doubtless mixed with other in their cow-horns which served as their powder-flasks and hung by their sides. The majority of their bullets consisted of spherical masses of lead, generally hammered into form and not moulded. Others were very roughly shaped and had a rough prominence on them, while a few were very carefully made.

The latter were generally surrounded by a piece of thin cloth sewn accurately on them. Between this and the bullet a powder of an herb supposed to be poisonous was placed. These were "doctored" bullets which the witch doctors had given them as being certainly fatal. From their fairly round and smooth form they were much more likely to do mischief than the other less carefully made ones. For these reasons, in our wounded we found the most varied appearances, courses, and effects produced. Except when the injury was produced by a Martini-Henry ball, as unfortunately took place in some of the cases herein recorded, the experiences gained of the nature of the injuries agree with those detailed in the books of old military surgeons of years gone by.

The most extraordinary of courses were taken, and the most trifling obstruction often caused what might have been a very serious injury to become a simple one; and, above all, the very large number of bullets lodged sometimes very superficially, and in not a few cases, after penetrating the skin, being stopped by the first bony obstruction, caused not the least damage thereto, and fell out on the garment being taken off for the purpose of examining the wound. All this proved that in the vast majority of cases the bullets were fired at considerable ranges from smooth-bore guns, charged with anything but large amounts of powder.

Later on, with the Boers we had quite a different sort of enemy and weapons to deal with. Trained from their earliest age to stalk deer and bring them down when in full retreat, naturally the very best rifles procurable were in their possession. For the first time in history the British Army was placed opposite a white race armed with weapons of modern scientific accuracy and firing cylindro-conoidal balls, and therefore for the first time were our men wounded in the manner in which they themselves are now wont to wound. The revolt commenced by the Boers using their own weapons—Westley Richard's, Express, and even Repeaters. A considerable number of Martini-Henry's had reached them through Zululand, which had been obtained after some of our defeats there in the previous year.

As the war went on, and calamities succeeded one another, they of course were able to put into the hands of even their boys Martini-Henry rifles, and they knew how to use them, too. When our troops met with disaster in the Zulu war, it meant total annihilation of all unable to escape, generally on horseback. In the Boer revolt, so far as the wounded were concerned, it was the same as if the action had been successful, or nearly so.

Assegai Wounds.

In nearly every instance in which our men were taken by surprise by the Zulus, death was the result of *assegai* wounds. It was only very rarely that any of our men escaped on occasions when the Zulus could use their favourite weapon. The following cases came under my observation:—

Mr W. B. E., an officer in the Natal Native Contingent, was escaping on horseback from the camp of Isandhlwana when an assegai hit him in the back of the thigh, "pinning him to the saddle." When galloping on he withdrew the weapon, and was seen next day by me at Helpmakaar. The wound presented the appearance of a simple wound made by a bladed instrument, did not injure any important part, and required nothing but a bandage to effect a cure.

Another case was that of Lieut. J. of the Scots Greys, who was hit by an *assegai* as he was furiously taking part in the charge at Ulundi. The *assegai* hit him on the sternum; and though he, with characteristic British pluck, thought it a trifle, it afterwards suppurated and was some little time in healing.

The next case is a very interesting one. Private J. H. M., of the 1st Battalion 3rd regiment Native Contingent, was present on the 12th of January 1879 at the attack on Sirayo Kraal, the first encounter between our troops and the Zulus. Several prisoners were taken and were being disarmed, when one of them, being irritated by our friendly Kaffirs, tried to force his escape, and, *assegai* in hand, stabbed right and left at everyone. This patient was one thus injured. A bandage was applied, and he was conveyed to Rorke's Drift for treatment. While there several outbursts of severe haemorrhage occurred from the wound, and, though the bleeding points were searched for by all the surgeons at that camp, it could not be permanently stopped, breaking out again after a day or more, or whenever the local means of arrest were withdrawn.

On the 26th of January he was sent to Helpmakaar, and I found a wound of a regular punctured nature in the lower end of the left ham, a little above the popliteal space. As there was no bleeding, I simply ordered the limb to be kept as quiet as possible. Next day, however, haemorrhage—which was found by two civil surgeons who attended to be almost impossible to control—took place. When I arrived, he had fainted, and his pulse could only just be felt. No further bleeding took place for two days, when it burst forth again. Assisted by Surgeon M'Gann and others, the patient being put under chloroform, I enlarged the wound to look for the bleeding vessels. Having made the incisions, I found a large cavity filled with coagulated blood extending up the limb and amongst the muscles; compression over the femoral during this procedure was maintained.

On relaxing this, after the clot was cleared out, numerous points of bleeding were seen, none of which could be seized for torsion or ligature. The patient was again almost pulseless and his face very pale. Raising the limb, prolonged digital and instrumental pressure all failing, it was agreed that ligature of the femoral was the only remedy left to us. I proceeded at once to do that. On reaching the sheath of the vessel the profunda was found to have a longer course than usual, and to be lying very close to the superficial femoral, both vessels being plainly felt pulsating.

On applying pressure with the point of one finger on the profunda branch, I found not a drop of blood escaped at the wound after the withdrawal of the tourniquet from the groin. I therefore adopted the lesser operation, and tied the profunda. The wound healed rapidly, and after the first two days, when he complained of slight uneasiness in the limb, there was nothing else to note. On the 15th of February he left Helpmakaar for the base hospital.

He afterwards returned to duty and joined "Buller's Horse," with which famous body he went through all the reconnaissances and battles, including Ulundi, without any inconvenience. This patient was one of those in the hospital at Rorke's Drift on the memorable 22nd of January, and managed, under fire, to hop out from one building to the other. He therefore had four marvellous escapes within a few days—first, that of the stab at Sirayo's Kraal; secondly, the escape under fire from the hospital at Rorke's Drift; thirdly, the frequent profuse haemorrhages; and fourthly, the operation.

A case of accidental *assegai* wound came under my observation. When the 2nd division found its way back to the Upoko River, after the Battle of Ulundi was over, athletic sports were held, one of the "events" being *assegai*-throwing. A great deal of interest, of course, was taken in this by all the members of the different regiments. The friendly Natal Zulus forming the Native Contingent regiment competed for the prizes. On one occasion an assegai was well, but wildly, thrown into the air, taking a high course, and descended with great rapidity amongst the ring of spectators, becoming transfixed in the upper portion of the calf of a soldier's leg. There was, of course, a sensational rush. When I got to him, he had withdrawn the weapon himself, and it was found the popliteal artery had just escaped.

General Remarks on Gunshot Wounds.

In wounds produced by round balls, or conoidal balls fired from smooth-bored guns, as in the Zulu war, the invariable slough appeared, and generally began to separate by the end of the first week. The case, however, is different with the modern rifle-bullet. I have seen so many instances of the healing process take place without any aid, after complete perforation of a thigh or arm, that I look upon the fact of a slough occurring as unusual. The wound of entrance and exit, also, differs in the two bullet injuries, the wound of entry in cases of cylindro-conoidal ones being frequently like those of exit in size and shape, and it would as often take a microscopist to detect the eversion or inversion of their lips.

Again, in the way of healing, almost in whatever line a round bullet travels, the wound of exit is the first to heal. This is as often not the case as otherwise with regard to the conoidal bullet injuries. I therefore look upon the simple muscular injuries produced by modern bullets as much less severe, and consequently less apt to be followed by the incidental plagues which nearly always show themselves in military hospitals in the field, than the old round ones.

I believe, also, the shock of a large round bullet, and the pain caused by its lodgement, to be a much more effective way of stopping the approach of an individual than a cylindro-conoidal bullet entering the same place, passing through at great velocity, and leaving a harmless little wound which heals by first intention, unaccompanied by any shock or pain, and which, I have even noticed, the individual never knew he possessed until attention was called to it.

When, however, a bone is injured, the great difference has to be considered. It is well known that a round bullet, in passing through a bone, is more local in its injurious properties than a conoidal one. When a shaft of a long bone is struck by a round bullet, long fissures and splitting up into fragments do not occur in the way they do when a conoidal one had hit a like bone. As regards the articular ends of the long bones, the difference is not so great between the effects of the bullets.

The great question at present seems to be, admitting that a femur is so reduced into fragments by a conoidal bullet passing through it, is it necessary to amputate the thigh, or will the fragments reunite, the periosteum, of course, being upon them? Sitting quietly with pen and ink in one's room, it is easy to imagine such union possible. When one reflects on what takes place in a case of a gunshot-shattered thigh, how, under the most advantageous circumstances, prolonged suppuration and the constant soaking of these bony fragments in pus must take place, it is necessary to think how, under these circumstances, this periosteum is to be made serviceable?

No; the line of practice of the future, I think, lies rather in the following direction:—Knowing the nature of a fracture of the femur from a conoidal bullet, the indication is, to cut freely down as early as possible after the injury, take away all the fragments lying loosely, leaving as much of the bone and periosteum as possible, then, making a suitable drain posteriorly, draw the limb together, put it up in some firm support, when a short, and, I doubt not, a fairly useful limb would be the result.

It scarcely requires me to follow out here the results of much of the "expectant" surgery it was my duty to witness, and afterwards form into what is generally called "conservative;" the cases speak for themselves. I cannot help pointing out, however, that in far the largest number of cases of gunshot injury, radical and immediate measures taken within the first few days after the receipt of the injury will very often suffice to save a limb or joint which is certainly doomed by the non-interference treatment. Free incisions down to the injury where there is comminution, and removal of every loose portion of bone or debris, will prevent any amount of irritative fever, prolonged suppuration, osteitis, and periostitis, and all the whole list of calamities which follows as certainly as day the night, if such is not done in the first instance.

Now, as regards the removal of bullets, it is generally thought, if firmly impacted in the heads of bone, for example, it is best to allow them to remain until they loosen and can be easily removed. I have seen the result of this treatment so often, and have always practised the opposite, that I have no doubt as to the latter being by far the safest course. In removing bullets, the first error which the surgeon who tries the operation for the first time commits is in making too small an incision through the tissues to get at them easily.

A small wound, and tearing with the blunt forceps, causes a nasty suppurating sore, while a free incision and simply extraction movement given to the instrument will make a clean wound which heals at once. In the British surgical field-cases bullet-forceps, formed with large spoon-shaped blades and with a joint resembling those on midwifery forceps, are found. These after one trial I discarded; and as long as I have one of the American tooth-shaped instruments and a good strong lever, as supplied in the excellent "cavalry surgeon's field-cases," I shall not use any other. The needlessly large wound which is necessary to be made in order to use the "regulation" kind, the difficulty in getting the points of the blades round the further end of an impacted ball, render it a useless instrument.

The small teeth of the American instrument, the narrow radius in which the blades open, the ease with which they reach any portion of the foreign mass, the security with which they hold the object, are all points of great consideration. It has been said that the danger consists in the fact that nerves, arteries, or other important structures have been seized and injured. This I cannot believe could occur except in the hands of one so manipulatively ignorant that any instrument would have its terror. In both wars there were numerous cases in which the discovery of the bullet was not always the easy matter it usually is. In no case did I find it necessary to use electricity, the porcelain-pointed probe generally clearing the doubt in such cases.

When a battle in which there have been a good number seriously wounded has taken place, it becomes a serious question as to the necessary treatment to be adopted—what cases should be treated by the "expectant," "conservative," or "operative" methods. Here, indeed, the whole specialty of army surgery comes in. Anyone can lop off a leg or arm: the schools teem with second year's students who can do this; but the thing which ought to distinguish the "army" from the "ordinary" surgeon is the knowledge of what injuries should be treated according to either of the above plans.

To the patient, and to the surgeon unacquainted with gunshot injuries, often the wounds externally look so trivial and the symptoms for some weeks so slight, that opinions are formed and sometimes expressed quite contrary to what the results finally show to be right. It is a very distressing thing to require to tell a poor wounded fellow, after suffering weeks of prolonged torture, that he must lose a joint or limb, after being assured it would most likely be saved. Such a thing must occasionally happen, yet with a little care these cases might almost always be avoided.

It was my fortune to visit the hospitals in Germany at the time of the triumphal entry, just after the Franco-German war. Again, shortly after peace was proclaimed between Russia and Turkey, I visited the former country. On both occasions I saw numerous operations of a more or less severe description, the result of the "expectant" surgery in cases unsuited for such treatment. Wounds through joints and bones, at first quite local, had become, by the processes so well known to surgeons, very extensive, and sacrifices had to be made in cases where earlier and less severe operative measures would have sufficed. To save as much as possible is the object of every surgeon, but not at the expense of life.

When I recall the cases in which the attempt was made, and is even now made, to save joints and limbs in the wars I served through, the more I feel that operative interference is far too little adopted. Now, though I say I think we do not operate enough, yet I would never sacrifice an upper extremity on account of a gunshot injury, unless in consequence of suppuration, osteitis, or periostitis rendering too large a portion of the shafts of the bones useless, and which only could occur as the result of previous expectant treatment. In my experience I have never seen a case of gunshot injury of the upper extremity in which "conservative" surgery—*i.e.*, the excision of the shoulder, elbow, or wrist, or even the resection of the shaft—could not have been done early in the history of the case, and so saved the limb. Cases of shell wounds are different.

The Dressing of Gunshot Injuries.

It is very difficult to understand what the term "antiseptic" means when applied to the dressing of wounds. I remember, when a pupil of the late Professor Syme, he taught us the theory of the germs in the air, and the practical way of keeping them out by means of putty in which carbolic acid was mixed, placed on a sheet of some metal. Then came an elaborate system of steam-sprays, innumerable coverings of gauze, solutions of varying strengths of carbolic acid, carbolic acid and oil, shellac plaster, and now we have solutions of chloride of zinc, boracic lint, and iodoform, with or without the spray.

Theory and practice seem to accommodate themselves in a strange way when some change takes place. Seeing it is so difficult even to keep one's self acquainted with the "latest" fashion of dressing wounds "antiseptically," I determined to arrive at a conclusion as to the best modern method of treating wounds, without reference to theory. And here let me say that the teachings of the illustrious Professor Lister helped me more than anyone else. As an army surgeon, I knew from personal observation that Mr Lister's mode of dressing wounds was quite impracticable in the field; and as I have always doubted the value of "spray" and "gauze," I was not sorry to adopt other means.

In both wars I have felt such confidence in my dressing, that though much tempted to use the elaborate system so often pressed upon me by surgical nurses of vast experience, I have never yielded. Had I done so, my results would certainly have been claimed by the advocates of the "spray" and "gauze." To keep quite clear of what is commonly called—not what Mr Lister and his followers call—antiseptic dressings, I avoided carbolic acid entirely. When it was used, it was only to wash out open wounds, and in a watery solution form. This was done after the supply of Condy's fluid, which I had previously used, ran short.

When sequestra of bone or bullets were removed, the wound was mopped out with Tenex—tarred tow; a suitable drain was invariably made, either by the wound itself or by a counter opening, and a tube inserted. Then the wound was closed, a piece of dry oiled silk as a protective placed over the wound, a good pad of loosely-opened Tenex placed over all, and secured by an ordinary triangular or roller bandage. No fluid, either in the form of spray or lotion, was, as a rule, used. If the parts surrounding the wound were dirty, then soap and water was applied; but the wounds were kept perfectly dry.

In excising a joint or removing a limb, much the same proceeding was adopted. The greatest attention was paid to drainage for two or three days after an operation; every point in which there was the slightest chance of effusion, or pus lodging, had a tube inserted. Rarely were the dressings removed the day after the operation, but generally on the second one. When the cases were not very severe, such as an ordinary excision of an elbow, amputation at the shoulder, thigh, or leg, the cases were quite healed in a fortnight; and with this method of treatment (if the operations be clone early after the injury) there are very few cases that could not bear transport from the locality of military operations to the reserve base in three weeks' time.

In one case I took an arm off at the shoulder-joint, and it was quite healed by the fourteenth day, on which the patient started, under my care, along with a number of others, for the base, and went all the way from Newcastle to Maritzburg—200 miles—taking fourteen days to traverse, and walking part of the way quite cheerily with the other members of the convoy. This shows what can be done in warfare, and is a more important fact, when reflected on by military medical organizers, than at first sight appears.

It is, therefore, both in the interest of the patient and the country that early operation in proper cases should be done. The wounds were dressed as frequently as necessity required. Some needed very few, while others, chiefly the shoulder smashes, from the implication of the scapula and its processes, required more. The temperature is always a delicate guide in the progress of the healing of wounds, and as to the necessity of opening to re-dress them.

While I am writing these pages, the following case is under my care, an officer's wife affected with scirrhus of the right breast. I removed the whole breast, and dressed it in the simple manner above described—oiled silk, Tenex, and drainage. It was only dressed three times, and was healed by the eighth day. On the tenth the patient was out driving, and on the twentieth day she went for a trip to Belgium.

I do not, for a moment, give this case for any other reason, than to show that this simple method of treating wounds is satisfactory. The healing of wounds is as much an act of nature as the birth of a child; and if meddlesome midwifery is bad, needless interference with wounds is equally so. Cover up any wound when once its lips are drawn together, place on it oiled silk—a substance with no medicinal virtue, only, being smooth and soft, it lies on the part without irritating the wounds, and allows nature's efforts, the more or less exudation of lymph or pus cells, to take place in or from the wound—and non-interference and union is the result. Such dressing, to the army surgeon, commends itself even more highly than to the ordinary civilian one.

Here we have an armamentarium of the most simple and easily conveyed description. The Tenex used by me for the dressing of the wounded from Rorke's Drift, and some of that at Ulundi, had served the purpose of a soft agent for packing the medicine-bottles in their boxes. With this, and an ample supply of oiled silk, which occupies but little space, and sufficient drainage-tubes, I want nothing more for the ordinary treatment of gunshot injuries. Boracic lint was used with benefit in foul sores. Sponges should never be used in military hospitals except to wash the surroundings of a wound.

The utmost cleanliness of hands, instruments, and wards or tents is, of course, imperative. Continentalists often forget this; hence the great contrast met with by them between antiseptic and non-antiseptic. For bringing the lips of a wound together I naturally used the catgut supplied liberally for the purpose in the Boer war. I regret it did not answer. Absorption took place before the wounds had firmly healed. On arrival in England, I found the great inventor had made another innovation to remedy this objection. Green catgut was now recommended, and possessed less absorbent properties. I still give the preference to the silver wire, and until these new things have been more thoroughly tried and their efficacy proved I shall not experiment any more with them.

In the largest number of bleeding-points one sees when performing an operation, catgut such as we had did well; but for ligaturing a main artery in field practice, he would be a rash man who would use catgut for such a procedure. In quiet hospitals at home, without the possibility of sudden excitements, such as always take place with, and more frequently without, cause, in war times, such might safely be done, but not in army service.

As regards drainage-tubes, those sent out to us were all made of dark vulcanised india-rubber. Now, as they nearly always parted with their colour when in use, it seems to me that the grey-coloured tubes are preferable. The old-fashioned tourniquet, with buckle, belt, and pad, was never used by me. In every case the simple elastic ligature of Professor Esmarch was found suitable. In this instrument we have received, next to the drainage-tube, the greatest boon to military surgery which the last quarter of a century has bequeathed.

Not half the assistants or anxiety need be associated with operative interference as before. The bloodless method (as taught by Esmarch) by the use of the elastic bandage, has been eclipsed by the equally satisfactory and much easier applied discovery of Professor Lister's, elevation of the limb for a few minutes previous to the application of the ligature, to arrest the circulation. This I found to answer every purpose, and the operations were almost bloodless.

Gunshot Injuries of the Head, Face, and Neck.

In *laager* fighting, such as at Rorke's Drift and Kambula, the heads and shoulders of our troops were chiefly exposed to the Zulus. Consequently, most of the severely wounded under those conditions received penetrating injuries to the head, which necessarily ended fatally. At Ulundi a Zulu chief called Stulumaan was taken prisoner after the action, and it was found he had been hit by one of our bullets. The missile entered behind the lobe of the right ear, and, passing internally across the cheek, lodged in the fold of the upper eyelid, from which it was removed.

No. 1112, Corporal J. L., of the 2nd 24th Regiment, when engaged in the defence of Rorke's Drift, received a bullet in his neck, near the posterior margin of the sterno-mastoid on the left side, about the upper portion of the middle third of its length. Only one wound, that of entrance, was present. He complained of great pain in the neck on the slightest movement. When in bed, the pillow caused an increase of this. He had lost almost all use of his arms and hands, especially the right one, which he described as "quite dead." Painful "twitchings" were experienced in the arms. Whenever he wished to move his head from the bed, someone had to support it between their hands before he could do so.

At Rorke's Drift several surgeons tried to find the bullet, but were unsuccessful. In the above condition he came under my care at Helpmakaar on the 26th January 1879, four days after the injury. Next day I put him under chloroform and made a prolonged attempt to find the bullet. The course I found it had taken was in a direct line with the spinal cord. I made a free opening in the middle line as far down the course as possible, and again attempted to reach the bullet. I found by digital examination now that the processes of two adjacent vertebrae were smashed.

I could also feel the spinal cord itself. Pressure thereon instantly caused the patient to turn pale and the pulse to be almost imperceptible, and necessitated the immediate withdrawal of the chloroform and the adoption of artificial respiration. I took away several pieces of the vertebral processes which were lying loose, but had to give up attempting to reach the bullet. The case continued much as described for some time. He was sent to the base hospital at Ladysmith, and on taking over the medical charge of that hospital a month later, I found my old patient much in the same condition. He was suffering greatly from the pain in his arms, and wished "to have them both off to relieve him from it." On examination, on making firm pressure, I found a distinct hard substance beneath the *ligamentum nuchae* which was not present on former occasions.

On consultation with the Surgeon-General of the forces, who happened to be on a tour of inspection at the time, I cut down upon it and enucleated an ordinary round bullet with a rather long rough process extending from its smooth surface. This wound healed rapidly, but the original one continued to discharge slightly for a long time. In a few days the pain entirely disappeared from his arms, and their use nearly returned. He was shortly after this sent home to England.

The following case illustrate injuries to the pelvis:—

No. 956, Private C. F., of the 58th regiment, was hit at Ulundi. A bullet from the enemy struck his ammunition pouch, which was attached to his waist-belt and held sixty rounds at the time. A hole was made in the pouch, and the cartridges fell through it on the ground. At the same time a bullet entered the highest point of the crest of the left ileum, and made its escape over the middle of Poupart's ligament on the same side, forming a long subcutaneous sinus. After the slough came away, the wound healed quickly.

Gunshot Injuries of the Shoulder.

In modern tactics the shoulder becomes a much more frequently injured region than any other except the head. Not many years ago it would have been thought cowardly to lie down and take every available means of shelter when advancing against an enemy, while now it is the recognised custom. At any field day in ordinary peace times the movements by "rushes" can be seen, and the prostrate positions assumed by the troops at intervals, as well as the rapid formation of shelter trenches by the free use of the spade. Such is the characteristic of modern "attack" against a civilized foe. The long range and the accurate aim of modern rifles as compared with the old smooth bore guns render such proceedings necessary.

For this reason, it is found that a large portion of our most serious cases are wounds of the most exposed shoulder, that is, the left one, in a fair stand-up open fight, and the right one, in *"laager,"* "recumbent," or "entrenchment" firing. In most of the *"laager"* fights in the Zulu war, as well as the engagement of the Ingogo in the Transvaal, the frequency of such injuries was considerable. In the first of these engagements the fighting took place from behind the shelter afforded by large bags of maize or earth which had been skilfully arranged for the purpose; while at the Ingogo numerous large boulders which fringed the border of the plateau held by our men, served a similar, though not so complete a purpose.

It is most important that settled opinions should be formed concerning the military surgery of the shoulder. If the eye be taken as the guide in forming an opinion as to the implication or non-implication of any joint, it is a very misleading one. This is almost as much the ease with regard to conoidal as to round balls. In the shoulder we have a complex portion of the framework to deal with. There is the ball-and-socket joint surrounded by numerous firm bony processes, the head and shaft of the humerus, the clavicle, coracoid, and acromial processes, and the spine and blade of the scapula.

Add to this the numerous strong muscles and tendons arising from or attached to any of these, and the difficulty of a bullet being able to penetrate the joint is seen to be considerable. Professor Longmore says, with regard to the shoulder and elbow joints, that "expectant surgery is more fatal, and the results less satisfactory, than after resection." As in all cases of injury near joints, the earlier the diagnosis as to the exact nature of the injury (by the most thorough physical examination if need be), and the earlier the right treatment is adopted, the less will be the sufferings of the patient, and the more useful the result of whatever is done.

There was a very common occurrence in the Boer war, of which several examples are here recorded, calling for serious consideration. Conoidal bullets hit at great velocity and penetrated the shoulder, often injuring the clavicle, some process of the scapula, and the blade as well, and then escaped. After the sequestra and bony debris had come away, by nature's aid, through the influence of suppuration, a certain degree of caries and necrosis was generally found to be present in and around such injuries. When such wounds are probed no loose bones are found, therefore the orthodox treatment is to let them alone.

Now, it is this treatment I wish to prove to be wrong. If the following cases, in which such symptoms were present, teach anything, it is that operative means should be adopted to remove these carious and necrosed portions of bone. They ought not to occur, but, being present, they should be at once removed. But then, after taking such parts away with bone-pliers or saw, what do we leave? say some. Certainly not uninjured, but healthy bone, which, if the rules of wound-draining be attended to, will at once go through the quick and natural course of healing. Contrast this with the months, even years, through which cases not so treated drag their weary course.

For a time, they partly heal up, and then start afresh in their cruel career, until one sequestrum after another is thrown off, and nature has effected a cure by the total destruction of all the bone in the neighbourhood. The limb all this time being useless, the muscles glue themselves together through the inflammatory exudations thrown out, muscular atrophy takes place, fixation of the joint results, and, with the exception of the fingers, the arm is of little or no service. The chances of one of the many severe inflammatory attacks, which accompany the blocking up the free exit of the pus from the presence of such fresh sequestra, being followed by any of the alarming symptoms of blood-poisoning is an additional danger. In addition, there is the constant open wound, the continual careful dressings and anxious attentions, and the drain on the system from the pus formed and evacuated, and the chances of erysipelas, etc.

Every surgeon with such cases under his care would consider the knife is cruelly withheld in their early history; and I have not met with a single such patient who would not willingly undergo anything to get radically well, so tired and disheartened do they become. Unfortunately, radical action then cannot do what it most certainly could earlier, namely, procure a useful limb. I shall now detail a few cases of gunshot injuries to the shoulder which occurred at Rorke's Drift and Ulundi in the Zulu war,

No. 1362, Private F. H., of the 2nd 24th Regiment, was hit, during the defence of Rorke's Drift, in the right shoulder. The bullet entered near the base of the scapula, having been fired from the hills opposite to which he was fighting. The bullet made its exit over the bicipital groove in the humerus. There was great swelling of the whole shoulder when seen by me on the 26th of January 1879, and ecchymosis. The tract of the wound was sloughing. Poultices and cold water sufficed to allay this, and the case did well.

Corporal C. S., of the 1st Battalion 2nd Co. Natal Native Contingent, was wounded at Rorke's Drift. The bullet hit the back of the head at the posterior margin of the left sternomastoid at its origin, and took a course towards the middle of the scapular base, where the bullet lodged subcutaneously, from which position it had been removed when I took charge of him on the 26th January. Here also the whole shoulder was greatly swollen and painful, requiring poultices.

This case, after the usual slough came away, got well.

No. 1240, Corporal W. A., of the 2nd 24th regiment, was hit, at Rorke's Drift, in the right shoulder. The bullet entered near the insertion of the deltoid muscle to the humerus, and made its exit at the upper and inner angle of the scapula. The bullet appears to have passed under the scapula, no bone or joint being touched. This wound sloughed and then very rapidly healed up.

Acting Assistant-Commissary D. was hit in the right shoulder at Rorke's Drift when busily engaged forming the "*laager*," which he had originally commenced, and to which was due the safety of the place. The bullet entered about half an inch above the middle of the clavicle, and made its escape posteriorly at the lowest border of the trapezius muscle. The course taken was curious, regularly running round the shoulder and down the back, escaping all the important structures. The wounds, like all those received at Rorke's Drift, were wide and open and sloughing when seen by me on the 26th January.

After the slough came away the usual Tenex was applied. The whole of the field medical equipment having been captured by the enemy at Isandhlwana, I had no antiseptic to use. I thought of quinine, which I knew was a wonderful preserver of animal tissues, and used a solution of that, experimenting in this case. It seemed to answer, as the wounds got well after being injected several times with it. My subsequent experience, however, is that the wound would have done as well without it.

No. 447, Private J. W., of the 1st 24th Regiment. This man had been left behind by his regiment (the one annihilated at Isandhlwana), as he was fulfilling the duties at Rorke's Drift of an hospital orderly. During the fight he was hit in the right shoulder. The bullet entered the deltoid muscle about its lower third anteriorly, and lodged opposite the surgical neck of the humerus posteriorly, where it had been cut out. On probing this wound no bone was felt, and after the usual sloughing it healed. In every case the projectile found was an ordinary round one, and the nature of the injuries tend to show that they were all produced by similar bullets.

No. 1979, Private W. B., of the 21st Regiment, in the square at the battle of Ulundi, was in the act of loading his rifle when he felt a thud on his shoulder. So great was this, as also the numbness which immediately succeeded in his arm, that at first, he thought it was completely blown off. The bullet entered immediately above the sterno-clavicular articulation on the right side, and, taking a transverse direction towards the acromion process of the scapula, lodged. From this position, after having to cut deeply, I removed it. It was a mass of lead roughly hammered into a round form. For some days the whole shoulder was ecchymosed and much swollen. The case recovered.

No. 564, Sergeant J. M'N., of the 94th Regiment, was in one of the reserve companies in the square at Ulundi, in its "rear face," and he left his place for a little to point out a body of Zulus coming down a hill to one of his brother sergeants in the front rank; while so pointing with his arm extended, he was hit in the shoulder, right over the head of the humerus. No wound of exit. Numerous attempts had been made to find the bullet. Though no probe could reach it, knowing it must be there, I freely opened up the locality, and found it very firmly impacted in the head of the bone, and, aided by the "elevator," extracted it. It was a large Enfield rifle bullet, which, from the absence of groovings on its surface, proved it was fired from a smooth bore gun.

GUNSHOT INJURIES OF THE ARM AND FOREARM.

The day, I believe, has come for the more extensive adoption of the practice of resection for gunshot injuries to the shafts of long bones. The experience of the Crimea, Indian Mutiny, and American wars was not in its favour, the cases thus treated almost invariably ending fatally. However, the use of counter-openings and drainage was not understood then as now, which entirely alters the case. I shall detail cases in which the immediate removal of the shattered fragments, and also where surgical interference of a more complex nature, was successfully practised.

Colonel B., of the 58th Regiment, was standing in front of his men forming a portion of the celebrated square at Ulundi. The Zulus attacked this portion in great force, crawling up amongst long grass. Suddenly he felt a stinging sensation in his right forearm, for which he could not imagine a cause. Very shortly after, Major H. of the same corps called his attention to the fact that his arm was bleeding. The bullet had entered the upper part of his forearm anteriorly, and, penetrating, made its exit in the middle of the forearm posteriorly. The entrance wound was the size of a shilling, clean and regular; that of exit large and irregular.

The whole of the ulnar shaft between the two wounds was smashed, and there was considerable haemorrhage. I removed the whole of the broken bone, controlled the bleeding, dressed it in Tenex, etc., and put on a splint. This officer made an excellent recovery, and two years after, when for six weeks sitting at the same mess-table together, I had the satisfaction of noticing the very slight diminution of power and use he suffered from after such a severe injury.

GUNSHOT WOUNDS OF THE HAND AND WRIST.

Cases of accidental injury to the hand, in the progress of campaigns, either when performing the duties of night piquet or before the enemy, are by no means rare. On several such occasions I have seen fingers torn or completely severed by a rifle being accidentally discharged either into the owner's limb or into that of a comrade. On one occasion, at the battle of Ulundi, my attention was directed to a severe case by the Sanitary Officer to the Forces. There had been a lull in the firing, and the soldier was resting on his rifle, the hand being upon the muzzle.

Something must have touched the trigger, as the weapon went off and made a great hole in the hand. Notwithstanding this I felt sure that immediate removal of all the injured bones, etc., would result in a serviceable limb. This I there and then did, afterwards effectually controlling the severe haemorrhage which naturally was present. This case, I afterwards learnt, made rapid progress; and though all the fingers were not of use, the majority were, and the hand was most serviceable.

Simple cases of taking off fingers I shall not allude to here, as in all such instances the injury had done most of the operation, and a pair of scissors generally did the rest. Conservative surgery, in such cases, has the most remarkable results.

There have been numerous cases recorded of the removal of one or two bones of the carpus after gunshot injuries such as occur as above described, but total excision of them as well as the joint, with articular ends of ulna and radius, are rare. According to no less an authority than Professor Longmore, the following case is the only one performed for gunshot injury on record in the annals of British Army surgery.

GUNSHOT INJURIES OF THE HIP AND KNEE--

A wounded Zulu, captured by Captain B. of the contingent at Ulundi, was seen by me on the field. The bullet had entered at the outer side of the patella and went right through the knee-joint, escaping in the popliteal space. I pushed the tip of my little finger into the joint and felt the articular cartilage. I reported the case to my chief, who gave me permission to operate. Circumstances occurred which prevented this, and he accompanied the convoy of wounded to Ladysmith base hospital, nearly 200 miles distant, where he arrived in such a condition that immediate amputation was resorted to, and he died.

Another case in a Zulu wounded at Ulundi came under my observation. For two months I was detained in Zululand after the war, and saw many of our former enemies come in to our camp, to get the written passes to enable them to return to their homes. Not a few of them were wounded. The number of simple penetrations of muscles was remarkable. I found one with the most distinct marks of a gunshot wound of the knee, which any one would have said, from the line of flight the bullet must have taken and from the situation of wounds of entrance and exit, must have penetrated the joint. The bullet hit the inner border of the patella, grooving it distinctly, and made its exit posteriorly half an inch internally to the tendons forming the outer upper margin of the popliteal space.

A month after the injury it was completely healed, the joint being perfectly mobile, without the aid of surgery. Through an interpreter he told me all about the progress of healing and the means adopted to get it well. There is a small flat-leaved orchid which grows very plentifully on the *veldt*. A leaf of this was secured on both wounds and changed occasionally: this was all that was done. A piece of oil-silk would have answered the same purpose and been followed by the same result.

Gunshot Injuries of the Ankle and Foot

Mr F. S., a non-commissioned officer in the Native Contingent Corps, a native of Switzerland, while in a most gallant manner—for which personal bravery he was awarded the Victoria Cross—defending the post of Rorke's Drift, was hit on the ankle by a bullet. The wound was a small one. The projectile struck just over the instep of the left foot, a little anterior to the outer malleolus. When I saw him four days after the injury there was very great swelling of all the tissues in the neighbourhood, both ankle and foot.

Poultices were kept regularly applied, and in two days evidence of diffuse suppuration was found, necessitating my making several long incisions into the tissues. After this was done and the poultices continued for some time, he made a very rapid recovery, and regained the use of his joint. The bullet must, in this case, have been an ordinary round one, which had ricocheted off some box or stone and struck the patient in the ankle.

Captain L., of the 58th Regiment. This officer was hit twice,—the only case of the kind which occurred at Ulundi,—in the arm, and in the ankle. He wore a pair of leather gaiters over his boots. On taking these off, the internal malleolus of the left ankle was found swollen and exceedingly tender. A very small opening existed, though none could be found in either boot or gaiter. A probe found a small splinter of the end of the bone broken off and loose. The joint soon got very much swollen, and evidence of suppuration being present, I had to freely incise the tissues, giving freedom to a considerable amount of pus.

Poultices were then kept regularly applied. For quite a year afterwards this patient limped when walking, but nothing serious occurred to the joint afterwards, which is now sound and well. This was a case of the usual gunshot injuries met with in Zululand, round balls fired at long range, with little ammunition to propel them. The gaiter and boot saved the ankle. Had he not been mounted, I should have thought it likely that the injury was inflicted by a spent bullet.

No. 999, Private R. M., of the 94th Regiment, was wounded at the engagement of Ulundi, while in the middle of the square. The bullet passed through the toe of his boot, entering the inner side of the matrix of the nail of the large toe of left foot, passing along its side into the sole of the foot, tearing up the tissues of the arch of the foot, and forming a wide, gaping wound, and lodging in the inner side of the *os calcis* without fracturing it. From this bone, after using considerable force with the lever, I extracted it, and the case did exceedingly well.

This case presents several points of interest,—the small entrance wound, the absence of any open track as far as the commencement of the plantar arch, and the presence from that locality, along the whole curve, of a wide, gaping furrow, and the lodgement of the bullet in the *os calcis*. The bullet, a well-preserved Enfield rifle one, must have passed into the toe in its normal axis of flight, and, when it lost part of its momentum, must have somewhat changed it in passing along the plantar arch, and then lodged.

Such injuries to the *os calcis*, unless freely drained from the commencement, really are more serious than one would at first believe. Bones of this nature readily take on internal carious action, and what was quite local becomes much extended and more severe. This case, for example, did well; the next one did not.

Gunshot wounds to the Thigh

No. 295, Private E. C, of the 94th Regiment, was in the square at Ulundi, and hit in the right thigh. The bullet entered at the apex of Scarpa's triangle, just avoiding the femoral artery, and, taking a course round the bone, came out on the other side exactly opposite. The wound, after sloughing, healed very soon, without any constitutional or other complications.

No. 1876, Private J. G., of the 58th Regiment, was in the square at Ulundi. Firing had just ceased, and he was turning round on the ground, he having lain down, when he accidentally came into contact with a comrade's rifle, which was loaded and lying close to him. It went off, the bullet entering the right thigh posteriorly about its middle, in the central line, and made its exit two inches above the outer side of the patella. Wound of entrance was small and clean, that of exit triangular and large, more than an inch long. A long, very painful sinus, followed by suppuration, was present. This after a time got well.

With regard to cases of fracture of the femur in gunshot injuries, I shall detail the case illustrative of the effects of the modern rifle and conoidal bullet. In the case I attended immediately after he fell, during the thick of the battle.

Lieutenant P., of the 13th Light Infantry, was hit in the engagement at Ulundi, and I saw him almost immediately afterwards. The bullet entered the right thigh about its middle, passing through it in a direct line without injuring vessel or bone, and entered the thigh of the opposite limb about its upper third, causing severe comminution of the femur, and then escaped on the other side. The wound in the right thigh healed, without a drop of pus coming from it, in a few days. The wounds were small, clean, and round, and no difference was perceptible between the entrance and exit.

Those in the left thigh were different, the wound of entrance being twice the size of that of the other limb, and that of exit being large, deep, and gaping, and there "was considerable haemorrhage present. I put the limb up in a long splint at the time, and immediately after the battle I wished to remove the limb. This was not agreed to, and I lost sight of him for two days. When seen then his leg was still in the splint I had put on, but the case had become more complicated. A considerable tumour, pulsating strongly, occupied Scarpa's space. Ten days after the injury the wound began to bleed alarmingly and all efforts failed to check it. The limb was then amputated—I assisting—but the patient died upon the table.

The following was the condition of the limb I found on making an examination afterwards. The whole of the femur, except a few inches near the trochanters and condyles, was fractured, and existed only in fragments, large, loose, sharp-edged and pointed pieces. The medullary canal was full of a fungoid mass smelling most foully, and all the fragments of bone were quite destitute of living covering.

An inch below where the profunda branch is given off by the femoral the main artery was cut half through, evidently by one of the sharp fragments of the femur, and a long dark clot was hanging from it. The tissues immediately in this vicinity were in a softened condition, the adductors and vastus muscles being pulpified and separated from one another, and the space tilled with blood-clot.

INJURIES TO GENERAL OFFICERS IN THE FIELD.

When one considers what a general of an army or a division in the field is, the immense interest which centres in any accident occurring during such periods to such officers is not to be wondered at. It has been my duty to treat two well-known general officers when serving in the field in South Africa. A short summary of their cases may be read with interest.

Major-General N., when he was collecting his division at Landman's Drift, on the Natal border, previous to the advance into Zululand, met with the following accident. He was out, mounted on a fine English horse he had brought from home with him, having a look at the nature of the country. As in most parts of South Africa, numerous ant-bear holes existed amongst the grass, and the native bred horses are very sharp in detecting and avoiding them. In this case the general's horse's foot went down in one, throwing the rider. I found he had broken his fibula, and there was the usual displacement of the foot in such injuries. Newspaper correspondents, staff officers, etc., all wanted information. The division might move any day—what was to be done? My medical chief and I had a consultation, and we kept the secret between us. The general had got a severe bruise.

When the swelling was subdued, I put the limb up in plaster of Paris. Fortunately, the force did not move for three weeks, and the general was able to transact his office duties in his tent. The order for advance, however, came, and, though in considerable pain, my patient was lifted on to his saddle each day. In this way he continued, and even commanded his division in Zululand and at the battle of Ulundi, with his leg in plaster of Paris. There was a little more callus than would have been thrown out under less adverse circumstances, and in consequence the ankle was weak and stiff for a long period. However, it got quite well, and he never complains of anything connected with his leg now.

Major-General D. L., who commanded the cavalry in the Zulu war, was afterwards sent out for a like, purpose to the Boer war. The peace negotiations had taken place, however, by the time he arrived in the country. When Sir Evelyn Wood was in Pretoria, General D. L. was left in command of the force around Newcastle. Returning on one occasion from the camp at Bennett's Drift to his quarters at the camp near Newcastle in the dark, his horse stumbled, and, being taken unawares, threw the rider, injuring his side. I found the whole of the injured side of the chest very painful, and the fifth rib at its junction with the sternum broken. The cartilage was evidently ossified.

The movement, causing constant slipping backwards and forwards on inspiration and expiration, was very painful. I put on a large cork, cut to fit the locality, and secured it along the whole side of the chest with stripes of adhesive plaster. Then a firm broad bandage was put round the chest, with shoulder-straps. This effected a cure. In a month all this constriction was removed, and the bone maintained its position.

THE HOSPITALS IN WHICH THE WOUNDED WERE TREATED.

The wounded from Rorke's Drift, on arrival at Helpmakaar, were accommodated in the end of a corrugated zinc shed. This was one of several, filled with commissariat stores, chiefly bags of maize. Many of them had been exposed to the heavy rains then prevailing before being stored, and were decomposing and giving off the most offensive smell. Long square boxes containing biscuits were arranged along the side of the building, and empty sacks laid over them. This was all the bedsteads and bedding obtainable for more than a fortnight, during which time stores were slowly making their way from the base of operations at Maritzburg.

The only medical stores in my possession at this time, with a garrison composed as stated below, was a field companion, a case containing pills, powders, bandages, and tourniquet, and usually carried suspended from the shoulder of an attendant, and a box containing eight bottles of brandy and ten of port wine. The usual printed label showing the contents of the pills and powders, etc., in the field companion had been removed, so that one had to trust to one's memory alone in using them.

	Officers.	Men
Royal Artillery,	4	66
1st 13th Regiment,	1	73
1st 24th Regiment,	7	110
2nd 24th Regiment,	0	45
Medical Department,	2	3
Commissariat Department,	1	6
Veterinary Department,	1	0
Mounted Infantry,	4	95
Mounted Police,	3	84
Natal Mounted Volunteers	4	49
Royal Engineers,	2	2
Mounted Basutos,	4	80
Total,	33	613

Thus, making a grand total of 646—with the exception of the garrison at Rorke's Drift, all that remained of the headquarters column—a large force to find one's self in medical charge of after one of the most unexpected disasters—Isandhlwana—our army ever encountered, and a very trying position for any medical officer to be placed in. This was augmented by about 600 more men a week after, belonging to the 4th Regiment.

The wounded after Ulundi were treated in the admirable double bell tents, and afterwards in hospital marquees. No better hospital could be found for surgical cases, provided they are stationary. However, for more than two weeks the camps were frequently being changed, and in consequence the wounded suffered not a little from the exigencies of service in such a country as we were operating in. How different is the case in Europe, where, even when an army is forced to retire, the wounded can be left behind in charge of their surgeons with perfect safety. All the cases treated in these tents did well.

Personally, I would prefer treating cases of severe gunshot injuries in a well-pitched marquee than in a hut with foul walls and uncertain ventilation. In the Boer war, the hospital at Newcastle to which I was appointed consisted of a series of thirteen square huts, the walls of which were formed of sunburnt bricks plastered with the gummy earth procured from ant-hills, so plentiful in the country. The roofs were thatch.

The huts were arranged regularly in four lines, three in each, with the odd one some little distance in the rear. These buildings had been used for a long time as the permanent barracks of the garrison, the separate one in the rear as the hospital. This hospital hut was called "No. 10," each of the huts having a number. The station, Newcastle, in the Zulu war had a notoriety for the numerous cases of enteric fever occurring at it, all the cases of which were treated in No. 10 hut. On the break-out of the revolt in the Transvaal the whole of these buildings were placed in charge of the Medical Department, to form their base hospital, and which, as I have said, all the wounded passed through on their way to Natal and England, as well as the majority of the sick at the station who required treatment.

No. 10 hut played an important part in the history of this hospital, being the one to which the most serious cases were removed. The patients in it fell to me as part of my duty. Naturally I had misgivings about it as regards the surgical success of treatment in such a building which had not even been whitewashed since its use as the "general" hospital of the garrison. The groans and agonies heard and witnessed in it were enough to give one an idea of what must have taken place on a larger scale in recent European wars, and made one feel how much we have, in every detail, to learn before we can plume ourselves as too many are apt to do at present.

Every case in this hut had subsequently severe surgical operations performed upon them, but not a single one died. It was indeed a contrast to see the poor fellows, minus a leg, arm, or joint, in about two months afterwards, all up and about, chaffing one another, and singing snatches of cheerful songs. Never did I feel the truth of the words of Goethe more, when he remarks:

> It is often said the world is ungrateful. For my part, I have never known it to be thankless when one has discovered the proper mode of rendering it a service.

The Bravest Deed I Ever Saw
By Archibald Forbes.

It was mid-December of 1878 when Sir Sam Browne's column, having occupied Ali Musjid and tramped on up the grim and sullen Khyber Pass, was settling itself down for the winter on the plain of Jellalabad. Lord William Beresford and myself only waited for the Christmas dinner of the headquarter staff, and then we rode down the passes together, blazed at by the Afghan hillmen all the way from Ali Boghan to Khata Khoostia, At Umballa we parted, Beresford to return to duty with the viceroy at Simla, while I made across the Bay of Bengal for Mandalay, the capital of native Burma, there to study the character and surroundings of King Theebau, While engaged in that somewhat barren operation, there suddenly reached me a telegram informing me of the catastrophe of Isandhlwana, and ordering me to betake myself to South Africa with all speed.

Beresford and I, when parting at Umballa, had trysted to meet next spring for the expected fighting on the way to Cabul; but the startling tidings of misfortune in South Africa disarranged that programme. At Calcutta I found a letter from Beresford, telling me that he had obtained six months' leave, that he was bound for Zululand, and that I should find him at Aden, waiting for the fortnightly steamer down the east coast of Africa. We duly foregathered in that extinct volcano crater, dodged wearisomely into every little Portuguese-Negro port along that coast—stagnant, fever-stricken, half-barbarous holes where, as it seemed, nobody was quite black or quite white.

Finally, we reached Port Durban about the middle of April, 1879, to find its roadstead thronged with the transports which had brought the reinforcements out from England, and the hotels of the place crammed with officers of all ranks and all branches of the service. Beresford belonged to the Cavalry arm—he was a Captain in the gallant 9th Lancers—and during the voyage to South Africa he was wishing with all his heart for a position on the staff of his old friend General Frederick Marshall, who was in command of the Regular Cavalry Brigade which had been sent out.

But yet better fortune was in store for my comrade. That resolute fighting man, Colonel (now General Sir) Redvers Buller, was in command at Kambula, far up in the remote Transvaal, of the irregular Volunteer Cavalry of Evelyn Wood's grand little fighting force, which had just gained a shining victory over a host of 20,000 Zulus. In one of the recent fights, Buller's staff-officer, Captain the Hon. Ronald Campbell, had been killed.

It was a peculiar and difficult post, which was vacant in consequence of his death, for Campbell was a man whom it was not easy effectively to succeed. The assignment rested mainly with Marshall; and on the night of our arrival he, knowing Beresford better than did most men then, obtained Lord Chelmsford's sanction for that fortunate officer's appointment to the post.

Beresford made no delay. Before breakfast on the following morning, he had got a kit together, bought his horses, requisitioned an Irish (very Irish) ex-trooper of the Royal Dragoons as groom, cook, and body-servant, and was ready for the long journey. A couple of hours later he was on the road, eager for duty.

Presently I, too, joined Wood's force up at Kambula, where I found Beresford too busy to do more than give me a hurried handshake. He was Redvers Buller's sole staff officer, and the force Buller commanded, some 800 strong, was the strangest and most mixed congeries imaginable.

It consisted of broken gentlemen, of runagate sailors, of fugitives from justice, of the scum of the South African towns, of stolid Africanders, of Boers whom the Zulus had driven from their farms. Almost every European nationality was represented; and there were men from the United States, a Greaser, a Chilian, several Australians, and a couple of Canadian Voyageurs. One and all were volunteers, recruited for the campaign at the pay of five shillings a day.

What added to the complication was that the force comprised some eight or ten subcommands, each originally, and still to some extent, a separate and distinct unit. Beresford had to arrange all details, keep the duty rosters, inspect the daily parades and the reconnaissance detachments, accompany the latter, lead them if there was any fighting, restrain the foolhardy, hearten the funkers, and be in everything Buller's right-hand man.

Buller was a silent, saturnine, blood-thirsty man, as resolute a fighter as ever drew breath—a born leader of men, who ruled his heterogeneous command with a stern hand.

Beresford, to the full as keen a fighter and as firm in enforcing discipline and obedience, was of a different temperament. He was cheery; with his ready Irish wit he had a vein of genial yet jibing badinage that kept queer-tempered fellows in good humour while it pricked them into obedience. In fine, he disclosed the rare gift of managing men—of evoking without either friction or fuss the best that was in the rough troopers. And, strangest of all wonders, the fellow whom all men had regarded as one of the most harum-scarum of mortals, was found to be possessed of a real genius for order and system.

At length, on June 1st, Lord Chelmsford's army wound down into the valley of the Umvaloosi, and there lay, stretched out beyond the silver sparkle of the river, the broad plain on whose bosom was visible the royal *kraal* of Ulundi, encircled by its satellites. Over the green face of the great flat there flitted dark shadows which the field-glass revealed as the *impis* of Cetewayo practising their martial manoeuvres.

Two days were accorded to the Zulu monarch in which to choose submission or a battle. It was desirable, meanwhile, to gain some acquaintance with the ground in our front, over which a final advance might have to be made. So, orders were issued that at noon of the 3rd Buller should make a reconnaissance across the river, without bringing on an engagement, since Cetewayo's "close time" was not yet up.

At the specified hour Buller and Beresford sat on horseback in front of Evelyn Wood's tent, waiting for their fellows to come on the ground. Presently Baker came along at the head of his assortment of miscreants; brave old Raaf brought up his miscellaneous Rangers; Ferreira, leading his particular bandits, was visible in the offing; and then Buller headed the procession of horsemen down towards the ford, Beresford remaining to see the turn-out complete and close up the command. Then he galloped forward to join the scouts; for it was, as ever, his place to lead the advance, Buller bringing on the main body.

There was no delay down by the Umvaloosi bank, where the scattered fire from the Zulus in the *kopjie* on the further side whistled over the heads of the horsemen—over whom, too, screamed the shells from the *laager*, which fell and burst among the crags where the Zulus lurked. The spray of the Umvaloosi dashed from the horse-hoofs as the irregulars forded the stream on the left of the *kopjie*, and then, bending to the left, took it in reverse.

The Zulu occupants of the rocks were quick to perceive their risk of being cut off, and hurriedly ran out into the plain through the long grass in front of the riders. Some fell as they headed for the nearest *kraal*, Delyango, out of which a detachment rattled the fugitives.

Nodwengo was found evacuated; and then the force—Beresford and his scouts still leading, the main body deployed on rather a broad front—galloped on across the open through the long grass in pursuit of the groups of Zulu fugitives. It really seemed a straight run in for Buller and Beresford as they set their horses' heads for Ulundi and galloped on.

Beresford, on his smart chestnut with the white ticks on withers and flanks, was the foremost rider of the force. The Zulu chief bringing up the rear of the fugitives, suddenly turned on the lone horseman who had so outridden his followers. A big man, even for a Zulu, the ring round his head proved him a veteran. The muscles rippled on his shoulders as he compacted himself behind his cowhide shield, marking his distance for the thrust of the gleaming *assegai*.

It flashed out like the head of a cobra as it strikes; Beresford's cavalry sabre clashed with it; the spear-head was dashed aside; the horseman gave point with all the vigour of his arm and the impetus of his galloping horse, and lo! in the twinkling of an eye, the sword point was through the shield, and half its length buried in the Zulu's broad chest. The gallant *induna* was a dead man, and his *assegai* stands now in a corner of Beresford's mother's drawing-room.

The flight of the groups of Zulus was a calculated snare; the fugitives in front of the irregulars were simply a decoy. Suddenly from out a deep watercourse crossing the plain and from out the adjacent long grass, sprang up a long line of several thousand armed Zulus. At Buller's loud command to fire a volley and then retire, Beresford and his scouts rode back towards the main body, followed by Zulu bullets.

Two men were killed on the spot. A third man's horse slipped up, and his wounded rider came to the ground, the horse running away. Beresford, riding behind his retreating party, looked back and saw that the fallen man was trying to rise into a sitting posture.

The Zulus, darting out in haste, were perilously close to the poor fellow, but Beresford, measuring distance with the eye, believed that he saw a chance of anticipating them. Galloping back to the wounded man, and dismounting, he confronted his adversaries with his revolver, while urging the fallen soldier to get on his (Beresford's) horse.

The wounded man bade Beresford remount and fly. Why, said he, should two die when death was inevitable but to one? The quaint resourceful humour of his race did not fail Beresford in this crisis; he turned on the wounded man and swore with clenched fist that he would punch his head if he did not assist in the saving of his life.

This droll argument prevailed. Still facing his foes with his revolver, Beresford partly lifted, partly hustled the man into the saddle, then scrambled up himself and set the chestnut a-going after the other horsemen. Another moment's delay and both must have been *assegaied*.

A comrade, the brave Sergeant O'Toole, fortunately came back, shot down Zulu after Zulu with cool courage, and then aided Beresford in keeping the wounded man in the saddle till the laager was reached, where no one could tell whether it was the rescuer or rescued who was the wounded man, so smeared was Beresford with borrowed blood.

It had been one of Ireland's good days; if at home she is the "distressful country," wherever gallant deeds are to be done and military honour won, no nation excels it in brilliant valour. Originally Norman, the Waterfords have been Irish for centuries, and Bill Beresford is an Irishman in heart and blood. Sergeant Fitzmaurice, the wounded man whose self-abnegation was so fine, was an Irishman also; and Sergeant O'Toole—well, there is no risk in the assumption that a man bearing that name, in spite of all temptation, remains an Irishman.

Going into Beresford's tent the same afternoon, I found him sound asleep, and roused him with the information which Colonel Wood had given me, that he was to be recommended for the Victoria Cross.

". . . . Defendant partly lifted, partly hoisted the man into the saddle."

"Get along with your nonsense, you impostor!" was his yawning retort as he threw a boot at me, and then turned over and went to sleep again.

But it was true all the same. As we approached Plymouth on the home-coming, the Prince of Wales, then in the Sound with Bill's elder brother Charles, was the first to forward the news that the queen had been pleased to give effect to the recommendation. Lord William was commanded to Windsor to receive the reward "for valour" from the hands of his sovereign.

But something more may be told. Beresford plainly told Her Majesty that he could not in honour receive recognition of the service it had been his good fortune to perform unless that recognition were shared in by Sergeant O'Toole, who, he persisted in maintaining, deserved infinitely greater credit than any which might attach to him.

Not less than soldierly valour can Queen Victoria appreciate soldierly honesty, generosity, and modesty; and so, the next *Gazette* announced that the proudest reward a British soldier can aspire to had been conferred on Sergeant Edmund O'Toole, of Baker's Horse.

Victoria Cross Recipients of the Zulu War, 1879

By Philip A. Wilkins

Teignmouth Melvill
(Lieutenant and Adjutant)
24th Regiment

On January 22, 1879, when the camp at Isandlwana was attacked by the Zulus and nearly every man killed, Colonel Pulleine, seeing the disastrous turn that affairs were taking, called to Lieutenant and Adjutant Melvill to take the Colours of the Regiment and endeavour to cut his way through the enemy to save them. His heroic conduct is described more fully in the record of Lieutenant Coghill (V.C.), with whom he was associated, and with whom, on the banks of the Buffalo River, he met his death.

Teignmouth Melvill, born in London on September 8, 1842, was the son of Philip Melvill, Secretary in the Military Department to the East India Company. Educated at Harrow, Cheltenham, and Cambridge, he graduated B.A. in 1865. Entered the Army in 1865, and received his lieutenancy December 2, 1868. Proceeded with his regiment to Malta, Gibraltar, and (in 1875) the Cape. Passed examination for Staff College and was ordered home to join that establishment when the Galeka War broke out, upon which he obtained permission to rejoin his regiment, and served through the suppression of the outbreak. At the commencement of the Zulu War, he joined the Headquarters' Column, and, with his regiment, took part in the attack and capture of Sirayo's stronghold on January 13, 1879.

Her Majesty the late Queen Victoria, as a mark of her appreciation and recognition of his heroic conduct, caused his name to be placed upon the Colour-Pole of the 24th Regiment, together with those of Lieutenants Coghill, Chard and Bromhead.

Nevill Josiah Aylmer Coghill
(Lieutenant)
24th Regiment

Nevill Josiah Aylmer Coghill, eldest son of Sir John Joscelyn Coghill, Bart., J.P., of Castle Townshend, Co. Cork, Ireland, was born on January 25, 1852.

He was educated at Haileybury, and passed direct commission in 24th Regiment; became *aide-de-camp* to General Sir Arthur

Cunynhame during the Galeka War, 1877, afterwards serving in a similar capacity to Sir Bartle Frere, who, at his own request, gave him six weeks' leave to join the fighting column in the Zulu War, under Lord Chelmsford.

He had been told off to act as galloper to Colonel Glyn on the unfortunate reconnaissance made from Isandlwana Camp, on January 22, 1879, but that officer, seeing he was quite lame, insisted he should remain behind and nurse his knee, injured while out foraging a few days before. He therefore remained in the camp, which, as soon as the Zulus had drawn off Lord Chelmsford and the main body of our troops, was attacked by an *impi* of 25,000 men, completely surrounded, and practically annihilated.

Colonel Pulleine, who was in command, seeing the desperate state of affairs, called to Lieutenant and Adjutant Melvill to take the Queen's Colour of the Regiment and endeavour to cut his way through the mass of Zulus, to prevent its falling into the enemy's hands. This order Lieutenant Melvill proceeded to carry out, and, with Lieutenant Coghill, spurred his horse over the rocky and dangerous ground to the Buffalo River, six miles distant. The direction chosen was the only one possible which gave any hope of success, for the road to Rorke's Drift was now seen completely blocked by dense masses of Zulus. As it was, they had to fight neatly the whole way, for the enemy, whose running powers enabled them to keep up with the horses, were *assagaing* from the saddle most of the fugitives who had followed these officers.

In company with one mounted soldier, Melvill and Coghill reached the Buffalo and plunged in, the soldier being at once carried away by the whirling stream and drowned. Coghill reached the Natal side in safety, and, turning round, saw Melvill, whose horse had been drowned, being carried down by the rushing torrent, and that the colour he had tried so hard to save, had been wrenched from his grasp and was floating away down the river. Though unable to walk owing to his injured knee, and knowing, as he did, that any accident to his horse meant certain death to him, with safety and life at hand if he chose to take them, yet Coghill refused to consider himself, and, turning his horse's head, rode back again into the stream to Melvill's assistance.

The Zulus kept up a hot fire upon both men, and shortly afterwards Coghill's horse was shot. With the greatest difficulty both managed to reach and climb the steep bank, and took shelter beneath some huge boulders. Higginson, an officer of the Natal Native Contingent, who had succeeded in escaping thus far from Isandlwana, saw them at this point and joined them, but both Melvill and Coghill persuaded him to save himself by flight, as, being unarmed, he could render no assistance and, when discovered, would only add another to the two lives whose tide was so nearly at the ebb.

Leaving them, he had gone some distance, when he heard shots fired, and looking round, saw them both surrounded by Zulus. Of their actual end no living man has ever borne witness, but when the search party under Major Black discovered the bodies of these brave men, a ring of dead Zulus around them bore silent testimony that they had sold their lives dearly and had fought it out to the last.

The queen, whose colour these officers had died to save, was quick to recognise such heroic bravery, and sent two wreaths to be placed on the arms of the cross which marks their grave by the Buffalo River, and later presented to the 24th Regiment a silver wreath to be hung on the Colour-Pole for ever, upon which were inscribed four names:—Bromhead and Chard, of Rorke's Drift, and Melvill and Coghill, of Isandlwana.

Samuel Wassall
(Private)
80th Regiment

With the exception of Lieutenants Melvill and Coghill and Private Griffiths (who was killed), this is the only man on the Victoria Cross list who was present at the terrible disaster of Isandlwana, January 22, 1879. When the camp was sacked and nearly every man massacred, there were a few fugitives who succeeded in reaching the Buffalo River, six miles away. Wassall had just commenced to ford the river when he saw one of his comrades, Private Westwood, being carried down the stream, almost certain to be drowned.

SAMUEL WASSALL

Though the Zulus were close behind him, without hesitation he sprang from his horse, which he tied up *to the Zulu bank* of the river, swam out to the man's assistance and brought him back to the shore. Then, again mounting his horse, he urged the animal across the river, dragging the exhausted man by the hand, and succeeded in getting him safely to the opposite side, in spite of a brisk fire kept up on him by the enemy, who had by then arrived at the river.

THE DEFENCE OF RORKE'S DRIFT (ZULU WAR)
January 22-23, 1879

John Rouse Merriott Chard
Lieutenant, Royal Engineers

Gonvill S. Bromhead,
Lieutenant, 2nd Batt. 24th Regiment

2nd Batt. 24th Regiment:
John Williams.	Private
Henry Hook	Private
William Jones	Private
Robert Jones	Private

William Allen   Corporal
Frederick Hitch   Private

James Henry Reynolds,
Surgeon-Major, Army Medical Department

James Langley Dalton
Acting Assistant, Commissariat and Transport Department.

Fc. Schiess
Corporal, Natal Native Contingent.

The Zulu War of 1879 is full of individual acts of heroism and devotion, and of situations of the gravest peril; yet, from among so much that is splendid in the behaviour of our troops against the fearful odds they had to face in that fierce conflict, the famous defence of Rorke's Drift stands out as one of the finest examples of discipline and valour ever recorded to the credit of British soldiers. Coming, as it did, within a few hours of one of the most terrible disasters which has ever befallen a British force—that of the Battle of Isandlwana, which was followed shortly after by the reverses sustained at Intombi and Inhlobane—the heart of the nation went out in admiration and gratitude to the little band of about a hundred men which held Rorke's Drift against 4,000 Zulus, whose natural ferocity and reckless disregard of death was rendered more dangerous by the confidence of recent victory.

On the morning of January 22, orders had come to Colonel Durnford to move up with all his command from Rorke's Drift to the camp at Isandlwana. Thus, the post was denuded of troops, a fact which is the more astonishing in view of its tactical importance as a point on the direct route from Zululand into Natal. The position was further left without any preparation for its defence, although it constituted a base for supplies, and an enormous quantity of provisions and commissariat was collected and kept there. The post was a mission station, and consisted of two buildings standing about thirty yards apart, the walls being constructed of sun-dried clay bricks, and the roofs of thatch.

The Mission House was, at the time, used as a hospital, and contained a number of wounded and convalescent soldiers.

The fate of Colonel Durnford and his men at Isandlwana is well known. After the massacre and complete annihilation of the force, the Zulus advanced towards Rorke's Drift with the intention of overwhelming the small guard which occupied it, and then a successful attack upon the garrison at Helpmakaar, fourteen miles distant, would have left them free to overrun and devastate the Colony of Natal.

About 3.30 p.m. Lieutenant Chard, R.E., the officer in command of the post, was on duty at the river superintending work on the pontoons, when he saw, in the distance, two horsemen riding hard for the drift. On reaching the bank they shouted to be taken across. They were Lieutenant Adendorff of the Natal Native Contingent, and a trooper, and were survivors of Durnford's force. They informed him of the disaster at Isandlwana, and warned him that the enemy were advancing on Rorke's Drift. The trooper then rode on to warn the garrison at Helpmakaar, while Lieutenant Adendorff remained and subsequently assisted in the defence. Lieutenant Chard was at once preparing to return, when he received a message from Lieutenant Bromhead, who was in command of the company of the 24th Regiment at the Post, asking him to return there immediately, which he proceeded to do after mooring the pontoons in midstream. Lieutenant Bromhead had also received warning of their peril from Captain Gardner, 14th Hussars, with orders to defend the post at any cost. Immediately the message was received, defences were erected, as far as was possible, in the time and with the materials at their disposal.

It was decided to form a *laager*, by connecting the two small buildings; with barricades, so that a square or oblong enclosure would be formed on two sides by the barricades, and at the ends by the walls of the two buildings, which faced each other. The barricades, to a height of four feet, were hastily constructed with bags of mealies and biscuit boxes. The buildings were loopholed, their interiors constituting, in a sense, two separate extensions of the central *laager*. A number of natives at the station deserted in a panic at the approach of danger, and this handicapped the construction of the defences in the loss of so much labour. Further, the garrison were thereby reduced to about eighty men, slightly reinforced by a few of the patients in the hospital who turned out to give what help they could.

While the defences were hurriedly being constructed—Mr. Dalton's energies being particularly noticed by Lieutenant Chard in his report—it occurred to the officers that they would necessitate dispositions too extended for the effective handling of the small force at their command, and therefore the *laager* was divided into half by a transverse barricade of biscuit boxes. The foresight which resulted in the construction of this extra defence ultimately proved the salvation of the little force from certain annihilation. So swiftly did the attack follow the warning received by the garrison, that only half an hour elapsed between the appearance of the fugitive horsemen at the *drift*, and the actual appearance of the enemy. Consequently, the garrison had not time to complete the *laager* before they were compelled to defend it for their lives.

About thirteen feet of the barricade connecting the two buildings remained unfinished on one side, and it was at this point that the fiercest fighting throughout the attack took place, preceding the retirement of the defenders into the completely finished half of the laager. Unfortunately for the defenders, cover for the attack, afforded by the trees of the mission orchard, ran right up to this gap in the barricade. It was about 4 p.m. when the first of the enemy came in sight. Private Hitch, of the 24th Regiment, posted as a lookout on the roof of the hospital, saw a Zulu on the crest of the hill and fired at him. This was the first shot of the action of Rorke's Drift.

The *laager* was situated at a short distance from a small *kopje* which rose above the mission buildings. On the other three sides stretched the bare undulating *veldt* which hid the river and was devoid of all cover beyond the hollows between rise and ridge. Near the *laager*, however, on the side of the *kopje*, a number of ovens afforded cover, while the orchard, already mentioned, also afforded advanced cover for the attack in the trees which grew right up to the gap in the barricade. No sooner had Private Hitch fired, than the Zulus emerged from the cover of the *kopje*. They extended swiftly and silently in the horn-shaped formation of Zulu attack, and, constantly preserving the direction of this curve, extended, under cover of the hollows of the *veldt*, until they completely encircled the little *laager* with its desperate defenders.

Then, with a yell, the circle closed in a combined attack upon the *laager*. The enemy advanced, firing, and attempted to carry the barricade with the rush of a sudden assault. As has already been stated, the weak point in the defences was the uncompleted portion of the barricade. Here the fiercest fighting took place through the desperate hours of succeeding attacks. It was a hand-to-hand conflict. The Zulus burst through the orchard trees till within a few yards of the gap, and hurled themselves repeatedly upon the men who held this point. And it was the bayonet work which held the gap.

Mr. Dalton's conduct at this point was exceptionally fine. He directed the fire of the men, and by his own unerring aim during the Zulu rush, and his courageous behaviour when they closed on the bayonet, contributed very considerably towards the repulse. The general nature of the attack, throughout, was a succession of desperate attempts to force and climb over the barricades, and the strain upon the defenders can be imagined under the stress of the circumstances in which they were placed. For twelve long hours, without cessation, this magnificent defence continued. The heroic bravery of the two young officers in command stimulated their men in the continual repulse of rush after rush of the fearless enemy.

Lieutenant Chard, standing in the centre of the *laager*, directed men from one point to another, as he saw that any particular part of the barricade required extra assistance. Lieutenant Bromhead bayonetted Zulu after Zulu, and, throughout the action, led his men where the attack was fiercest. But a much more serious and terrible defect in the defence, due under the circumstances to, perhaps, a venial want of foresight rather than to want of time, became apparent when the attack developed. It has already been stated, that the two mission buildings constituted extensions of the *laager* formed in the square by barricades connecting the two. Therefore, each of these buildings was truly outside the *laager* altogether.

Moreover, the doors of the mission house—used as a hospital—were so arranged that the inmates could only gain exit in the face of the enemy's attack, when they would find themselves outside the barricades of the *laager*. With the exception of a tiny window in the wall opening into the *laager*, no communication could possibly be made between those in the hospital and their comrades. This window, moreover, could not be reached from any of the rooms, as, with one exception, there was no interior communication from one to another of the several rooms, which all opened outwards towards the enemy. Now the terrible situation of the sick and helpless men in this building when the attack developed, can be fully realised.

On three sides of them surged their fierce relentless enemy; yet escape from room to room was impossible, and the wall not only barred them from refuge into the *laager*, but shut them effectually from the succour of their comrades. Private John Williams was posted with Privates Joseph Williams and Horrigan in one of these isolated rooms, having three patients under their care. For upwards of an hour, they held the door against the Zulus, John Williams working to cut a hole in the partition to enable him to get his patients through to safety.

At last, the Zulus forced the door, and dragged out Joseph Williams and Horrigan, and killed them, together with one of the patients; but John Williams contrived to get the other two through the wall and joined Henry Hook, who was in a room farthest from the *laager*, with six wounded men under his care. These two men rescued every one of their charges by the exercise of splendid valour and devotion. The doors of the hospital were blocked up with mealie-bags, and the attack upon both doors and windows was defended by Hook and Williams, for some time, by rifle-fire through loopholes, which the former had made with a pickaxe in the wall of the building. But at last, the door was carried, and the Zulus attempted to rush into the room. While Hook held the door singlehanded against the enemy, Williams moved the patients out of this room into the next one nearer the *laager*. (This was the only room having communication with the next by a door.)

Hook retreated last, carrying in his arms one of the patients whose leg was broken. The enemy rushed the room, and again Hook held the inner door, while Williams, with the pickaxe, attacked the partition wall of clay bricks to make an aperture large enough to enable them to continue their escape. Happily, the door of this room, which opened outwards, resisted the attacks of the enemy to batter it in, so that Hook's attention was concentrated in the defence of the inner door by which they had entered. By now the roof of the building was in flames. The Zulus, tying lighted material to *assagais*, had flung them on to the thatch, which caught readily, and the interior soon became filled with smoke, in the choking fumes of which this desperate conflict continued.

When, at last, Williams had succeeded in breaking through the wall, the party retreated into another room still nearer the *laager*, while Hook again retreated last with his disabled comrade in his arms, only to turn again and defend this aperture against the rush of their pursuers, while Williams once more attacked the wall leading into the last room that now divided them from refuge in the *laager*. The retreat into this room was successfully accomplished. They were now in the room nearest to the *laager*, but their only means of exit was through the small window to which reference has already been made.

This window, too small to allow a man to pass through, much less to drag wounded men through it, had to be enlarged by Williams with the pickaxe. Hook defended the aperture till all had passed through with safety while the Zulus stabbed at him through blinding and almost suffocating smoke. When the window was enlarged, Williams lifted the patients through into the *laager*. Then he himself followed, pulling Hook after him, just in time to evade a final rush of the Zulus.

The fact that the enemy were now in possession of a building actually commanding the *laager*, would have proved a matter of extreme peril for its defenders, had not a greater part of the blazing roof fallen in with a crash upon its inmates, very shortly after its evacuation by the British. Many of the Zulus perished in the blazing ruins of the roof, their charred and roasted bodies being subsequently discovered. Meanwhile an equally heroic action had been enacted in another part of the hospital by William and Robert Jones. Seven patients were under their care, and these two men defended them to the last, succeeding in saving six of them. The seventh, Sergeant Maxwell, was delirious, and when his brave comrades had dressed him, he refused to be moved.

After saving the other six, Robert Jones returned to save him by force, but found the Zulus had stabbed him as he lay on the bed. William Allen and Frederick Hitch kept the open space between the hospital window and the inner defence clear, enabling the patients to be brought safely across from the burning building.

Under a raking fire they held their post against terrible odds, and both received severe wounds, but persevered in their heroic duty. Later on, when so badly wounded as to be almost incapacitated, they braved the bullets and rain of spears showered all around them, and carried ammunition to their comrades during some hours of the defence.

Amid the hail of missiles which beat upon the gallant defenders of the barricades there was one heroic figure moving from point to point, taking no active part in the defence, and with no excitement of battle to sustain him. It was Surgeon-Major James Henry Reynolds, who worked calmly and devotedly, ministering help to those struck down. During those long hours of desperate battle, he earned his Cross repeatedly, and when not actually attending to the wounded, busied himself in carrying ammunition to those at the barricade. His example of cool bravery was the admiration of all.

Another brave man among many was Corporal Schiess, of the Natal Native Contingent. He noticed that one Zulu in particular was doing great damage from behind an ant hill, crept along the barricade far out, and under fire, and after a short time was able to shoot this Zulu marksman. Before he returned, he disposed of two others in a similar way. Three times he leapt on to the top of the wall of sacks, stabbed a Zulu and sprang back, in spite of the fact that he had just come out of hospital when the attack commenced, having been previously severely wounded in the foot.

The garrison had now been forced to retreat behind the inner line of defence into the half of the *laager* against the opposite mission building, and a breach made in the barricade of this half, to render possible the retreat of the garrison with the sick, had to be desperately defended throughout the remainder of the attack. Night had now fallen. The Zulus upon all sides continued, with unabated fury, their combined attack upon the remaining portion of the *laager*. The blazing roof of the hospital threw a lurid glare upon the scene, and showers of burning sparks fell in a fierce rain upon the conflict and confusion beneath, while high into the air rose a great volume of smoke, flaming with the reflection of the fire underneath, and shone in the night, visible from far in the surrounding country. It was this glare that attracted the attention of Lord Chelmsford and his force, telling them of the attack upon Rorke's Drift, and filling them with apprehension for the fate of their comrades of the garrison.

To the last this terrible conflict remained a hand-to-hand struggle against odds. The Zulus swarmed into the space between the inner barricade of the hospital, and attempted, by force of numbers, again and again to overwhelm the garrison. But hard pressed as they were, their daring spirit remained undiminished; after hours of hopeless battle, men were found to follow Hook, in a charge through the mass of their foes, to bring in the water-carts, abandoned in the retreat, the necessity for which was absolute, to mitigate the suffering of the sick and wounded men within the *laager*. This brave act was successfully accomplished without any loss to this sortie of a forlorn hope.

Until 4 o'clock in the morning the fighting continued. Then, after some desultory firing, the enemy withdrew over the hill. Fearing a fresh attack, the position was strengthened, the weapons of the dead Zulus were collected, and a message was sent to Helpmakaar for reinforcements. About 6 a.m. another large body of Zulus appeared in sight, but shortly afterwards Lord Chelmsford's column was sighted coming towards the post. The heroic little garrison was relieved. 'The total number present during the defence was eight officers, ninety-six non-commissioned officers and men, and thirty-five non-commissioned officers and men sick. Their losses were fifteen killed and two died of wounds received. The official number of Zulus killed is given as 350, this being the number found around the defences, but many more were afterwards found some distance from the post, bringing the number up to 600.

John Rouse Merriott Chard
(Lieutenant, Afterwards Colonel)
Royal Engineers

This officer was in command of the Rorke's Drift Post on January 22, 1879, when, with about a hundred men, mostly of the 24th Regiment, the position was attacked by 4,000 Zulus. Throughout the entire defence, which lasted from 4 p.m. till daybreak next morning, Colonel Chard directed the operations with the most heroic bravery. The lieut.-general in command of the troops reported that "had it not been for the fine example and excellent behaviour of these two officers (Lieutenants Chard and Bromhead), under the most trying circumstances, the Defence of Rorke's Drift Post would not have been conducted with that intelligence and tenacity which so essentially characterized it"; also "that its success must, in a great degree, be attributable to the two young officers who exercised the chief command on the occasion in question."

The Defence of Rorke's Drift will go down to posterity as

one of the finest examples of British heroism, and the names of Chard and Bromhead will hold a prominent position in the annals of the British Army. The late Queen Victoria caused their names to be inscribed on the Colour-Pole of the 24th Regiment, together with those of Lieutenants Melvill and Coghill, who fell so heroically on the banks of the Buffalo River on the same day, while endeavouring to save the Colours of the Regiment from the enemy after the Massacre of Isandlwana.

Colonel Chard, son of Mr. W. W. Chard, of Pathe, Somerset, and Mount Tamar, Devon, was born in 1847. Educated at Plymouth New Grammar School, Cheltenham, and Woolwich, he entered the Royal Engineers in 1868. He was stationed at Bermuda for some time, ultimately going to South Africa on the outbreak of the Zulu War. After the Defence of the Drift, for which, in addition to the Victoria Cross, he was promoted captain and brevet-major, he became ill of fever, and went to Ladysmith to recruit his health, but recovered sufficiently to take part in the Battle of Ulundi. Towards the end of 1879 he was ordered home, and on his arrival at Plymouth was met by a telegram from the late queen and received by her at Balmoral. He retired from the service in August, 1897, and died at Hatch Beauchamp Rectory, near Taunton, Somerset, on November 1, 1897.

Gonville S. Bromhead
(Lieutenant, Afterwards Major)
24th Regiment

In the Defence of Rorke's Drift Post, on January 22, 1879, Lieutenant Bromhead was associated with Lieutenant Chard, and the eulogistic remarks made by the lieut.-general in command on that officer, were made to apply equally to him. By his splendid example of courageous bearing, he inspired his men in the magnificent defence of the barricade, where, with rifle and bayonet, he assisted to repel the terrific and continuous attacks made for hours by the Zulus.

His name, together with those of Chard, Melvill, and Coghill, are inscribed upon the Colour-Pole of the 24th Regiment, and will go down to posterity associated ever with one of the grandest achievements of British arms. In addition to being awarded the Victoria Cross, he was promoted captain and brevet-major. Was the son of Sir Gonville Bromhead, Bart., and died in Lucknow, India, on February 10, 1891.

James Henry Reynolds
(Surgeon-Major, Now Lieut.-Colonel)
Army Medical Department

On January 22, 1879, during the Defence of Rorke's Drift, Lieut.-Colonel Reynolds behaved with conspicuous bravery, attending to the wounded under a heavy cross-fire from the Zulus on the hills above the post, and a continual shower of *assagais* from those attacking the barricades. When not actually engaged in his humane task, he carried ammunition to the men from the magazine.

Son of Mr. L. Reynolds, J.P., of Dalyston House, Granard, Ireland, Colonel Reynolds was born at Kingstown, Dublin, on February 3, 1844. Educated at Castle Knock and Trinity College, Dublin, he entered the Medical Staff Corps as assistant-surgeon, March 31, 1868, becoming surgeon March 1st, 1873; surgeon-major (for distinguished field service), January 23, 1879; lieut.-colonel, April 1, 1887; and attained substantive step (brigade-surgeon lieut.-colonel) December 25, 1892, retiring in 1896. Served in the Kaffir War of 1877-8, and in Zulu War; besides Rorke's Drift, was present at the Battle of Ulundi.

Possesses the South African Medal, with three dates, 1877-8-9—being equivalent to three clasps, and also the Gold Medal of the British Medical Association for his services at Rorke's Drift. During his second years' service received the approbation of the commander-in-chief (Lord Sandhurst), for services rendered during a severe outbreak of cholera in India in the 36th Regiment. Colonel Reynolds is now, 1904, (although on retired list) in Medical Charge of the Royal Army Clothing Factory, London.

James Langley Dalton
(Acting Assistant)
Commissariat and Transport Department
(afterwards Commissariat Staff Corps)

The successful defence of Rorke's Drift on January 22, 1879, was in a great measure due to this officer, who, on hearing the news that the Zulus were marching on the post, devoted his energies and resource to the construction of the barricades. He was at the corner of the hospital when the first onslaught was made by the dense mass of Zulus, and his unerring aim and cool courage did much to contribute to the repulse of, and heavy loss inflicted on, the enemy at that point. One Zulu had sprung on to the barricade, and, having seized the rifle of one of the defenders, was about to *assagai* him, when Dalton rushed forward and saved the man's life by shooting the Zulu.

During the defence he was very severely wounded, but continued at his post until the Zulus retired. In spite of the invaluable work done by Dalton, the War Office ignored his merits, and it was not until many months after—in November, 1879—that they were awakened to the fact that his bravery had been overlooked, and he would have been left unrewarded had not the facts been laid before Parliament, and pressure of public opinion been brought to bear in his favour.

Dalton had been a sergeant-major in the British Army before the war. He died at Portsmouth in April, 1887.

William Allen
(Corporal, Afterwards Sergeant-Instructor of Musketry)
24th Regiment

To this man's undaunted bravery at the Defence of Rorke's Drift, January 22, 1879, when, with Frederick Hitch, he held a most dangerous and difficult position, the removal of the wounded and sick patients from the burning hospital across to the Inner Defence was able to be accomplished. Severely wounded, he still held his post, raked by a heavy fire from the Zulus on the adjacent hill.

When the wounded had been removed and his post was no longer tenable, he served out ammunition to the holders of the. barricade.

Unfortunately, this brave man is no longer on the list, having died some few years ago (as at 1904).

Frederick Hitch
(Private)
2nd Batt. 24th Regiment

On January 22, 1879, at the Defence of Rorke's Drift, Hitch was associated with William Allen (V.C.) in a most courageous defence of a dangerous and important position. By their steady fire the two men held open the communication between the Hospital and the Inner Defence, enabling the wounded to be carried across, when the Zulus had set light to the thatched building.

He was very badly hit by a roughly-made Zulu bullet, which inflicted a fearful gash in his shoulder, no less than thirty-six pieces of bone being taken away afterwards from the wound. He was presented with the Cross by Queen Victoria at Netley Hospital on his return in the summer of 1879.

Born at Southgate in Middlesex, November 28, 1856. Previous to the Zulu War, he had served through the Kaffir War of 1877-8, and since leaving the army has held various positions of responsibility, chief among them that of one of the "Right of the Line" Corps of Commissionaires, stationed at the Imperial Institute, and also at the United Service Institute, Whitehall. Hitch, though his arm has lost a great deal of its former power, may now often be seen in London, driving his smart cab, with which (possessing two horses of his own) he makes a comfortable living.

Henry Hook
(Private)
24th Regiment

The heroic conduct of Private Henry Hook on January 22, 1879, and his superhuman efforts in saving the wounded from the burning hospital will be found fully related in the account of the Defence of Rorke's Drift Post.

He was born at Churcham, Gloucestershire, and served for five years in the Monmouthshire Militia before joining the 24th Regiment. Served through the Kaffir War, 1877-8, and for his bravery at Rorke's Drift was presented with the Victoria Cross by Lord Wolseley on August 3, 1879. Has served in the Volunteers, and at present (1904) is sergeant in the 1st Volunteer Battalion Royal Fusiliers, and one of the staff at the British Museum.

Robert Jones
(Private)
Batt. 24th Regiment

Decorated for conspicuous bravery and devotion to the wounded at Rorke's Drift, January 22, 1879. Privates Robert and William Jones, posted in a room of the hospital facing the hill, kept up a steady fire against enormous odds, and while one worked to cut a hole through the partition into the next room, the other shot Zulu after Zulu through the loopholed walls, using his own and his comrade's rifle alternately when the barrels became too hot to hold owing to the incessant firing.

By their united heroic efforts six out of seven patients were saved by being carried through the broken partition. The seventh, Sergeant Maxwell, being delirious, refused to be helped, and on Robert Jones returning to take him by force he found him being stabbed by the Zulus on his bed. Robert Jones died in London only a few years ago, (as at 1904.)

William Jones
(Private)
2nd Batt. 24th Regiment

To the heroic efforts of this man and his namesake Robert Jones, six out of seven patients were saved from the burning hospital at Rorke's Drift on January 22, 1879. The fate of the seventh, together with the courageous defence of both) these men, in a room of the building, against tremendous odds, is described in the record of Robert Jones.

F. C. Schiess
(Corporal)
Natal Native Contingent

The heroic share of Corporal Schiess in the splendid Defence of Rorke's Drift was only tardily recognized by the authorities, and the same pressure was brought to bear upon them as was necessary in the case of James Dalton (V.C.), before his undoubted merits were rewarded. By birth a Swede, he was one of the wounded in the hospital when the news was brought that the Zulus were marching on the drift, and in spite of a severe and painful injury to his foot, he came from his bed and took part in the heroic defence.

His conduct at the barricades was brave to a degree. On one occasion he leapt on to the wall of mealie-bags, stabbed a Zulu, and sprang down again, repeating the performance three times in succession.

John Williams
(Private)
2nd Batt. 24th Regiment

At the defence of Rorke's Drift, January 22, 1879, John Williams was posted with two other men in a distant room of the hospital, and by his heroic bravery and devotion was the means of saving the lives of two patients. When the Zulus had fired the hospital, he broke a way through the partition and succeeded in getting them through into the next room. His courageous conduct, when afterwards associated with Private Hook (V.C.), is detailed in the chapter on the Defence of Rorke's Drift.

Anthony Booth
(Colour-Sergeant)
80th Regiment

After the appalling disaster of Isandlwana seven weeks previously, it was inconceivable that any body of our men should have formed a *laager* at any place in Zululand without adequate precaution against surprise.

Yet such actually happened on March 11 and 12, 1879, when about twenty wagons, carrying provisions for the garrison at Luneberg, were *laagered* up on the Intombi River, only a solitary sentry being placed on watch during the night, and in spite of the fact that Umbelini, a notoriously evil-disposed Zulu chief, was close at hand in his *kraal*.

Besides the convoy-guard, there was only a company of the

ANTHONY BOOTH

80th Regiment under Captain David B. Moriarty, as a protection, this officer having taken the handful of men out of Luneberg to meet the wagons a day or so earlier. In the middle of the night the sentry was set upon, but contrived to fire a shot and warn the camp.

Four thousand Zulus were, however, upon them, and a general massacre ensued. A few survivors on the opposite bank of the Intombi River opened fire, but 200 of the enemy got across. The lieutenant in command of this small party of survivors rode off to Luneberg for assistance, leaving them without any commanding officer, but Booth rallied his men, ten only in number, and showed so bold a front, that, though the enemy followed for three miles, he was able to bring his little party back to Luneberg and even secure the safety of a few more who escaped from the slaughter on the left bank.

His resolute valour was the means of saving the lives of any who eventually reached Luneberg, for had he not acted with such presence of mind and conspicuous courage in the face of terrible odds, not one man would have lived to tell the tale.

Henry Lysons
(Lieutenant) 2nd Batt. The Cameronians (Scottish Rifles); Now (1904) Lieut.-Colonel, 1st Bedfordshire

On March 28, 1879, Sir Evelyn Wood, V.C., in command of the mounted men, taking part in the assault of the Inhlobane Mountain, noticed that much loss was being caused to our men by some Zulus who had taken up a strong position in some caves, from which they commanded the spot where some of our wounded were lying.

He therefore ordered their dislodgment. Some delay taking place in carrying it out, Captain the Honourable Ronald Campbell, Coldstream Guards, with Lieutenant Lysons and Private Edmund Fowler, "advanced in a most courageous manner over a mass of fallen boulders and between rocks which led to a cave in which the enemy lay hidden." There being only room for one man to pass at a time, they had to advance in single file, and the first to reach the cave was Captain Campbell.

On seeing him the Zulus fired, shooting him dead, upon which Lysons and Fowler sprang forward, and with great gallantry drove them from their stronghold. Afterwards Lysons remained at the cave's mouth while Captain Campbell's body was carried down the hill.

Lieut.-Colonel Lysons, son of the late Sir Daniel Lysons, of

Crimean fame, was born at Morden, Surrey, on July 13, 1858. Educated at Wellington, he joined the 90th Light Infantry in 1878, serving through the Zulu War as A.D.C. to Sir Evelyn -Wood, V.C., taking part in the affairs of Zungen Nek, and the Inhlobane Mountain, and the Battles of Kambula and Ulundi, being twice mentioned in despatches and obtaining medal and clasp. Served through the Soudan War, obtaining medal, clasp and bronze star with the Egyptian Army.

Edmund Fowler
(Private) 90th Perthshire Volunteer Light Infantry (The Scottish Rifles); Now (1904) Sergeant the Royal Irish

This gallant soldier was associated with Lieutenant (now, 1904, Lieut.-Colonel) Lysons, in a most courageous act at the Inhlobane Mountain, Zululand, March 28, 1879. Fuller details are given in the record of that officer.

Redvers Henry Buller, C.B.
(Captain And Brevet-Lieut.-Colonel, now (1904) General, The Right Honourable, G.C.B., G.C.M.G., P.C.) 60th Rifles

The Zulu War of 1879, though successfully carried out in the end, was responsible for terrible loss of life during the short time occupied in forcing the Zulus to submission. The disaster at Isandlwana was terrible enough, that at Intombi followed soon after, and the affair at the Inhlobane Mountain narrowly escaped

REDVERS HENRY BULLER, C.B.

equalling the first-named in appalling consequences. Hearing that vast herds of cattle were on the top of the mountain, a raid upon them was arranged, and, on March, 28, 500 mounted: men set off to bring them down. The ascent of the side approached was so steep, that it was hardly passable for horses, but they succeeded in gaining the summit, and had commenced to drive the herds together, when Sir Redvers Buller saw, about six miles away, a force of 20,000 Zulus advancing upon him.

This *impi* was known to be "on the way" from Ulundi, but it was never imagined that it could compass the distance in so short a time. There was now nothing for our men but a hasty retreat, and down the precipitous paths they had ascended (the easier road on the other side, which they had intended to use being now blocked by the enemy) men and horses struggled, fell, and crowded together.

The advanced Zulus promptly fell upon them, *assagaied* the horses, and speared every man they could reach, and it was during this terrible time that Captain Buller performed the many heroic acts for which he was deservedly awarded the Cross.

Captain D'Arcy, Lieutenant Everitt, and a trooper of the Frontier Light Horse, were all, one after another, rescued by him from the ferocious Zulus, when their horses had been shot or stabbed to death. Rallying his men, he rode, time after time, at the hordes of the infuriated enemy, and by his personal courage, cool behaviour, and undaunted resolution, held them in check and covered the retreat. Captain Thomasson, in his work on the Zulu Campaign, says that Buller is known to have saved six men that day, but it would be impossible to tell how many more owed their lives to his orders and example. Streatfield, another chronicler of that war, says that:

> Buller was a splendid worker, and never seemed to tire, however great the amount of hard work, and wherever the stiffest amount of work was, he was sure to be found. In action, if you could ascertain for certain where most bullets were flying, you would be pretty safe in betting that Buller would be in the middle of it.

Born December 7, 1839, Sir Redvers Buller is the son of the late James Wentworth Buller. Educated at Eton, he entered the 60th Rifles in 1858, serving in the China War, 1860; Red River Expedition, 1870; Ashanti War, 1874; Kaffir War, 1878; Zulu War, 1879; Boer War, 1881, acting in the latter as Chief of Staff. Was in Intelligence Department during Egyptian War, 1882, taking part in the Battles of Kassassin and Tel-el-Kebir, for which he was mentioned in despatches, received the medal and clasp, 3rd class Osmanieh, Khedive's Star, and was created K.C.M.G. Served in Soudan Expedition, 1884, mentioned twice in despatches, and promoted major-general.

Was chief of staff in Soudan (Nile), 1884-5, again mentioned in despatches and created K.C.B. quartermaster-general, 1887; Under-Secretary for Ireland, 1887; adjutant-general, 1890-7, and in command at Aldershot, 1898-9. On the outbreak of war in South Africa in 1899, commanded the forces at the commencement of the troubles in that country, and, later on, acted as general officer commanding in Natal, conducting the operations for the relief of Ladysmith, which, with that dogged and resolute way so characteristic of him, he successfully accomplished.

William Knox Leet
(Major, Afterwards Major-General, C.B.)
1st Batt. 13th Prince Albert's Somersetshire Light Infantry

On March 28, 1879, the fighting on the Inhlobane Mountain, under Sir Evelyn Wood, was so severe that a retirement was deemed advisable. During the retreat the Zulus continuously harassed our men. The 13th Light Infantry formed part of the small force.

Towards evening Lieutenant A. M. Smith, Frontier Light Horse, had his horse shot from under him, and, being closely pursued by the enemy, was on the point of being speared, when Major Leet, galloping to his rescue, took him up behind him, riding with him under rifle-fire and a shower of *assagais* to a place of safety.

During the Indian Mutiny General Leet served with marked distinction, both with his battalion under Lord Mark Kerr, and as a staff officer to several columns towards the end of the campaign, being twice mentioned in general orders. Served in South Africa, 1878, against Sekukuni, and also in the Expedition to Mandalay, 1886-7, in both latter campaigns being mentioned in despatches.

Was in 1887 created a Companion of the Bath, and died on

June 29, 1898, aged 65. (Born November 3, 1833.)

Edward Stevenson Browne
(Lieutenant, now (1904) Brigadier-General, C.B.)
1st Batt. 24th Regiment

Decorated for his bravery at Inhlobane Mountain, in Zululand, March 29, 1879, when, during the disastrous retreat of our force, he twice rode back towards the pursuing Zulus and assisted an unmounted man to escape.

Brigadier-General Browne entered the army in 1871, and since 1902, has commanded the 5th Army Corps at York.

Lord William Leslie de la Poer Beresford
(Captain, Afterwards Colonel, K.C.I.E.)
9th (Queen's Royal) Lancers

Previous to the Battle of Ulundi, which broke the Zulu power and brought that sanguinary war to a close, a reconnaissance was made across the White Umvolosi River on July 3, 1879. The cavalry having pushed far out towards Ulundi, thousands of Zulus, hidden up to that moment in deep hollows, opened a brisk fire on our men. The "retire" was sounded, and at that instant Sergeant Fitzmaurice, of the 24th, was thrown from his horse, severely injured and partially stunned, and, the Zulus being now only a few yards away, his fate seemed sealed.

Lord William Beresford then rode back, cut his way to the

LORD WILLIAM LESLIE DE LA POER BERESFORD

man, took him up on his horse and brought him away safely. This task was rendered all the more dangerous and difficult owing to the fact that Fitzmaurice twice nearly pulled him off the saddle, but Sergeant O'Toole rendered valuable assistance by helping to keep the man on the horse, at the same time checking the advance of the nearest Zulus with his carbine.

O'Toole was deservedly awarded the Victoria Cross also, thanks to Lord William speaking on his behalf, for when commanded to Windsor to receive the decoration, he told Her late Majesty that he could not in honour receive the recognition of his services unless it were shared in by Sergeant O'Toole, who, he generously affirmed, deserved infinitely greater credit than any which might attach to himself, and the next *Gazette* announced O'Toole's reward.

Colonel Lord William Leslie de la Poer Beresford, third son of the Rev. John de la Poer, fourth Marquess of Waterford, was born on July 20, 1847. Educated at Eton, he entered the 9th Lancers in 1867 as cornet, obtained his commission as lieutenant in 1870, and his captaincy in 1876. Was an *a.d.c.* to Lord Lytton, Viceroy of India, from the end of 1875 to October, 1881.

Served through the Jowaki Expedition, 1877-8, this being his first active service.

Besides the Zulu War, he served with the gallant lancers in the Afghan War, being present at the capture of Ali Musjid, and from 1881 to 1894 was Military Secretary to the successive Viceroys of India, Lords Dufferin and Lansdowne. Became major in 1884, and served with the Burmese Expedition, being mentioned in despatches and receiving brevet of lieut.-colonel. Became colonel in January, 1891. Died December 28, 1900.

Edmund O'Toole
(Sergeant)
Frontier Light Horse

In the Zulu War of 1879, a reconnaissance was made, prior to the Battle of Ulundi, on July 3, 1879. When ordered to retire, vast hordes of Zulus advancing towards the mounted men, Sergeant Fitzmaurice was injured by his horse falling and rolling on him.

Lord William Beresford rode back and took him up in front of him, but the enemy were now only a short distance from them and O'Toole kept them in check, shooting many with his carbine. Fitzmaurice, however, was so stunned by his fall that he could not keep upon the horse, and nearly dismounted Lord William, upon which O'Toole threw away his carbine and together they were able to rescue him. (See also account of Lord William Beresford.)

Cecil D'Arcy
(Captain)
Frontier Light Horse

On July 3, 1879, during the reconnaissance before Ulundi by the Mounted Corps, Trooper Raubenheim, of the Frontier Light Horse, fell from the saddle as the rest were retiring. Notwithstanding the proximity of the Zulus, who were rushing towards them, Captain D'Arcy waited until his companion had mounted behind him and then proceeded to ride away, but the horse kicked both men off. Raubenheim was stunned, so D'Arcy tried to lift the man into the saddle again, heroically making several attempts, though the Zulus were getting nearer and nearer; but at last, finding he was powerless to do so, he was obliged to leave him. It was a miraculous escape for Captain D'Arcy as, when he started to save himself, the Zulus had actually closed upon him.

Captain D'Arcy's life was saved by Sir Redvers Buller, V.C., during the Zulu War.

THE BASUTO WAR AND OPERATIONS AGAINST SEKUKUNI, 1879 AND 1881

Peter Brown
(Trooper)
Cape Mounted Rifles

This Colonial trooper was awarded the Victoria Cross for a particularly humane and courageous act at the storming of Moirosi's Mountain, Zululand, April 8, 1879.

The following letter, which appeared in a Cape newspaper, gives the details of his heroic act and the subsequent disposal of the Victoria Cross he so well deserved. 'The second paragraph appeared in the *Cape Argus* of August, 1895, but the first bore no name or date when it came into the author's hands, though probably it issued from the same source—

1

It may interest you to hear how Peter Brown won his

Victoria Cross. Everybody who knows the circumstances under which he got it believes that no man ever deserved the decoration better than he did, if as well. He was a rough, ignorant, but excessively manly and kind-hearted man; exactly the sort of man so well described by the late Sir Hastings Doyle in his well-known poem, '*The Private of the Buffs.*' I am certain that Brown did not know of the existence of such a decoration as the Victoria Cross when he performed the signal act of valour that got it for him, and this, of course, made his conduct all the more admirable.

He was one of the advanced party of stormers in the assault made on Moirosi's Mountain stronghold, on the 8th of April, 1879. In rushing up to the assault, several men (officers, non-commissioned officers and privates) fell, killed and wounded. 'Three wounded men crept to the shelter of a small rock that lay in the middle of a perfectly open space, not twenty yards from the lower tier of *schanzen*. The stormers had passed on to the left of this open space, and were trying to scale defences on the flank of the position, when these three men began to cry piteously for water.

It appeared to be certain death to go to them, as the open space, where this sheltering stone lay, was completely swept by the fire of all the *schanzen* on that part of the mountain. Their screams, however, became quite heart-rending, and after a minute or two Brown said with an oath, 'I can't stand this any longer; has any one any water?' He was handed a tin canteen half full of water, and he coolly walked across the open space, knelt down beside the rock, and, without making the slightest attempt to shelter himself, began to pour water into the mouth of one of the wounded men; while doing this a bullet broke his arm; he quietly picked up the canteen and went on pouring the water into the man's mouth with his other hand, and almost immediately a second bullet struck him in the leg, and he fell over amongst the men to whose help he had gone.

It is impossible to imagine an act of more deliberate self-sacrifice, coupled with absolutely dauntless bravery, than that performed by Peter Brown.

(Signed) J. M. Grant,
Lieut.-Colonel Commanding C.M.R.

2

From the *Argus* (Cape), August, 1895—

At a recent Parade sale, Trooper Brown's Victoria Cross, together with the '77, '78, '79 war medal and clasp, were put up to auction, and knocked down to a bidder at twenty-five shillings. Twenty-five shillings was the exact price of the rarest distinction that can be conferred on a Briton for doing his duty on the field of battle. The purchaser, a captain in the Cape Town Highlanders, who says he would give his own right hand for such a distinction, purposes presenting the Cross and medal to the commanding officer of the C.M.R., and in so doing he is taking the only right and proper course. The little story is its own moral, and we leave our readers to follow out the reflections which it may awaken. Of one thing we may be certain—that the dead trooper's Cross and medal will not again come beneath the hammer of the auctioneer. The commanding officer of the C.M.R. will see to that.

Robert: George Scott
(Sergeant, now (1904) Lieut.-Colonel)
Cape Mounted Rifles

Decorated for a particularly fine act of courage and devotion on April 8, 1879, during an attack on Moirosi's Mountain. The enemy were concentrating a very severe fire upon our men from behind a line of stone barricades, and it was impossible for the Colonials to reply in any effective manner. Seeing the serious state of affairs, Robert George Scott, then a sergeant in the Colonial Corps, volunteered to creep up to the enemy's defences and fling time-fuse shells into their midst.

He, first, caused all his men to retire under cover, lest any shell should burst prematurely—by which precaution he probably saved many of their lives—and then, under a hail of lead, deliberately advanced under the enemy's defences, and twice attempted to throw the shells over. 'The second time, owing to some defect in the fuse which he had lighted, the shell burst almost in his hands, blowing the right one to pieces, and severely wounding him in the left leg.

During the Boer War, 1899-1902, he served with the Kimberley Light Horse.

Edmund Baron Hartley
(Surgeon-Major, now (1904) Colonel, C.M.G.)
Cape Mounted Rifles

Decorated for his great bravery in attending the wounded during the unsuccessful attack on Moirosi's Mountain, Basutoland, June 5, 1879. Corporal A. Jones fell, severely wounded, and, in spite of the very heavy fire from the enemy, Surgeon-Major

Hartley crossed the open ground and carried the wounded man to shelter. Having done this, he continued ministering to the other injured. among the storming party, exposing himself freely and fearlessly during his devoted duties.

Colonel Edmund Baron Hartley (C.M.G. 1900) has been Principal Medical Officer, Cape Colonial Forces, since 1878. Son of Dr. Edmund Hartley. Was born on May 6, 1847, at Ivy Bridge, Devon, receiving his medical education at St. George's Hospital, London. M.R.C.S. England; L.R.C.P. Edinburgh. From 1867 to 1869 was a clerk in H.M. Inland Revenue; 1874-7 was district surgeon in Basutoland, joining, in the latter year, the Colonial Forces, with which he served during the next four years in the Galeka, Gaika, Moirosi, Tembu and Basuto Campaigns. He next saw active service in 1897, in Bechuanaland, where he was wounded; and later, in 1900, in South Africa, against the Boers. For his services he was created C.M.G.

Francis Fitzpatrick
(Private)
94th Regiment
(Now, 1904, 2nd Batt. Connaught Rangers)

Sekukuni's Town was the stronghold of a native chief in South Africa who caused us much trouble to reduce and capture in 1879, long after the Zulu War was ended. and out of which it arose. On November 28, Lieutenant J. C. Dewar, King's Dragoon Guards, fell severely wounded. He was, with the exception of Private Fitzpatrick and Private Flawn (to whom the Victoria Cross was also awarded), practically alone, having under his command only six of the native contingent.

These were proceeding to carry him down a steep hill, when suddenly about forty of the enemy, spear in hand, appeared in pursuit, whereupon the wounded officer was dropped and deserted by all but the two Irishmen, one of whom bore him on his back, while the other fired at the oncoming enemy. Alternately, one bearing and the other defending, he was eventually carried off into safety.

Thomas Flawn
(Private)
94th Regiment
(Now, 1904, 2nd Batt. Connaught Rangers)

At the attack on Sekukuni's Town, South Africa, on November 28, 1879, Flawn, with Private Fitzpatrick (V.C.), saved the life of Lieutenant Dewar, King's Dragoon Guards. Further details of this gallant act are given in the record of Private Fitzpatrick (V.C.).

John Frederick McCrea
(Surgeon)
1st Regiment, Cape Mounted Yeomanry

On January 14, 1881, during the action against the Basutos at Tweefontein, near Thaba Tsen, Surgeon McCrea behaved with very great bravery and devotion to the wounded. The enemy had charged with the greatest determination, forcing the *burghers* to retire with a loss of sixteen killed and twenty-one wounded.

Among the latter was a man named Aicramp, who had been shot and lay some considerable distance away, but McCrea went to his assistance under a heavy fire, and, with the help of Captain Buxton, of the Mafeteng Contingent, carried him to the shelter of an ant-heap, and then returned for a stretcher. While again crossing the open space he was severely wounded in the right breast by a bullet, but still continued in his duties with the ambulance, and carried many wounded from the field.

He paid little attention to his own injury, and was forced to dress it as well as he could later on, as no other medical officer was present. The *Gazette* stated that, had it not been for his exertions, the sufferings of the wounded would have been greatly aggravated and many more lives lost. He died in Africa in the summer of 1894.

ALSO FROM LEONAUR
AVAILABLE IN SOFTCOVER OR HARDCOVER WITH DUST JACKET

AN APACHE CAMPAIGN IN THE SIERRA MADRE by John G. Bourke—An Account of the Expedition in Pursuit of the Chiricahua Apaches in Arizona, 1883.

BILLY DIXON & ADOBE WALLS by Billy Dixon and Edward Campbell Little—Scout, Plainsman & Buffalo Hunter, *Life and Adventures of "Billy" Dixon* by Billy Dixon and *The Battle of Adobe Walls* by Edward Campbell Little (*Pearson's Magazine*).

WITH THE CALIFORNIA COLUMN by George H. Petis—Against Confederates and Hostile Indians During the American Civil War on the South Western Frontier, *The California Column, Frontier Service During the Rebellion* and *Kit Carson's Fight With the Comanche and Kiowa Indians*.

THRILLING DAYS IN ARMY LIFE by George Alexander Forsyth—Experiences of the Beecher's Island Battle 1868, the Apache Campaign of 1882, and the American Civil War.

INDIAN FIGHTS AND FIGHTERS by Cyrus Townsend Brady—Indian Fights and Fighters of the American Western Frontier of the 19th Century.

THE NEZ PERCÉ CAMPAIGN, 1877 by G. O. Shields & Edmond Stephen Meany—Two Accounts of Chief Joseph and the Defeat of the Nez Percé, *The Battle of Big Hole* by G. O. Shields and *Chief Joseph, the Nez Percé* by Edmond Stephen Meany.

CAPTAIN JEFF OF THE TEXAS RANGERS by W. J. Maltby—Fighting Comanche & Kiowa Indians on the South Western Frontier 1863-1874.

SHERIDAN'S TROOPERS ON THE BORDERS by De Benneville Randolph Keim—The Winter Campaign of the U. S. Army Against the Indian Tribes of the Southern Plains, 1868-9.

GERONIMO by Geronimo—The Life of the Famous Apache Warrior in His Own Words.

WILD LIFE IN THE FAR WEST by James Hobbs—The Adventures of a Hunter, Trapper, Guide, Prospector and Soldier.

THE OLD SANTA FE TRAIL by Henry Inman—The Story of a Great Highway.

LIFE IN THE FAR WEST by George F. Ruxton—The Experiences of a British Officer in America and Mexico During the 1840's.

ADVENTURES IN MEXICO AND THE ROCKY MOUNTAINS by George F. Ruxton—Experiences of Mexico and the South West During the 1840's.

AVAILABLE ONLINE AT **www.leonaur.com**
AND FROM ALL GOOD BOOK STORES

ALSO FROM LEONAUR
AVAILABLE IN SOFTCOVER OR HARDCOVER WITH DUST JACKET

THE FALL OF THE MOGHUL EMPIRE OF HINDUSTAN by *H. G. Keene*—By the beginning of the nineteenth century, as British and Indian armies under Lake and Wellesley dominated the scene, a little over half a century of conflict brought the Moghul Empire to its knees.

LADY SALE'S AFGHANISTAN by *Florentia Sale*—An Indomitable Victorian Lady's Account of the Retreat from Kabul During the First Afghan War.

THE CAMPAIGN OF MAGENTA AND SOLFERINO 1859 by *Harold Carmichael Wylly*—The Decisive Conflict for the Unification of Italy.

FRENCH'S CAVALRY CAMPAIGN by *J. G. Maydon*—A Special Correspondent's View of British Army Mounted Troops During the Boer War.

CAVALRY AT WATERLOO by *Sir Evelyn Wood*—British Mounted Troops During the Campaign of 1815.

THE SUBALTERN by *George Robert Gleig*—The Experiences of an Officer of the 85th Light Infantry During the Peninsular War.

NAPOLEON AT BAY, 1814 by *F. Loraine Petre*—The Campaigns to the Fall of the First Empire.

NAPOLEON AND THE CAMPAIGN OF 1806 by *Colonel Vachée*—The Napoleonic Method of Organisation and Command to the Battles of Jena & Auerstädt.

THE COMPLETE ADVENTURES IN THE CONNAUGHT RANGERS by *William Grattan*—The 88th Regiment during the Napoleonic Wars by a Serving Officer.

BUGLER AND OFFICER OF THE RIFLES by *William Green & Harry Smith*—With the 95th (Rifles) during the Peninsular & Waterloo Campaigns of the Napoleonic Wars.

NAPOLEONIC WAR STORIES by *Sir Arthur Quiller-Couch*—Tales of soldiers, spies, battles & sieges from the Peninsular & Waterloo campaigns.

CAPTAIN OF THE 95TH (RIFLES) by *Jonathan Leach*—An officer of Wellington's sharpshooters during the Peninsular, South of France and Waterloo campaigns of the Napoleonic wars.

RIFLEMAN COSTELLO by *Edward Costello*—The adventures of a soldier of the 95th (Rifles) in the Peninsular & Waterloo Campaigns of the Napoleonic wars.

AVAILABLE ONLINE AT **www.leonaur.com**
AND FROM ALL GOOD BOOK STORES

ALSO FROM LEONAUR
AVAILABLE IN SOFTCOVER OR HARDCOVER WITH DUST JACKET

THE 9TH—THE KING'S (LIVERPOOL REGIMENT) IN THE GREAT WAR 1914 - 1918 by *Enos H. G. Roberts*—Mersey to mud—war and Liverpool men.

THE GAMBARDIER by *Mark Severn*—The experiences of a battery of Heavy artillery on the Western Front during the First World War.

FROM MESSINES TO THIRD YPRES by *Thomas Floyd*—A personal account of the First World War on the Western front by a 2/5th Lancashire Fusilier.

THE IRISH GUARDS IN THE GREAT WAR - VOLUME 1 by *Rudyard Kipling*—Edited and Compiled from Their Diaries and Papers—The First Battalion.

THE IRISH GUARDS IN THE GREAT WAR - VOLUME 1 by *Rudyard Kipling*—Edited and Compiled from Their Diaries and Papers—The Second Battalion.

ARMOURED CARS IN EDEN by *K. Roosevelt*—An American President's son serving in Rolls Royce armoured cars with the British in Mesopotamia & with the American Artillery in France during the First World War.

CHASSEUR OF 1914 by *Marcel Dupont*—Experiences of the twilight of the French Light Cavalry by a young officer during the early battles of the great war in Europe.

TROOP HORSE & TRENCH by *R.A. Lloyd*—The experiences of a British Lifeguardsman of the household cavalry fighting on the western front during the First World War 1914-18.

THE EAST AFRICAN MOUNTED RIFLES by *C.J. Wilson*—Experiences of the campaign in the East African bush during the First World War.

THE LONG PATROL by *George Berrie*—A Novel of Light Horsemen from Gallipoli to the Palestine campaign of the First World War.

THE FIGHTING CAMELIERS by *Frank Reid*—The exploits of the Imperial Camel Corps in the desert and Palestine campaigns of the First World War.

STEEL CHARIOTS IN THE DESERT by *S. C. Rolls*—The first world war experiences of a Rolls Royce armoured car driver with the Duke of Westminster in Libya and in Arabia with T.E. Lawrence.

WITH THE IMPERIAL CAMEL CORPS IN THE GREAT WAR by *Geoffrey Inchbald*—The story of a serving officer with the British 2nd battalion against the Senussi and during the Palestine campaign.

AVAILABLE ONLINE AT www.leonaur.com
AND FROM ALL GOOD BOOK STORES

www.ingramcontent.com/pod-product-compliance
Lightning Source LLC
Chambersburg PA
CBHW030358100426
42812CB00028B/2759/J